THE
CASE
AGAINST
COLLEGE

Other Books by the Author

The Invisible Scar

Born Female

The Crowding Syndrome

*Everything a Woman Needs to Know to Get Paid
    What She's Worth*

THE CASE AGAINST COLLEGE

by

Caroline Bird

edited by

Helene Mandelbaum

DAVID McKAY COMPANY, INC.

NEW YORK

4/11/77 Eastern 6.64

To my granddaughter Andrea

THE CASE AGAINST COLLEGE

COPYRIGHT © 1975 BY CAROLINE BIRD

Library of Congress Cataloging in Publication Data

Bird, Caroline.
    The case against college.

    Bibliography: p.
    Includes index.
    1. Universities and colleges—United States.
2. Universities and colleges—United States—Costs.
I. Title.
LA227.3.B57   378.73   74-25721
ISBN 0-679-50519-9

MANUFACTURED IN THE UNITED STATES OF AMERICA

Acknowledgments

I wrote this book out of my concern for young people, and they in turn—hundreds of them—contributed in large measure to its realization. I talked with them when I lectured on campuses from the University of California at Davis to Green Mountain College in Poultney, Vermont, as well as in the courses I gave at Russell Sage, and the New School for Social Research. Many more—in and out of college—spoke, not only to me but also to students who were doing independent study projects for credit under my guidance in colleges as diverse as Kirkland and Hamilton in Clinton, New York, and Wright State University in Dayton, Ohio. The names of students, interviewers and interviewees are listed alphabetically in the notes for chapter 1.

Margaret Sanborn, Vassar '73, coordinated the student interviews, and her fine ear for quotable dialogue has enriched the text. She has also kindly given us permission to use material from her article, "You're in the Navy Now!" in *Seventeen* (November 1974).

As on two previous books, Helene Mandelbaum was in charge of intellectual law and order. She helped me mold hundreds of pages into a rational structure, patiently querying me when I was elliptical, and pruning me when I went off the deep end. Marjorie Godfrey kept administrative and fiscal law and order out of the scores of books, people, phone bills, and odd jobs involved in what turned out to be a much more ambitious research project than we expected. Elizabeth Bennett, a reference librarian, kept the research material—books, interviews, tapes, articles—in order through many changes of direction, and verified every fact in the book. The project owes a great deal to my husband, Tom Mahoney, whose aim for obscure facts is deadly and accurate. He and Harold Mandelbaum provided husbandly support in many ways. Esther Vail patiently and cheerfully typed the manuscript through several metamorphoses.

Stephen G. Necel of the Empire National Bank of Poughkeepsie, New York, and his trusty computer were the statistical athletes who projected the value of a college education in money.

The editors at David McKay, Eleanor Rawson, John Hartnett, Grace Shaw, and Judith Steer, and Bantam editor Toni Burbank helped sharpen the argument. The analogy between college and the True Church elaborated in chapter 6, "The Liberal Arts Religion," is a direct response to an eloquent editorial memorandum by Toni Burbank.

Professors, college administrators from presidents to admissions officers, psychiatrists, placement officers and deans, and students of higher education have been generous in talking to me when I've bothered them, but none is, of course, responsible for my heresies. I want particularly to thank Jeanne Ballantine, Wright State University; Nina Baym, University of Illinois, Urbana-Champaign; Ivar Berg, Columbia University; David P. Campbell, Center for Creative Leadership, Greensboro, North Carolina; Marvin D. Dunnette, University of Minnesota; Abbott L. Ferriss, Emory University; Shirley Johnson, Vassar College.

Also Fritz Machlup, Princeton University; David S. Mundel, Harvard University; Alan C. Purves, University of Illinois, Urbana-Champaign; Reynolds Price, Duke University; Jane Ranzoni, Vassar College; David Riesman, Harvard University; Gordon Sabine, University of Iowa; Rita Simon, University of Illinois, Urbana-Champaign; Paul J. Taubman, University of Pennsylvania; Martin Trow, University of California, Berkeley; Sheldon White, Harvard University.

Also Jean Aldrich, Bennington College; Samuel Babbitt, Kirkland College; Warren Bennis, University of Cincinnati; Mary G. Bodel, Vassar College; Newell Brown, Princeton; Sterling Chaykin, University of California, Davis; Theresa Chow Clements, City University of New York; John R. Coleman, Haverford College; Bridget Cosper, Kirkland College; Father John Cuddigan, Creighton University, Omaha, Nebraska; John M. Duggan, Vassar College; Robert Ehrmann, University of California, Los Angeles; Mary Louise Farley, State University of New York, New Paltz; Richard Gummere, Columbia University; Don Hagerty, University of California, Davis; Carol M. Hedderly-Smith, University of Washington; Martin Hunter, College of Dayton Art Institute, Dayton, Ohio; Mary Alice Hunter, Vassar College; Susan Hurd, Kirkland College; Dorothy Knoell, California State Department of Education, Sacramento, California; John W. Kraft, Community College of Allegheny County, Pittsburgh, Pennsylvania; S. Malin, Harvard University; Brother Martin, University of Dayton; William Matthis, College of Dayton Art Institute; Joan McCall, National Association of Women Deans and Counselors, Washington, D.C.; Sterling McMurrin, University of Utah, Salt Lake City.

James O'Connell, Iona College, New Rochelle; Patricia Ollson, Augsburg College, Minneapolis; Joan Orr, Community College of Allegheny County, Pittsburgh; Dabney Park, Jr., Florida International University, Miami, Florida; Ruth Rinard, Kirkland College; John D. Shingleton, Michigan State University; Kenneth W. Stetson, Northeastern Illinois University, Chicago; Rebecca Stickney, Bennington College; Michelle Stimas, Babson College, Wellesley, Massachusetts; Ruth Van Doren,

The New School for Social Research, New York City; Barbara Wells, Vassar College; James Wilson, Wright State University; and Harrison Wright, Swarthmore College.

Librarians and resource people in government and private agencies spent many hours patiently directing us to research data on colleges, college students and young people of college age compiled by the Census, the Department of Labor, the Carnegie Commission on Higher Education, the U.S. Office of Education, and many private foundations as well. I wish especially to thank Joan Murphy, Margaret B. Hubbard, and Frances Goudy of the Vassar College Library; Jane McGarvey of Adriance Memorial Library in Poughkeepsie; and Rhea Tabakin of the Institute of Life Insurance Library.

Also Susan A. Camardo, University Information Services, SUNY Buffalo; Larry A. Green, National Association of College Admissions Counselors, Skokie, Illinois; Diane Haspel, The Wharton School, University of Pennsylvania; Linda J. Shepard, University of Michigan.

Government resource people who tracked down information or straightened me out include: Dave Bayer, Department of Health, Education and Welfare, Washington, D.C.; Fred Beamer, U.S. Office of Education, Washington, D.C.; Patricia Bommilino, Bureau of Labor Statistics, Washington, D.C.; Charles W. Bray, U.S. State Department, Washington, D.C.; Paul Glick, Bureau of the Census, Washington, D.C.; W. Vance Grant, U.S. Office of Education, Washington, D.C.; Alice Hansen, U.S. Office of Education, Washington, D.C.; Charlotte Hoffman and Patricia Hopson, Department of Health, Education and Welfare, Washington, D.C.; W. T. Hudson, Office of Civil Rights, U.S. Coast Guard; George Lind, U.S. Office of Education, Washington, D.C.

Also John J. Mallen, Jr., Committee for Economic Development, New York City; Patricia Mapp, Department of Industry, Labor and Human Relations, Madison, Wisconsin; Larry Mead, U.S. Office of Education, Washington, D.C.; Jacob Mincer, National Bureau of Economic Research, Washington, D.C.; Roger W. Ming, New York State Education Department, Albany, New York; Arthur Norton, Bureau of the Census, Washington, D.C.; Greg Senseney, U.S. Office of Education, Washington, D.C.; Lewis Siegel, Bureau of Labor Statistics, New York City; Skee Smith, U.S. Office of Education, Washington, D.C.; Emmet Spiers, Bureau of the Census, Washington, D.C.; Murray Weitzman, Bureau of the Census, Washington, D.C.; Meyer Zitter, Bureau of the Census, Washington, D.C.

Research specialists who helped include: Steven Bailey, American Council on Education, Washington, D.C.; Nancy Beck, Educational Testing Service, Princeton, New Jersey; Gail Fishgold and Leslie Houck of the College Scholarship Service, New York City; R. A. Hinckley, National Opinion Research Center, University of Chicago; Mary Conway Kohler, National Commission on Resources for Youth, Inc., New York City; James Maxey, American College Testing Program, Iowa City, Iowa; Alexander Sidar, College Entrance Examination Board, New York City; Ken Young, American College Testing Program, Washington, D.C.

Authorities in business, media and in secondary education who gave us information include: William M. Ellinghaus, President, New York Telephone, also Dominic Carbone and Syndee Feur of that company; Douglas Bray, Amy R. Hanan, Thomas L. Putalik, and Mary Reinart, AT&T, New York City; Edward F. Babbott, Summit High School, Summit, New Jersey; Glenn Bassett, General Electric, New York City; A. Bruce Bergquist, The Dynamy Program, Worcester, Massachusetts; Joan Breibart, ITT, New York City; Benjamin Cohn, Board of Cooperative Educational Services, Yorktown Heights, New York; A. J. Fritz, Jr., General Electric, Schenectady; Rita Gillmon, The San Diego Union, San Diego California; Jane Newitt, Hudson Institute, Croton-on-Hudson, New York; H. Overstrom, General Electric, Schenectady, New York; W. J. Reusch, Bethlehem Steel Corp., Bethlehem, Pennsylvania.

Friends who gave generously of their own views include: Sol Kimball, Professor of Anthropology at the University of Florida, Gainesville; James McClellan, Professor of Education at SUNY Albany; Leslie Koempel, Professor of Sociology Emeritus at Vassar; Leonard Sayles, Professor of Business Administration at Columbia; and my son-in-law, John Paul Barach, Professor of Physics at Vanderbilt.

The resources suggested for readers who wish to pursue alternatives to college were assembled by Marjorie Godfrey and Margaret Sanborn, under the guidance of Rosalie Tucker, Readers' Services Librarian Emeritus, Vassar College.

Caroline Bird
Poughkeepsie, New York

Contents

PART I

THE
YOUNG
AS
VICTIMS

1

The College Mystique

This is a book about what happens to young people when they get out of high school.

It is about college only because college is where we put as many of them as possible to get them out of the way. It isn't about education, really, or the virtues of an educated citizenry. It is not about the value of college for those young people who love learning for its own sake, for those who would rather read a good book than eat. They are a minority, even at the big-name prestige colleges which recruit and attract the intellectually oriented. For them college is intellectual discovery and adventure.

But a great majority of our nine million postsecondary students who are "in college" are there because it has become the thing to do or because college is a pleasant place to be (pleasanter at least than the "outside," sometimes called "the real," world); because it's the only way they can get parents or taxpayers to support them without working at a job they don't like; because they can't get any job at all; because Mother wanted them to go; or for some other reason utterly irrelevant to the courses of studies for which the college is supposedly organized.

It is dismaying to find, as I did, that college professors and administrators, when pressed for a candid opinion, estimate that no more than 25 percent of the students they serve are really turned on by classwork. For the other 75 percent, college is at best a social center, a youth ghetto, an aging vat, and at worst a young folks (rhymes with old folks) home, a youth house (rhymes with poorhouse) or even a prison. However good or bad it might be for the individual students, college is a place where young adults are set apart because they are superfluous people who are of no immediate use to the economy and are a potential embarrassment to the middle-aged white males who operate the outside, or "real," world for their own convenience.

EDUCATIONAL HUCKSTERING

This segregation of the young began, as many evil institutions do, with the noblest of motives. We believed at the end of World War II that a grateful nation owed every veteran a chance at a college education. Older and eager to make up for lost career time, the veterans who used their G.I. Bill of Rights proved what educators had long contended: that millions of potential lawyers and doctors were working out their lives as factory hands and taxi drivers simply because they didn't have the money to go to college. During the affluent and expanding 1950s, we became convinced that a college education should be available to *every* qualified high-school graduate regardless of ability to pay. After the Russians beat us to space in 1957, it became patriotic as well as noble to promote advanced education, particularly in the sciences.

Educators tapped the bottomless reservoir of national defense appropriations to fund lavish research and educational development programs aimed at "catching up." We overlooked the fact that all other nations, including Russia, educate at public expense only as many of the most talented young people as the economy actually needs. Just as we were the first nation to aspire to teach every small child to read and write, so we were the first and remain the only great nation that aspires to *higher* education for all.

It was a generous ideal in the best American tradition: a door open to talent wherever it occurred. And in grandeur the concept paralleled the nineteenth-century vision of a nation united by railroad tracks from coast to coast. The ideal was especially popular, of course, with the politically articulate middle class in the 1950s and '60s when their families were having trouble finding places in existing colleges.

Americans pride themselves on implementing impossible dreams. In the 1960s we damned the expense and built the great state university systems as fast as we could, blinking at waste and graft as we went. And like the building of railroads, the building of a state-supported college system offered riches for contractors, power for a new class of administrators, employment for many workers languishing in dead-end jobs, rising land prices for property owners—something, in short, for everyone. The effort transformed the landscape. Small farming and shopping centers that used to be dots on the map, like Mount Pleasant, Michigan, home of Central Michigan University, blossomed into glittering new cities—great plush youth ghettoes of high-rise dormitories sitting in the middle of cornfields. In 1974 Dr. Ernest Boyer, chancellor of the State University of New York, estimated that students could take over the communities of New Paltz, Fredonia, Oneonta, Geneseo, Old Westbury, Plattsburgh, and Potsdam if residency rules permitted those who were eighteen and over to vote in local elections.

Education became a mammoth industry. In the 1970s institutions of higher education were spending more than $30 billion annually. And though tuition rises priced thousands of students out of the colleges their parents had attended, the taxpayers were still providing more than half of all the money spent on higher education.

But in spite of these huge sums, less than half the high-school graduates were going on to higher education, raising a new question of equity. Is it fair to make all the taxpayers pay for the minority who actually go to college? We decided, long ago, that it is fair for childless adults to pay school taxes because everyone, parents and nonparents alike, profits by a literate population. But does the same reasoning apply to *higher* education? Would college for everyone benefit society enough to be worth it? We will not try to answer that question in this book; we are concerned here only with what college can and cannot do for individual students. It is interesting to notice in passing, however, that those who argue the public value of a college education are very apt to be the affluent, college-educated parents who have always sent their children to college—even when they had to foot the whole bill themselves. Social critics who are concerned with social equality have begun to point out that state-supported higher education is regressive taxation of the majority of noncollege users—who are more likely to be poor—for the benefit of the children of the middle-class.[1]

The response from educators has been to ask for more. They have argued that simple justice requires tax-supported higher education for *every* high-school graduate, and damn the expense. But the expense would be formidable. Fritz Machlup, an economist who specializes in putting dollar values on knowledge and human capital, has estimated that universal schooling to age twenty-two would have cost $47.5 billion in 1970–71,[2] a year in which corporate profits aggregated $35 billion and the total proceeds of agriculture, fisheries, and forests came to $25 billion. And as costs, both total and per capita, have continued to mount faster than per capita personal income, even the establishment-oriented Carnegie Commission on Higher Education, organized in 1967 to study higher education and its future in the United States,[3] has conceded that there is a limit to what the taxpayers are willing to spend for higher education—and the limit is in sight. Programs for getting *everybody* into college turn out to cost more for each full-time student than programs for educating the traditionally collegebound. By dint of remedial instruction, counseling, tutoring, and extra financial assistance, SEEK (Search for Education, Elevation, and Knowledge) has been helping educationally and economically disadvantaged New Yorkers through the free-tuition City University of New York. But the program costs an average of $2,500 per student in books, stipends, services, overhead, and financial aid, in addition, of course, to the $800 CUNY spends per student on instructional costs in general.

Equality has begun to look like a prohibitive luxury, particularly now that colleges have all they can do to keep their regular programs afloat. Predictable demography has caught up with the empire builders. The power-hungry academics built plants on the assumption that enrollments would continue rising indefinitely. Only a few demographers in the Census Bureau had pointed out, and then mostly in footnotes, that the "market" could not continue to grow at the boom rates of the 1960s, but that the rate of growth would have to decline as the war-boom babies moved out of college and into the job market.[4] That's exactly what happened. While few colleges would confess to actual vacancies, observers estimated that another half million students could have been accommodated each year in the early '70s at a time when inflation was pushing costs up at unprecedented rates. College administrators began to panic.

Most have turned to the hard sell. Admissions officers have put down rugs, put on help, and retained Madison Avenue public relations and advertising firms to woo applicants. Catalogues have grown fatter, glos-

sier, and more pictorial. Kent State University in Ohio
bought time for radio commercials. In 1973 Northern
Kentucky State College borrowed the giveaway tech-
nique used to promote toothpastes. During Christmas
vacation, when students were free to move around outdoors, they launched 200 helium balloons, 103 of
which carried scholarship offers on the basis of finders
keepers.

Some colleges offered tuition rebates to students who
recruited other students. High scorers on the Scholastic
Aptitude Tests administered by the supposedly non-
commercial College Entrance Examination Board
found themselves the target of high pressure direct mail
and telephone solicitations from respectable colleges,
and the very highest scorers of all were offered scholarships even when they did not need the money. And as
the economy cooled down, big corporations were
slower to recruit executives, and the headhunters turned
to the college field. One entrepreneurial operator in
Boston was said to have charged colleges $100 for each
freshman procured and enrolled.

The Madison Avenue campaigns sell colleges like
soap, promoting those features that market analysts
think the customers really want: innovative programs,
an environment conducive to meaningful personal relationships, and a curriculum so free that it doesn't sound
like college at all—"We shape our curriculum to your
individual needs." But pleasing the customers is something new for college administrators, and many alumni
and parents blame the financial crunch for what they
feel to be an undignified if not immoral capitulation to
student whim.

Colleges have always known that most students don't
like to study and are, at least part of the time, ambiva-
lent about the college experience as a whole, but they
have never thought it either right or necessary to pay
any attention to these student feelings. Then, in the
1960s, students rebelling against the Vietnam War and

the draft discovered that they could disrupt a campus completely, and even force cancellation of the hated final examinations. News of riots discouraged donors and applicants, and so, when it didn't cost too much in money or power, administrators acted on some student complaints.

But what nobody really understood was that the protests had tapped the basic discontent with the idea of college itself—a discontent that did not go away when the riots subsided. Students now protest individually rather than in concert. They turn inward and withdraw from active participation. They drop out to travel to India or to feed themselves on subsistence farms. Some refuse to go to college at all.

Most, of course, have neither the funds nor the self-confidence for a constructive articulation of their discontent. They simply hang around college because they can't think of anything better to do. As the costs of college to parents, taxpayers, and students themselves have escalated, as jobs for college graduates have begun to dry up, many people—on campus and off—have become disturbed by the mood of college students and have begun to pay more attention to what students themselves are saying about the college experience.

THE MOOD ON CAMPUS

The unhappiness of young people is nothing new. Like everyone else, I have always assumed that many young people have personal problems. And, like everyone else, I expected them to cope with these problems on an individual basis. But as I traveled around the country speaking at colleges, I was overwhelmed by the prevailing sadness. It was as visible on campuses in California as in Nebraska and Massachusetts. I encountered just too many young people who spoke little—and then only in drowned voices.

Sometimes the mood surfaced as diffidence, wariness, or "coolness," but whatever its form, it began to look like a defense mechanism, and that rang a bell. This is the way it used to be with women! Like everyone else in the 1950s and 1960s, I used to think that the troubles of women were personal, to be dealt with by psychoanalysis if necessary. Now we all recognize that the malaise of women and blacks are normal responses to the limited role society has assigned to them. I began to suspect that the same thing was happening to young adults: just as society has systematically damaged women by insisting that their proper place was in the home, so we may now be systematically damaging eighteen-year-olds by insisting that their proper place is in college.

Campus watchers everywhere know what I mean when I ask why students are so sad, but they don't agree on the answer. My first thought was that it might be an expression of the drug culture. But the mood survived the decline of drugs. Students were as withdrawn in 1974, when a national magazine announced the end of the drug culture, as they were several years earlier when drug usage made daily headlines.

During the Vietnam War, sadness could be ascribed to the draft. But peace did not revive enthusiasm for the future. Students, as well as their mentors, frequently blame "the mess the world is in." This isn't convincing. The world has always been in a mess and never more so than when everyone was optimistic in the so-called Gay Nineties of the last century and the misnamed Roaring Twenties of this one.

"Affluence," say parents and older folks. Young people are jaded and sated because they have received too much too soon, and there's nothing left to look forward to. They are used to instant gratification, and since unlimited wishes cannot be instantaneously gratified, they are doomed to chronic disappointment. But there is more envy than logic to this diagnosis. Whatever affluence does to people, it ought not to make them as cast down as Watteau's clown. On the contrary, in a recent psychological study "having money" is identified as the only factor that reliably correlates with happiness.[5]

A more rational theory, advanced by a forty-year-old college professor, is that his students are sad because of their permissive upbringing. He says that parents have been too lazy or timid to teach children how to get along with people, so they have grown up to be monsters their own parents can't bear to have around the house. And if your own mother is against you, who can be for you?

I don't buy the moralistic undertone of the hard-hat, law-and-order attack on permissiveness, but that bit about parents fearing, hating, and rejecting their grown children sounds plausible to me. The mood that worries me, come to think of it, is exactly the mood of a person jilted in love.

Are young people being rejected on a mass basis in supposedly youth-oriented America? Do we really hate our young? Are we covering up this hate and fear when we talk about how much we love them, how much we are sacrificing for them? Are the kids really living off the fat of the land, suffering from "too much, too soon"? Or do we glorify, envy, and pet them—and send them to college—in order to put them down and leave them out of the so-called real world, the same as we do to women? Is there anything else or anything better we can do for them except send them to college?

This book is the record of what I found out when I tried to answer these questions with the journalistic tools of my trade—scholarly studies, economic analyses, and historical record, the opinions of the specially knowledgeable, conversations with parents, professors, college administrators, and employers, all of whom spoke as alumni, too. Mainly, it reports what hundreds of college students on campuses all over the country, and young people not in college, told us in 1973 and 1974.[6]

My unnerving conclusion is that students are sad because they are not needed—not by their own parents, not by employers, not by the society as a whole. They were not, for the most part, unwanted babies. Their fate is more awkward. Somewhere between the nursery and the employment office they became *unwanted adults*. No one has anything in particular against them. But no one has anything in particular for them either, and they don't see any role for themselves in the future. There are too many people in the world of the 1970s already, and we do not know where to put newcomers. The neatest way to get rid of a superfluous eighteen-year-old is to amuse him all day long at a community college while his family feeds and houses him. This is not only cheaper than a residential college, but cheaper than supporting him on welfare, a make-work job, in prison, or in the armed forces.

RELUCTANT STUDENTS

The enormity of our hypocrisy about the young is not readily apparent. We assume that we are sending them to college for their own best interests and sell them college the way we sell them spinach—because it's good for them. Some, of course, learn to like it, but most wind up still preferring green peas. College students are forced to eat spinach—to go to college—even when they don't like it.

Educators admit as much. Nevitt Sanford, a distinguished student of higher education, says students feel they are "capitulating to a kind of voluntary servitude."

Some of them talk about their time in college as if it were a sentence to be served. A Mount Holyoke graduate of 1970 told us that she would have to write a long essay to explain exactly what Mount Holyoke had done to her and her friends. "For two years I was really interested in science," she said. "But in my junior and senior years, I just kept saying, 'I've done two years, I'm going to finish.' When I got out I made up my mind that I wasn't going to school anymore, because so many of my courses had been bullshit. I was just really miserable."

If students feel they are being coerced, it's hard to tell exactly who is coercing them. Parents, of course, are the nearest culprits. Shirley Ann Lee is a black student who feels it's up to her to "put her best foot forward" at Wright State University in Dayton, Ohio, because her mother gave her the opportunity to learn.

"My mother had the chance to go to college, but she gave it up so that her sister and brother could go instead," Shirley Ann told us. "Since I've gotten here, it's not that I thoroughly want to quit, but sometimes you feel down and say like 'I want to take a week away from school.' But I didn't want to quit or anything like that. I think that would hurt my parents."

How parents feel about college is sometimes the key to whether a student applies, goes, and stays. Educators are very much interested in the reasons why students go to college. Because their bread and butter depends on it, they have done extensive market research on their potential customers.[7] They have weighed the impact of place of residence, the income and occupations of parents, the type of secondary school, and even the influence of a young person's peer group. But to some questions there are no answers. Very few people know exactly why they go. However, the studies do suggest some interesting patterns. A big survey of more than 10,000 Wisconsin high-school seniors showed that for all I.Q. levels and both sexes, youngsters from families of limited income whose parents talked up college to them were more apt to plan on going than classmates from affluent families whose parents didn't seem to care whether they went or not.

If parents don't push, high-school counselors may conceive it to be their duty to do the pushing for them. They talk about their responsibility to "detect" and "motivate" scholastically able "college material." And when confronted with youngsters who don't know what they want to do with themselves, counselors who don't know what to do with them either can export the sticky problem to college on the ground that while college may not help the undecided student find his path, it probably won't do him any harm.

During the 1950s and 1960s, high-school counselors pushed and shoved the reluctant into college with a clear conscience. Society needed to "save talent." Parents called up counselors to beg them to help persuade children who were balking at the idea of more school. School authorities eager to increase the ratio of their graduates going "on" to college approved this pressure. Ben Cohn, who supervises guidance counselors for the Board of Cooperative Educational Services in the Northern Westchester-Putnam area of New York State, says that counselors who felt that a youngster was being railroaded into college tried to give him adult support for his intuition against it by urging him to go along with what his parents so badly wanted "just for one year."

When railroaded freshmen get into trouble at college, the college psychiatrist frequently blames the high-school counselor. An occasional problem at selective women's colleges is the bright girl who did very well in high school but never really wanted to go to college. The guidance counselor who "saved" her from the domesticity for which her parents reared her isn't around when she goes to pieces in the competitive environment of the preprofessional campus he chose for her.

Debbie Lewis entered Kirkland, an experimental women's college in upstate New York, because "my mom thinks of college as a step between high school and marriage." That's all right with Debbie, but she didn't bargain for a campus where every other woman is headed for graduate school. Debbie is quite frank to say that she "isn't the kind of person who can benefit from a liberal arts education," and she has the spunk to rebel. "This is too unreal," she told us. "It isn't what I want to do." Debbie thinks she might like to be a cabinetmaker, but she quickly adds she might not be dedicated enough to undergo a seven-year apprenticeship. "Actually, there isn't anything I'm dedicated to. For me it's more important to develop personal things than to have a career."

For every woman pushed into unwonted ambition, there are, of course, a dozen men, and in the unisex world of the young, more of them have now become liberated to join Debbie in asserting that "it's more important to develop personal things than to have a career." Debbie's male analogue has long been the staple client of the psychiatrists of good men's colleges. Classically he is a sensitive, intellectually gifted, and socially isolated young man who feels he cannot bear to carry on the family business or carve out the distinguished career his parents hope for him. The pressure on young males to succeed may be more important than any hormonal fragility in explaining the high suicide rate of male college students. Now that women are expected to succeed, more of them break under the pressure too, and the suicide rate of young women, particularly young black women, is rising.

Luckily, the picture is changing somewhat. Parents who have read up on the latest theories are ashamed to pull and haul on their young the way they used to do. Ben Cohn says that sophisticated Westchester County, New York, parents now tell the high school counselor, "I want my kid to do what he really wants to do." But what they really do, he adds, is to apply the pressure in a more subtle way.

An important and not-so-subtle pressure is, of

course, financial. Many families are happy to support their children only as long as they are in college. "College is like welfare," one Bennington dropout explained. "It's what you do when you run out of money and have to go back to your parents for help."

The more thoughtful college psychiatrists don't like to blame parents. "It's the whole society—the whole system that pushes them into college," says Dr. Jane Ranzoni, a psychologist at Vassar. Students say as much themselves. While a substantial proportion told us, in response to the direct question, that they were in college because their parents wanted them to go, many others couldn't identify any particular person or force that impelled them. "I really don't know why I came," one student told us. "It's just something everybody does. My family went and all my friends, so I came, too." "The name locks you in," said a Wellesley student.

The pressure of what "everybody" does is both visible and measurable. According to the same study of high-school graduates that established the importance of parental encouragement, those who live in a poverty neighborhood are less likely to go to college than those who have no more money but who live in a more affluent neighborhood where it looks as if everyone really did go.

Reluctant students who come to college primarily because they can't get up the courage to do anything else may stick it out for the same reason, beefing no more than drafted soldiers. A Russell Sage junior who told us she stayed on because of "the tears of my mother" added that she would have disregarded those tears if she could have found a friend to go jobhunting with. "I just couldn't see myself getting off a bus all alone in a strange city with $50 in my pocket and looking for a policeman to ask where the Y was," she said, obviously disgusted by her own timidity.

Students often say college is an alternative to a far worse fate. They are sticking it out because it is "better" than the army, better than a job—and it has to be pretty bad before it is worse than staying at home.

Student after student told us what college counselors told us, too: The main thing college does for students is to get them away from home without having to break with their parents or earn their own living. In his book *No Time for Youth*, Joseph Katz reported the results of a massive psychological study that followed students through four years of Berkeley and Stanford.[8] A high proportion felt that physical separation from their families was what really changed them. This was true even for the great majority who wanted the same sort of life as their parents were leading.

Students aren't belligerent about this. Some seem surprised at their own answer. "What did I learn in college, really? Well, I learned to do things on my own. At college there are no parents to get you up in the morning and tell you when to study."

Occasionally, of course, college is an alternative to an intolerable home situation. We talked to several students who were glad to be in college because their parents were separating. Steve is the youngest of his family, and both of his parents were married very young. By the time he was in high school, he was the only one left at home. "When they weren't taking out their frustrations on each other, they were inflicting them on me. Sure, I'm glad to get away from home. I don't exactly like college, but it's better than the hassles I'd get at home."

One student we talked to was breaking away from the religious faith of his family and welcomed a chance to "get off by myself and think things out." Many like the feeling of freedom. "At college you don't have to tell anyone where you are going and when you are coming back," one woman exulted. More women than men mentioned personal freedom to come and go— testimony to the perpetuation of a double standard of parental supervision. The prospect of freedom to experiment sexually looms large, but no larger, perhaps, than freedom to choose friends, clothing, manners, and language without explaining them.

Most students want autonomy, not a quarrel with their parents. Shirley Ann Lee, the student whose mother wants her to learn, thinks she got more out of going to a residential college far from home. "Here your attitudes and all your views change because you have the last word on what you're going to do," she told us. "A lot of my friends are still home. They're independent, but they're not really independent. Like right now, I say, I'm going to do this. And I make the last decision. I still have my parents' views—they will always be with me—but right now I have my own views and my own attitudes. So when I get my degree, I'm going to be happy, but I'm going to say, 'Hey, Mom. *I* did it.' "

College is a graceful way to get away from home. It is also a graceful way for a parent to push an overly dependent young one out of the nest. Richard Baloga, the son of a policeman, describes himself as shy. Going away from home to Wright State University in Dayton, Ohio, "forced me out of my freshman shell. I wanted to drop out because I was homesick. I was down here at college and my girl was back home."

Richard's freshman homesickness is classic, and his policeman father handled it in a straight-armed way that seems to have worked for a son brought up to it. "My father straightened me out," Richard related. "He said, 'Don't think about now, think about the future.' I hate school. I don't like it now any more than I ever did. But at the same time the underlying feeling to do it for my father made it worthwhile. It gave me a reason to go." This is, of course, growing up by the book, and it does happen. College sometimes turns the neat trick of getting a young person away from home while doing exactly what the home folks wanted him to do all along.

Many students frankly told us that they were in college because they couldn't find a job. "I'd go again for really poor reasons," Candy Chayer, an eighteen-year-old freshman at Augsburg, said. "I have no options. Some kids have gone through high school taking courses that prepared them for jobs right after high school, but I never did that. College was the only 'job' I could get when I was through with high school."

The economy of the 1970s is biased against beginners in two ways. First, they are hurt by the changing economic structure—there are fewer "entry" jobs which lead to promotion. Young people used to start working as office boys, assistants, apprentices, go-fors, and learners in whom employers invested training. Now machinery does much of the routine work which made it possible for beginners to earn as they learned. Most of the new jobs for beginners that were created during the 1960s and '70s are service jobs—waiting on people who have money to spend in hotels, restaurants, gas stations, retail stores, banks, hospitals, resorts, and the schools that service young people themselves. With few exceptions, these jobs are unskilled, low-paid, routine, and, above all, dead-end.

Second, young people are hurt by cyclical unemployment. When the economy is expanding and employers are hiring, beginners get a chance. When the economy falters, or even if expansion slows, employers don't hire new people. That's why teen-age unemployment is more volatile than the unemployment rate of family heads, the rate most frequently quoted. During the slower growth of 1974 the unemployment rate of teenagers fluctuated around 20 percent.

In Pittsburgh, a West Virginia Wesleyan junior who couldn't find a job during the summer of 1973 after applying to "all the department stores, a health spa, drugstores, and supermarkets" reported that "a lot of kids I know are going to summer school because they can't find a job." College has become a glamorous and

expensive way for the affluent society to keep its unemployed young people off the streets. In 1974, William
James McGill, the president of Columbia, warned
against the danger of using universities "as storage
houses for bored young people."

College is, at the least, a voluntary, rather than an
involuntary, servitude. A senior at Augsburg College
told us what went through his mind when he thought
about quitting college. "God, studying is really a drag,
and, gee, it would be neat to earn money and always
have enough money to spend, to be on your own, but
you know it's really kind of a dream. Besides, who
wants to work when you've got four years to get your
head together?"

A substantial number of students on every campus
feel a little like Daniel Sanderson did when he told us
that "college is a wonderful life compared with prison."
Danny was busted for selling a half-pound of marijuana
to an undercover policeman. Instead of the parole his
family expected for a first offender, he wound up behind bars. After two and a half years, he was chosen
for an experimental program under which selected prisoners are given an educational furlough, and went to
Wright State University. Like many other college students, he would like to quit college and travel, but his
case is rather special. If he quits before his term is up,
he'll be sent back to jail.

The remarkable thing about Danny is not that he is a
furloughed prisoner. It is that he sounds and feels so
much like the other students who are glad to be in
college primarily because of the fate from which college
is saving them.

How many are reluctant? Estimates depend on how
reluctant you have to be to be counted. The conservative Carnegie Commission estimates 5 to 30 percent.
Sol Linowitz, former chairman of the board of Xerox,
who was at one time chairman of a special committee

on campus tensions of the American Council on Education, found that "a significant number were not happy with their college experience because they felt they were there only in order to get the 'ticket to the big show' rather than to spend the years as productively as they otherwise could."

There may, of course, be nothing very new about this reluctance except the seriousness with which educators now take it. Students have always wished themselves away, especially when examinations loom and the work piles up. As one student told us, "Clerking in the drugstore, I'd at least have my evenings." "Academics" are generally held a "drag," or as another student put it, "College wouldn't be so bad if it weren't for all the studying you have to do."

Older alumni will identify with Richard Baloga, the policeman's son who stayed in school even though he "hated it" because he thought it would do him some good, but fewer feel this way every year. Daniel Yankelovich has surveyed undergraduate attitudes for a number of years, and reported that in 1971, 74 percent thought education was "very important," but just two years earlier, in 1969, 80 percent had thought so.[9]

The doubters don't mind speaking up. Leon Lefkowitz, chairman of the department of social studies at Central High School in Valley Stream, New York, interviewed 300 college students at random and reports that 200 of them didn't think that the education they were getting was worth the effort.[10] "In two years I'll pick up a diploma and I can honestly say it was a waste of my father's bread," one of them said.

"I don't think I was cut out for college," another young man told us. "I thought of dropping out, but what would I have done? I just don't know. I'd probably have just bummed around for a while until I got myself straightened out." It would be cruel to tell this overearnest young man that his predicament is not

unique. A majority of the population "bums around"
this way from birth to death—and without noticeably
straightening themselves out.

As a sociologist explained to me, you don't have to
have a reason for going to college—it's an institution.
If I understand him correctly, an institution, sociologi-
cally speaking, is something everyone accepts without
question. The burden of proof is not on why you go,
but why anyone thinks there might be a reason for *not*
going. The implication—and some educators express it
quite frankly—is that an eighteen-year-old is too young
and confused to know what he wants to do, let alone
what is good for him. Later on, you'll be glad you went.
Most successful and happy people seem to have gone to
college, so why take a chance with *your* life?

Mother knows best. The reasoning recalls the dubious comfort administered by nineteenth-century mothers of reluctant brides: "You're too young to realize
that every woman has to be married to be happy, but
you'll see. In time you'll learn to love him."

It has always been comfortable for people to believe
that authorities like Mother or outside specialists like
educators could determine what was best for them. I
don't agree. I believe that what is good for me is what
feels good for me. I believe that college has to be
judged not on what other people think is good for students, but on how good it feels to students themselves.
Specialists and authorities no longer enjoy the credibility former generations accorded them. Patients talk
back to doctors and are not struck suddenly dead. Clients question the lawyer's bills and sometimes get them
reduced. It is no longer so obvious that adolescents are
better off studying a core curriculum that was con-
structed when all educated men could agree on what
made them educated, or that professors, advisors, or
parents can be of any particular help to young people in
choosing a major or a career.

It is now safer to assume that people have an inside

view of what's good for them. If a child doesn't want to go to school some morning, better let him stay at home, at least until you find out why. Maybe he knows something that you don't know.

So with college. If high-school graduates don't want to go—or if they don't want to go right away—they may perceive more clearly than their elders that college is not for them. High-school graduates see college graduates driving cabs and decide it's not worth going. College students find no intellectual stimulation in their studies and drop out or stop out with the encouragement of college authorities.

And if students believe that college isn't necessarily good for them, you can't expect them to stay on for the general good of mankind. Young people may be more altruistic than their elders, but no great number are going to spend four years at hard intellectual labor, let alone tens of thousands of family dollars, for "the advancement of human capability in society at large," one of the many purposes of higher education invoked by a Carnegie Commission report.[11] Nor do any considerable number of them go to college to beat the Russians to Jupiter, improve the national defense, increase the Gross National Product, lower the crime rate, improve automobile safety, or create a market for the arts—to mention some of the benefits taxpayers are supposed to get for supporting higher education.

Nor should we expect young people to go to college to bring about social equality—even if it could be attained by putting everyone through four years of academic rigor. On the contrary, this seems to be a very roundabout and expensive way to narrow the gap between the highest and the lowest in our society. And it is worse than roundabout. Equalizing opportunity through universal higher education subjects the whole population to the intellectual mode natural only to a few. It violates the fundamental egalitarian principle of respect for the differences between people.

The simple thesis of this book is that college is good for some people, but it is not good for everybody. The great majority of high-school graduates aren't sure what they want to do. They, and their parents, need some realistic help in deciding whether the promotional claims for the product college are what they want to buy.

PART II

THE
COST

2

The Cost to Parents

Anywhere you go, any way you count it, a college degree costs more money than entering freshmen and their parents think it will. Never mind how much taxpayers and rich alumni kick in. What students are expected to pay comes as a rude shock even to the best-heeled families. For families in more modest circumstances, the costs can be overwhelming.

I met Dave Luback in California. When I asked a group of students what the rising cost of college was doing to their parents, he gave me his mother's phone number. Bearded, articulate, responsive, and wholeheartedly contemporary, Dave is one of those winners in the rough and tumble of undergraduate politics who sounds more mature at nineteen than many people in his parents' generation.

Yes, getting up the money for college was a terrible problem, Mrs. Luback told me. "We try not to think about it," she said. "But of course we end up by thinking about it all the time."

Dave's sister is also in college. Their father earns $16,000 a year as a foreman. According to the College Scholarship Service, which makes such calculations, the Lubacks ought to be able to pay about $4,400 toward the expenses of two children in college at the same time. But they can't. The result is that they are going deeper and deeper into debt—all of them.

By the time Dave gets his M.D., he'll owe various student loan programs and banks close to $15,000. As soon as Linda gets her B.S. she will have to start paying back the $2,000 she borrowed from the Crocker National Bank to go to a fashionable school in the East for her freshman year. "That eastern school was a disaster," Mrs. Luback confided. "By Christmas, Linda was telling us that she would turn into a prostitute or a drug addict if she didn't get out of that place." The Lubacks persuaded her to stick the year out, but they had to increase their loan at the bank to pay the January phone bill incurred while the decision was being made.

"They have high ideals, and they are both outstanding students," Mrs. Luback says, warming to her favorite subject. "They've always been good at school, and we've always urged them to shoot for the top. Even in high school, Dave won a trip to Tokyo. Of course, they both have campus jobs—it's part of the financial loan package—but they like to do the nice little extra things that will help them later on." Dave is helping a professor do research, even though he doesn't get paid for it. Linda spends a lot of time serving in student government. And she was chosen to be an interne in Washington one semester—the only extra she had for that was her air fare from California.

The $4,400 the Lubacks have to pay out of pocket is just about 40 percent of their children's college expenses. Theoretically, financial aid covers the rest. Linda is at Scripps College, where tuition, room, and board, and the college's estimate of personal expenses, including books and travel, amounted to $5,150 in 1974, and Dave is at Stanford, where it costs $5,500. Both of them work during the summer in an electronics factory near their home, but neither of them was able to get steady enough work through the summer to clear the $500 that the College Scholarship Service thinks students should be able to contribute out of summer earnings.[1]

"They aren't extravagant, either of them, but it's hard for them because the other students where they go are wealthy. . . ." Mrs. Luback's voice trails off as we sit having coffee on the torn plastic chairs of her dinette set. Overhead a raw electric wire hangs down where the ceiling light should be. She follows my eye upward and shrugs. "Oh, that. We're so used to it now that we don't notice. After the fire, the insurance company took the low bidder and we were never able to get them to come back to finish the job."

Ruth Luback remembers the date of the fire and will to her dying day. It happened just before Linda was to go east for her freshman year. A loose wire somewhere started it and then there was an explosion that destroyed the garage and both their cars and the kitchen and all their appliances—it would cost more than $25,000 to replace everything, and of course the insurance didn't cover it all. The insurance company gave them $500 right away for a new washing machine, but it was six months before they got the kitchen working again, and all that time they had the expense of eating out.

"We tried to save for college," Mrs. Luback explained, "but it all went—even before the fire. Harold had to have an operation that wasn't covered by the medical insurance where he works. Now we're on the Kaiser-Permanente health plan, and a good thing, too, because the doctor found a clot in my leg—he says it's due to nervous strain—and that sounds as if there might be more big bills any day now. I'm supposed to take it easy."

The College Scholarship Service made an adjustment for the fire. "The Parents Confidential Statement goes into everything," Mrs. Luback says. "There's a place where you have to tell about your savings, your pension, the mortgage, the make of car you drive—it goes into much greater detail than the income tax, and it's hard to fill out. Most families don't keep all the numbers they want. The worst is, you can't get by on what they say the expenses will be. There are so many extras, like the long distance calls and trips home. It sounds niggling, but even parcel post runs up when you have to send them bulky parcels all the time.

"Some of our friends here in Anaheim think we're crazy. We could send them to Cal colleges for much less. But they're both so bright, we think they deserve the best. At Berkeley and the state schools the classes are so big that some of the students don't even see the professor—they have to watch the lecture by television from an overflow room. Now where Linda is, she's taking one course where she is the only student—and she has two professors all to herself!"

Ruth Luback's faith is in her children. She perks up when she talks about their achievements and their future, but most of the time she seems to be wondering how things got off the track. She and her husband have always tried hard to do the right thing. Mrs. Luback insists that Harold is a good man in his company— better, she says, than the young college fellows who have been jumped over him. But in 1974 he was still making the $16,000 a year to which he was raised at the height of the Vietnam War boom.

Harold went to work for the company right out of high school during World War II. His father had died and he had to support his mother. Ruth went to college for two years, but she quit after the war when returning veterans literally pushed civilians out of the popular courses because they had preference for the places available. She worked as a secretary until the children came, but never thought about returning to work until they were both in high school and able to take care of themselves when they came home. By then, however, she had to take care of her mother, who wasn't well enough to live alone. Ruth's mother is living in a nursing home, but now Ruth isn't well enough herself, and the expenses keep mounting.

For Ruth and Harold, the "good old days" were the years when the children were in high school and $16,000 looked bigger. Now Ruth takes a pocket adding machine along to the supermarket to be sure she isn't piling too many high-priced impulse items into her cart. She hasn't bought a new dress for a year. The cars they lost in the fire were bought new, but they have learned to get along ever since on a single used one.

"The truth is, we're drowning. . . . We're frightened. We can't see any way out."

"What do Dave and Linda say about it?" I couldn't help asking.

Ruth Luback didn't answer right away. "I don't know," she finally said. "They don't say much, and we don't bring it up."

Ruth Luback is not her right name, and the names of the colleges have been changed. But everything else, including the dollar figures, is accurate. A week after she promised to give me a Parents Confidential Statement to use as an example, she told me she couldn't do it.

"Harold says it's too risky," she explained. "Even if you change our name, the story might be traced to us. We can't afford to jeopardize the children's future. . . ."

"But what could happen?" I asked, genuinely curious.

"Well, they are both going to need loans and scholarships for years to come. . . ."

"And you are afraid that they might not get help because you had talked to a reporter?" I pushed.

"Yes. It could happen," she answered. "You hear all sorts of things. They both have California state scholarships, and we know that our governor is cutting back funds for education. . . . We're afraid. . . . We just can't take the chance."

THE PRICE OF A DEGREE

During the 1970s college costs rode the crest of inflation. They rose faster than personal income, faster than real estate prices. Between 1970 and 1974, for instance, the College Scholarship Service reported that average costs for students living at home and commuting to four-year private colleges rose 55 percent, compared with a rise of 36 percent for students commuting to four-year public colleges, and 34 percent for those attending two-year public community colleges.[2] The rises were somewhat lower for resident students, although the absolute charges were, of course, higher. In spite of highly publicized plans for expanding federal and state financial aid, there simply wasn't enough financial aid to go around. According to one estimate, no more than 2.7 million of the nine million students enrolled in institutions of higher education in 1973 received financial aid.[3]

Mercifully, perhaps, few families look the costs full in the face at the outset. Like the Lubacks, they just stumble into them. Most Princeton graduates of 1976, for instance, will be shocked to hear that the diploma handed to them at their graduation ceremony carries a price tag of $34,181 to the student, in addition to the investment made by taxpayers and philanthropists who support Princeton as an institution.[4]

There is nothing theoretical about that $34,181. In 1972–73, tuition and fees, room and board and personal expenses, including books and college travel estimated by the college, amounted to $5,130; these charges rose to $5,380 the next year, and $5,730 the year after that. Allowing for a 5 percent increase in 1975–76—no more than the increases in previous years—we arrive at a total cost for the four years of $22,256.[5] So many students stop or drop out during the course of a four-year career that parents are advised to throw in another third of a year as a margin, but let's assume our student goes straight through. Somehow, he and his parents have to come up with $22,256 to pay Princeton, buy books, get to the place, and keep him in the minimal pocket money Princeton administrators "suggest."

If you're thinking our student could have shaved those costs by spending less than the $650 suggested for personal expenses, books, and travel, forget it. As a matter of fact, while Princeton increased its tuition costs every year and its room and board costs every year but one, the college held the estimated personal expenses of students at the $650 figure, blithely disregarding such inescapable facts of student life as the rising price of textbooks and the increase in train fare between anywhere and Princeton Junction.

But this $22,256 is not the full cost. Legally speaking, a high-school graduate eighteen years old is considered an income tax deduction for his parents only under special circumstances. He's supposed to be self-supporting. According to the Census Bureau, a male eighteen-year-old high-school graduate earned an average of $5,834 in 1972. Those bright enough to get into Princeton probably would have been able to earn more, but never mind. The point is that attending Princeton is considered a full-time "job," so that while most students pick up odd jobs for extra spending money, they aren't expected to be full-time earners during the nine-month college year. That means that for three-fourths of the year, a student has to go without the money he would have earned if he were *not* in college. In 1972 this foregone income came to three-fourths of $5,834 for an eighteen-year-old, or $4,376.[6]

Counting foregone income sounds like the calculation of the woman who tried to convince her husband she was making money when she resisted the urge to buy a new hat. But it can become real as suddenly as a collegebound student can become the sole support of someone else. Michael Perper's father died two days before he was to leave for Colorado State College to prepare for a career in forestry. A few months later Michael was earning a living wage as a steamfitter's apprentice in New York City. He could look forward to earning $9.50 an hour as a journeyman steamfitter, more than is available in the woods.

If our Princeton-bound high-school graduate went straight to work instead of to college, he would have to feed, house, and keep himself supplied with pocket money, but he would be able to live a lot better—or at least he would have more money to spend on living— than the amount budgeted for maintaining him at Princeton. Whatever the psychological rewards of living on the Princeton campus (many students prefer to live off-campus), the dollar facts are that a student would have more to spend if he were employed full time in the labor force.

It is possible to calculate in cold numbers how much of the income a student would otherwise have earned he gave up in order to be a Princeton student. By deducting the room and board ($1,480) and personal expenses exclusive of books and travel to Princeton ($321) from the money he could have been expected to earn for the nine months ($4,376), we find that in 1972–73 he would have been exactly $2,575 ahead if he had taken a job instead of entering Princeton. His sophomore year, when he was nineteen, he would have been able to earn more, and he would have sacrificed $2,943, according to census figures. Foregone income for the four years 1972–76 adds up to $11,925. Add that to the official Princeton expense budget and the total is $34,181.

Princeton costs more, but the investment is considerable even at community colleges. A student can't really "save" much by living at home. An eighteen-year-old has to eat, sleep, and store his gear somewhere. When college is not feeding and housing him, his parents feel his presence financially at the supermarket checkout counter and in cars and phone bills.

In my home town of Poughkeepsie, New York, Dutchess Community College told freshmen entering in 1974 that they would need, for the year, $660 for tuition and fees and $2,000 for subsistence at home, personal expenses, and transportation to and from classes —an expense that usually means adding a car to the family. At the rate of $2,660 for the year, plus 5 percent more for 1975–76, a Dutchess Community Associate of Arts degree, Class of '76, will cost $5,453. If the Dutchess student had chosen to work and pay his parents the room and board suggested by the college for students, he would have had a bit more money left over to spend than the Princeton student would have had, but only because room and board at home and transportation for commuting turns out to be about $230 less than the Princeton living expenses.

These are the extremes. The colleges which enrolled the largest number of freshmen headed for a four-year degree in the fall of 1974 were the tax-supported colleges and universities which mushroomed, in building and enrollment, during the 1960s. Although a few were "free" to residents so far as tuition goes, most charged fees which even in California, the most generous state, were running between $100 and $200 a year. According to the College Scholarship Service, the average costs at four-year public institutions for freshmen entering in 1974 were $541 for tuition and fees, $1,116 for room and board. Add another $743 for books, clothes, transportation, and spending money, and the tab for the year comes to $2,400 for resident students. For nonresident students room and board at home is estimated at $704, making a total cost of $2,085.

Figuring that the CSS budgets for resident and commuter students at four-year state institutions will continue to rise as they did between 1970 and 1974 at an average rate of about 8.5 percent a year, the total cost of a four-year education in 1978 for resident students at state schools will be $10,894 and $9,464 for those who attend a state school and live at home.

Counting everything, including foregone income, an education at state-supported colleges comes to about half the cost of four years at Princeton, but it's still an impressive sum. And foregone income alone is a large enough amount to keep ghetto students from attending free-tuition, tax-supported colleges. In order to attract *them*, the College Scholarship Service thinks it may become necessary to pay *their families* some part of the financial support they are losing because an able-bodied young breadwinner has chosen to learn instead of earn.[7] Inner-city blacks can afford to go to "free" colleges only when they can't get paying jobs.

UNIFORMITY OF SACRIFICE

The "rich" have other problems. Rising college prices can bankrupt the well-to-do as fast as the medical bills which they are charged because they look as if they should be able to pay. Take the Johnsons. They are as real as the Lubacks, but their income is considerably higher.

The Johnsons look as if they had it made. Eric Johnson is an engineer earning $24,500 at IBM, which puts him in the top 5 percent of all salaries. The family lives in a substantial brick house in a wooded residential section of Poughkeepsie, New York, with three cars in the driveway, walls full of books, and the expectation that they ought to be able to send any or all of their five children to good colleges.

It wasn't until Cathy, the first to go, was accepted at Vassar, that the Johnsons realized how much college charges had risen. Luckily, IBM had moved the family to Poughkeepsie that year, so Cathy was able to get by on the money they had budgeted for college by living at home, even though that meant losing out on some of the unique experiences of that predominantly residential college. During Cathy's last year, her oldest brother John was entering Alfred University, and a year later the second son, Peter, headed for Worcester Polytechnic Institute.

The Johnsons had begun to look around for help. Like the Lubacks, they had read of scholarships going begging, only to find that you had to be an American Indian, or a war orphan, or a Cuban refugee to qualify. Cathy was an outstanding student, and they had hoped she could "win" a scholarship that would lighten the family load. The best known are National Merit Scholarships, widely publicized by the donor corporations, which include Mr. Johnson's employer, IBM. However, while this program provides more merit-based scholarships than any other, the program can help only 3,000 near-geniuses. They are a tiny drop in the bucket. In the 1970s, about three million college students were receiving aid of some sort—and in a typical year, 1972–73, for example, only one-third of those who applied for aid actually received any.[8]

The Johnsons quickly discovered that the huge sums supposedly available for college students weren't going to be much help to a family in their income bracket. John's expenses at Alfred were $2,800 for tuition and $850 for room and board, plus the inevitable travel to remote Alfred, New York, as well as pocket money. Although John won a New York State Regents Scholarship, his father's income was so high that he was given only $375 of the $1,500 he could have received if the Johnsons had less money. And since Peter was planning to attend an institution outside of New York State, he couldn't get any state help at all towards the $4,936 Worcester Polytechnic Institute now costs.

How rich is rich? Financial aid is supposed to go to those who need it. Whether grant or loan or student job, it is awarded on the basis of the gap between what the family and the student can be expected to contribute and the "student expense budget" prepared by the college the student will attend.

In order to be sure that every family with a child in college will be aided on a strictly equal basis—the principle is "uniformity of sacrifice"—the needs analyses for almost all colleges are calculated by the College Scholarship Service (CSS), an arm of the College Entrance Examination Board which prepares and administers the famous Scholastic Aptitude Test. (American College Testing, a similar service for small Midwest colleges, works the same way.) CSS designs the forms and every year processes through its computers more than a million applications.

The principles guiding CSS are noble: uniformity of sacrifice, need rather than merit in determining the amount of aid, safeguarding the interest of the student regardless of the behavior of the parent. But anomalies haunt the application. Does a family loaded with debt "need" more aid than a factory worker who has been driving a cab weekends for years to build up a college fund? Yes, says CSS. Shocking, say those who have saved.

The operative document in needs analysis is a forbidding form called "Parents Confidential Statement." It looks like the long form of the income tax return, but it actually demands much more information. The form is complicated in an effort to be absolutely fair and to take into consideration all the myriad factors which make financial circumstances different. The Lubacks, for example, were able to get more financial aid because of the fire.

At Vassar, the Parents Confidential Statement is required of all students applying to live at Ferry House, a small, chummy dormitory where a few students can save a little on room and board by doing all their own cooking and housekeeping. Cathy Johnson, who lived there one year, says that a physician whose daughter wanted to join them took one look at the form sent to him as a routine measure and vetoed the plan: "I don't care where you want to live," he is reported to have snorted. "I just won't answer those questions."

It is easy to see why. A father or mother who runs a business is required to list all assets and the rate at which they are depreciated, as well as all income and expenses, including nontaxable expenses. Specifically "all gifts, inheritance, bequests, child support, military subsistence and quarters allowances, allotments, and aid from friends or relatives." In addition, the instructions go on to say, "include an estimate of other income such as free housing, food, and services." They want to know how much life insurance the head of the family carries and whether he has a retirement plan.

The computer makes allowances for the age of the parents, and there's also consideration for "such emergency or extraordinary expenses as payments for alimony, child support, uninsured natural disaster, termite control, unreimbursed tuition for your education [the *parents'* education, that is], nursing-home care, funerals, legal fees, water, street, and sewer assessments (installation only), and unreimbursed moving expenses." But the instructions warn, "Do not include such expenses as payments for home appliances and furnishings, cars, medical insurance, retirement plans, contributions, commuting expenses, household help, and car repairs."

In order to show parents what's expected of them, the applications for 1974–75 included a filled out sample—the Parents Confidential Statement as it might have been submitted for student Mary Brown.

From it the computer learns, among other intimate details, that Mary Brown lives with her father, a fifty-year-old sheet-metal worker, her mother, a forty-nine-year-old part-time typist, and her younger brother and sister in a termite-prone house that the Browns bought for $8,600 in 1950 and have insured for $12,000, al-

though they put its present market value at $15,000.
We know it is termite-prone because the Browns are
claiming an emergency expense of $30, explaining, in
the proper space, that "we live in an old house and
must have termite inspection each year." Other items
disclose that Mr. Brown has to pay $90 union dues,
that he owes part of a hospital bill for his daughter's
operation, and that although he received a raise to
$10,000, his wife's income will be lower because "due
to ill health, she will not work as many hours this
year." The upshot of all these figures is that the Browns
would be expected to pay $1,237 toward Mary's col-
lege expenses, and Mary herself should contribute $975
from earnings, savings, and gifts.

CSS merely establishes need. How much Mary gets,
and what proportion will be in the form of grants,
loans, or work–study jobs will depend on which school
she chooses, and the school she chooses may depend in
turn on the "mix" of the aid package it offers.

Very little of the financial aid comes in the form of a
direct grant—what used to be called a "scholarship"
and is now called a "gift" to distinguish it from aid that
is ultimately borne by the student in the form of a loan
or a job. And the "gift" portion of the package is
limited. It's up to the colleges to allocate the aid from
the resources they have and give it to the students they
most want. The Lubacks and families like them can't
always save much money by sending their children to
state schools. The private colleges may give a student
more aid than he or she could receive at a state school.
The general idea is that need depends on the expenses
of the school, and aid depends on need.

This sounds fine in theory, but it raises trying problems in practice. One student we talked to thinks that
the aid she expected when her father lost his job did not
come through because they still owned their house. Financial aid officers would deny this, but since there is

never quite enough money to go around, judgments have to be made which are worrisome enough to the recipients to warrant the squeamishness of the Lubacks.

In 1974 Susan Beaver's father, a pharmaceutical salesman earning $12,000, was afraid that his next raise would cost more than it was worth in financial aid for his two daughters in college. Susan was at Kirkland, receiving financial aid amounting to $2,841, far more than her older sister at the Fredonia branch of the State University of New York, because Kirkland costs more. She *thinks* that she came out better because at the state schools "they have so many kids who need financial aid."

Susan has epilepsy, so her financial aid packet includes a $1,000 New York State grant for disabled students in addition to a $750 Kirkland grant, a $1,000 student loan, and a federally funded Basic Educational Opportunity grant amounting to $91. This last is an odd amount because anything more than $100 would be subtracted from the $750 outright gift. It's the same with her campus job. Kirkland allows her to work at the college for up to $350 and keep it "for herself," but if she earns any more, they'll deduct it from her grant. Campus jobs are counted as part of financial aid and doled out on the basis of need, like work relief jobs during the Great Depression.

Needy students who get little or no aid are likely to be in college because their parents are willing to sacrifice above and beyond the standard of sacrifice prescribed by the intricate formulas of the College Scholarship Service. Mothers go back to work. Fathers borrow on their life insurance or moonlight. The Johnsons have switched to powdered milk, but you can't save much on food when you have seven to feed. They're talking about selling their house in order to generate the cash to send Peter to Worcester Tech.

"It is just like starting all over again, like the first

days we were married," one mother says. "It isn't easy, but it is simple. We don't *change* plans for trips. We just don't *go*, period. We just give up everything."

But not every parent is willing to "just give up everything" or even what the College Scholarship Service figures they ought to give up on the basis of the Parents Confidential Statement. A lot of middle-income parents are simply giving up *college*. In the spring of 1974, private colleges were alarmed at the decline not only in applications for admission, but even more ominously, in applications for *financial aid*.

Alberta Arthurs, Radcliffe dean of admissions, financial aid and women's education, thought the decline might be due to misinformation on the part of middle-income parents. They've been "led to believe that they can't afford a Harvard or Radcliffe education and that scholarships are reserved only for the very low income groups. That simply isn't true." Admissions officers of Ivy League private colleges began to think about expensive public relations programs to "inform" parents in the $12,000 to $18,000 bracket that there was "plenty of money" for middle-income students.

Privately, the college hustlers admitted that the reluctance of parents was more serious than "ignorance" which could be overcome by a program of "education" (public relations). "Middle-income parents simply don't like to fill out the forms," one officer told us. When interviewed, some of them blurted out what seems closer to the truth: "For middle-income families, a college education competes with a second car, a color television set, or a vacation—and college may lose."

Quite so. College is worth more to some middle-income families than to others, and the attempt to shame families into sending their kids to college when they'd really rather have a second car bodes no good for child or parent. It is chilling to consider the undercurrent of resentment the abstemious Lubacks must feel toward their two children or the burden of guilt children must bear every time they "goof off" for a few days.

Some parents take extreme measures and get enough financial aid for their children by removing themselves from the scene completely, like the men who desert their families to make them eligible for welfare. A student is "emancipated" when he receives less than $600 support from his parents and does not appear on their income tax return as a dependent. The financial need of an emancipated student is judged on the basis of the Students Confidential Statement (SCS) alone, instead of on the SCS plus the PCS (Parents Confidential Statement).

Sometimes a student is emancipated by a financially sophisticated parent. The parents of one student, who were far too rich to warrant any scholarship help at all, arranged for her to be self-supporting so that she could qualify for a student loan. She maintained herself during the summer by doing chores around the yacht club for her room and board. As soon as her loans come due, after graduation, her father intends to pay them, and he will be ahead of the game because he will have invested her tuition money in treasury notes or certificates of deposit that return him more than twice as much as his daughter has to pay in interest for her government-subsidized student loans.

All "emancipated" students aren't welfare cheats, of course. Some are genuinely estranged from their parents. After graduating from high school, young people increasingly put distance between themselves and their homes, and many simply don't ever return. Other emancipated students want to spare their parents the financial sacrifice of putting them through college. And still others are making the logical response to the familiar clincher of parental authority: "As long as you live under this roof, you'll do as I say. When you are on your own, you can do as you please."

Whatever the circumstances, emancipation is rising.

Two-thirds of sixty-three institutions who reported to CSS on the financial aid outlook for the fall of 1974 called the increase in applications from self-supporting students "dramatic." The rise can be attributed, in part at least, to the rigors of the Parents Confidential Statement and the dubious concept of uniformity of sacrifice.

The concept sounds fair, but "uniformity" means that you get only as much help as someone else thinks you need. In effect, that "someone else"—the educational establishment—tells you how to spend your money. It's not surprising that some people have begun to rebel against this attempt to enforce the same values and priorities on all.

You can argue about how much parents ought to pay, but the fact of the matter is that there's a limit to what any particular parent is willing to sacrifice, and when that limit is reached, that parent will duck out. What concerns us here is that more and more parents are reaching that limit, and as they do, more of the costs of college are coming out of the hides of the students themselves.

3

The Cost to Students

College students are supposed to be a privileged class. Establishment voices are always telling them so, in the same admonishing tone that is still used to remind women how much better off they are "really" than men. And, like women and other victims of discrimination, some students gratefully buy whatever psychic comfort is available. How can they possibly think they are being badly treated when they have such bright futures ahead of them?

Feminists will recognize the fallacy. Like the image of the pampered wife, the facts are otherwise for many of the supposedly carefree college students. They pay in money for much of their own education—and, as we shall see, through the nose. They pay even more dearly in the loss of independence and status that goes with their "privileges."

COLLEGE STUDENTS IN DEBT

In the fall of 1973, Friendly's Steak and Sundae Shop in Longmeadow, Massachusetts, the company's only complete dinner restaurant, appointed its first woman shift supervisor. Diana Coleman, Russell Sage '73, got along fine with the men she supervised, and she peppered her boss with just the kind of fresh-eyed suggestions that big business hopes to get from college trainees. But she was not training to become a manager.

"I have absolutely no desire to make Friendly's a career," Diana wrote me, "but since I so desperately need the money and the job is near enough home so that I can bank most of what I earn, I must put up with it for a while. Meanwhile, without offending anyone, I am trying to dream up some sort of sociological study on the Friendly Corporation to make my time more interesting and worthwhile."

Diana was the star student in a class I taught at Russell Sage. She was a sociology major headed for graduate school, and that's where she would have been a year later, if she had had only herself to consider. Diana's plight is a cautionary tale for middle-class students whose parents are too proud to apply for financial aid. Her father, a college professor, flatly refused to divulge the information demanded on the Parents Confidential Statement. Instead, Diana and her father and her mother agreed to split her expenses three ways. Diana's mother met her part of the bargain by going back to work, but Diana was never able to earn enough of her third, so she had to borrow $1,500 from a family fund. She's working at Friendly's to pay the fund back in time for her sister's first year in college.

Nobody knows how many students graduate with debts to their families that must be repaid to send a younger brother or sister to college, but we do know about their debts to institutions. As of June 30, 1973, 3.5 million students owed $4.8 *billion* to banks which had lent them money under the federally backed Guaranteed Student Loan Program, and 2.4 million students owed their colleges and schools $2 billion that had been lent to them under the National Direct Student Loan Program.[1] All this money—and the totals are growing —is ultimately owed to Uncle Sam, who lets students take ten years to pay at interest rates so far below the commercial price of money that banks don't really like to bother servicing the no-risk loans.

Nobody likes to saddle young people with debts that force them to take jobs they don't want, but with the deepening crunch on money for college students, loans have become an indispensable part of every aid package. Programs backed by the government aren't supposed to lend more than $10,000 to any one student, and most financial aid officers try to hold the debt down to half that much, but a student who can wangle outside loans in addition—and not always from members of the family—can easily graduate owing more. In California, where debt seems to come more easily than in other parts of the country, I heard of medical and law school couples who expected to owe as much as $30,000 on their two degrees. Out of their first paychecks, they would have to start repaying $200 a month.

Doctors and lawyers and engineers may be able to carry sizeable mortgages on their lifetime earnings, but the government backs loans to students in all majors, and, of course, to both sexes and all races, regardless of differences in lifetime earnings expectancy. In Modesto, California, a divorced mother supporting two small children complained to me that she could not get a loan big enough to cover child care while she pursued a two-year Associate of Arts degree in creative writing. I was shocked that she was incurring any debt at all for a program which was not likely to pay off. What she clearly needed, at least while her children were small, was a vocational course that would improve her immediate earning power, but there was nobody to tell her this. The financial aid officer was not supposed to consider her major, and the academic advisor paid no attention to her financial responsibilities. I could not help thinking that she would never be able to pay anything back on the loans she already had, and the taxpayers would be the eventual losers.

A banker told me that her bank was not pursuing students who didn't pay their loans. "We expect the defaults to grow worse," she added. "Teachers and social science majors can get loans, but they can't get jobs. A lot of these loans will just *never* get paid." As of February 1974, nearly 7,000 students had filed in bankruptcy, and many others couldn't pay because they were on welfare. Defaults were only 1 percent of all loans, but the dollars and students involved doubled between September 1973 and February 1974.[2]

Low-income students who need loans most desperately are often so afraid of debt that they will quit school rather than borrow. They've seen friends and relatives trapped by installment payments and they want none of it. In 1974, for instance, Nikki Turner was thinking of quitting the Dayton Art Institute "because of the money." She likes art, but she isn't sure she can make a living at it, and she doesn't want to have to go to work with the responsibility of a debt hanging over her head. Many women don't like taking out loans that a future husband might legally have to assume.

But men dread debt, too. "I didn't know why I was in college," a male dropout told us. "And I didn't see going into debt to find out. I figured I could sort out my mind just as well doing a nine-to-five job that would leave my mind free."

For those who don't want to go into debt, jobs are the final resort, and more students every year are coming to it.

STUDENTS AT WORK

"Work–study" jobs doled out by colleges as part of the financial aid packet underwritten by the federal government are supposed to be related, if possible, to the student's academic work, but in 1974–75, those who needed aid were "awarded" such jobs as campus guards, cafeteria workers, janitors, snow shovellers, and chapel bell ringers. Some were doing "scut" work, shelving books in the library, sweeping out the laboratories, and feeding the white mice, which can be interpreted as "educational" only because they bring the worker into environmental contact with the intellectual life.

Some work–study jobs are obviously "boondogles," the term coined in the Great Depression of the '30s for creating jobs for the unemployed by thinking up work that really did not need to be done. But as colleges grow big, they have come to depend on this reservoir of cheap help. Employing students at cut-rate wages appeals to efficiency–minded administrators; it's like heating the house by burning the garbage. College costs would be higher if there were not this device for getting students to do "their own" work—as housework done by housewives used to be called. In order to maintain this form of support for higher education, the minimum wage rise signed into law during 1974 provided that full-time students working no more than twenty hours a week may be paid 85 percent of the legal minimum.

Summer employment used to be regarded as optional, at least so far as colleges were concerned. Now summer earnings are programmed into the financial aid package as part of the Students Confidential Statement. Upperclassmen are expected to *clear* $600 towards their college costs, a neat trick if you have to pay commercial rates for your room and board. Hence the popularity of live-in resort jobs, especially resort jobs in places like Cape Cod where a certain amount of resorting is available after work.

When times are good, this is fine. But the slightest downturn hits the travel and resort market hard. In the summer of 1974, resorts from the Berkshires to the Poconos to Yellowstone in the West were hiring fewer college students, and the U.S. Immigration and Naturalization Service ruled that foreign students would not be allowed to earn during the summer because there were not enough summer jobs to go around for our own.

Before the big boom in enrollment, students who "worked their way through" were regarded as local heroes. Their diplomas were more valuable to some employers on the theory that their willingness to work demonstrated unusual ambition and self-discipline. And people who employed undergraduates felt they were doing something noble, like contributing to the United Fund. It was easy to feel this way, when the only students who worked were the few poor boys who were ambitious enough to aspire to college. Rich boys didn't do it.

Now all kinds of students earn, and not just those on formal financial aid. In 1973, a third of all full-time undergraduates were in the labor force, working an average of sixteen hours weekly for women and twenty hours for men. The College Scholarship Service was dismayed to report that many more California students from the upper brackets were earning bigger sums than in the 1960s. According to one California dean, "the folks at home just aren't shelling out."

Students would like rewarding or career-related jobs, but very few of them get to work in museums, on newspapers, for travel agencies or research organizations, or as companions to rich families on their travels abroad. And only a select handful get apprentice-type jobs handed out as a public relations gesture by a small number of organizations such as Bethlehem Steel.

With these rare exceptions, college students work strictly for the money. Protected socially in their status as students, and generally less snobbish than their parents, undergraduates do not scorn the manual or the menial. A male student found he could earn up to $1,000 one summer shoveling grain out of Great Lakes transports. Students are commendably adaptable as recruits to the labor force. One undergraduate prized her part-time job as ticket taker in the local movie theater because, like babysitting, it permitted her to study on company time.

"It's hard, physical work, and you sleep good every night after it," a student at Marist College who sanded my living room floor in Poughkeepsie said. "I spend every summer doing this work for my uncle. The pay is good, but I'm glad when school starts." Construction work, available in the summer, is the high end of student employment. It pays so well that it is beginning to attract women students for whom the highest-paying traditional job has long been that of "cocktail waitress" in a good "lounge" or "club" where patrons are free with their tips.

Far more typical of the student population is John Bianchi, a student at Bernard Baruch College in New York City. He was living at home with his mother, an office worker, and his father, a cab driver, and working in a supermarket, earning $40 a week at the minimum wage of $1.85 an hour sweetened by tips. Because supermarkets are open for long hours, they provide work that fits college schedules. John broke into the newspapers, and out of what has become a student job ghetto, when an elderly recluse whose groceries he had delivered willed him a fortune estimated at $50,000. When reporters caught up with him, John had been promoted to cashier, and was earning $95 a week.

Student employment is so essential that nobody likes to think hard about what it is doing to students, the labor force, and the attitude of the next generation towards career work. Employers have begun to count on students for the dead-end work against which blacks and women have rebelled. The student job ghetto also supplies the part-time and seasonal workers who can be hired and fired as needed to iron out employment peaks and valleys in the growing service industries such as hotels and restaurants.

The parallel between the economic role of blacks, women, and students is not exact, but is instructive.[3]

When you cut through the layers of prescriptive piety evoked by any consideration of the status of the young, you can recognize the similarities. Like the old "nigger jobs," the pay for "women's jobs" and "student jobs" is based on demographic status rather than on economic contribution. These jobs do not come with pensions, sick leave, medical insurance, overtime, or the other fringe benefits which now amount to 26 percent of compensation in "regular" industrial jobs.[4] They are seldom unionized.

Ugly labor practices, reminiscent of the Great Depression, have begun to appear. A mother in Detroit and another in Cleveland asked me what government agency they could contact about the minimum wage law. Both complained that their teen-agers had been working long hours at less than legal pay during busy summer weekends at local hotels and restaurants.

Unions fear the competition of cut-rate student workers. The first formal protest came from postal workers. The U.S. Post Office has pioneered equal opportunity. It was the first big employer to offer blacks promotion, and one of its do-good programs has been the employment of students part time to help them earn their way through college. But in the fall of 1973, the number of student workers was limited by agreement with the American Postal Workers Union.

Another way to protect the regular workers is to require employers to pay students the full union or minimum wage. Resorts were among those who lobbied for the exemption of students from the minimum wage law. They claimed they had been using fewer students in part because the minimum wage had been raised to the point where it was cheaper to hire older and more experienced workers instead. At Ohio University, full-time, nonacademic employees supported part-time student workers who struck for recognition of a student workers union in 1974.

The most important thing about the employment of

students is that it makes the status of students less special. "It's getting harder and harder to distinguish between the students who are working to earn their way through school and the students who are going to school in the time they can spare from their jobs," a student counselor at Allegheny College in Pittsburgh observed. "Both are part time. And both may do the same kind of paid work. It's a matter of emphasis, I guess."

Students who work their way through college at the dull, dead-end jobs they would have had if they had not gone to college learn to support themselves without expecting much from the job but the paycheck and the sociability that goes with routine jobs. They may simply carry over these attitudes to the very similar jobs available to college graduates of the 1970s. The student job ghetto that is now a part of the college experience may be turning students away from the Protestant work ethic. Instead of inspiring working-class students to pursue careers, college may be teaching the striving middle classes to invest less of themselves in the job and more of themselves in "living a little." Most of the undergraduates who defined themselves as "prelaw" in 1973 and 1974 were quick to explain, when I asked them why, that they didn't intend to practice. "My father knows nothing about art. All he knows is law," one of the many exemplars of the New Vocationalism told us. "I want to be a lawyer, but I don't want to be a lawyer like that."

For most students the really important thing about paid work is that it makes you an adult. The term "adult" crops up frequently in student talk and in odd ways. "How old do you have to be to be 'adult'?" I asked a twenty-two-year-old Dartmouth senior who spoke as if he were not one.

"No special age," he said. Legally he's right. You can vote and serve in the armed forces at eighteen, and since the passage of the Twenty-sixth Amendment some states have conferred other rights on eighteen-year-olds, but in many states a man who can vote can't marry without parental consent, nor can he sign a contract. But legal rights were not what he had in mind.

"When will *you* become an adult?" I asked.

"When I don't have to ask my father for money anymore," he blurted, shame-faced.

On campus, "adult" means self-supporting.

Can a student become an adult by earning all his expenses, including his tuition, without any scholarship aid? Pressed for the definition, most students give a dubious yes, adding that of course you can't earn all your keep and go to school full time. A student who is "really" self-supporting passes out of the status of studentry and becomes an adult who happens to be going to school. He or she is no longer one of us, but one of "them"—the adults.

Students who share part of the economic costs also bear the psychological cost of continued dependence. Parents who sacrifice to send their children to college do not always realize the burden of guilt they unwillingly saddle on their children. Listen to students talk, and it comes up all the time.

Susan Beaver wasn't sure, when she was first accepted, that she wanted to go to Kirkland. "I decided that it really wasn't what I wanted to do, because I didn't know where I'd be going, and I really felt like a burden to my parents because I've cost them so much in medical bills," she recalls. "I felt that somebody who was so unsure about what she wanted to do shouldn't go to college. I thought maybe I should wait." She ended by going, though, because Kirkland "appealed to me," but she admits she feels guilty about what her mother and father go through to send her—and particularly about the raise her father isn't sure he wants because it may disqualify her for aid. If it wasn't for college, the raise would mean more comfort for her parents.

"They feel their scraping is worth the effort, and that's another pressure," she adds. "I can't let them down. I enjoy college, but enjoyment is almost secondary to knowing that I've got to stay in here and have to make it."

When I asked my Russell Sage students to project what they thought they would be doing when they were as old as their mothers, a surprising number cited the cost of college as a reason why they would have few children or none. An educational system that would not strap parents figured in several of their utopias. Students concerned about the sacrifice their parents are making want to have a good and clear reason for exacting this sacrifice. It makes them uneasy the minute they feel, like Susan Beaver, that they "don't know where they're going."

For many sensitive middle-class students, the burden is more than they can bear, so they drop out to prove they can make it on their own. "Dave saw his leave as a challenge to himself," a case history of a 1974 study of leaves of absence from Harvard begins, "to see what he could do with a year off, and whether, in fact, he could support himself during that time."[5]

Independence—proving they could be their own persons—figured heavily in the reasons given by a majority as to why their stopping out was successful. "It was wonderful to be completely self-reliant, to be successful at work and to make it on my own," said a Harvard senior. Somewhat relieved, most students who take time off to test their self-sufficiency come back to college with renewed self-confidence and direction. Many, however, told us frankly that while college is a pleasant place to be—and beats working—it would not be worth it if they had to pay for it themselves.

"You can meet new people and learn how to get along with them anywhere," said a Lafayette undergraduate. "College is the only place you can do it without having to earn a living."

A student who worked as a common laborer digging the foundation for a faculty house recalls the sudden envy with which he regarded classmates walking by his trench. "There they were," he remembers thinking, "walking around with nothing to do but have fun." Once out of the ditch and back in class, however, he wondered why he was bothering with college at all.

"If I had to pay for it," one student told us, "it would be a lot more serious for me than it is now," and he adds that his situation is such that he really doesn't have to worry about earning a living.

Those who do, take a much more critical view. Sheila Feldman looks back on the University of Buffalo with mixed feelings. Although she is an associate editor on a magazine—a job coveted by most college graduates— she isn't sure she would go to college again to get the degree that led to the job, "especially if I had to pay for college myself. On balance, I'm glad I went, but it was good for me mainly because my parents were willing to pay for it."

Students who have to pay a large part of their own way in college understandably demand more of it and are discouraged more easily than those who are paying for their education in psychological dependence alone. Brown University's financial aid officer thinks that this explains the drop in applications for financial aid, particularly in the Ivy League colleges which have been offering more of the aid than formerly in the form of loans and jobs. Rather than work, middle-class students have been going to state colleges where they can make it without applying for financial "aid."

But no matter how little money is available on campus, it is more than many young people could otherwise get. College can be a form of welfare for students who are literally paid to go. Most people forget that the biggest single nonfamily source of money for college expenses is, of course, the G.I. Bill of Rights, which provides living expenses for veterans. The third biggest source, after the programs administered by the Office of Education, comes from Social Security payments to dependents which end at age eighteen unless the recipient is attending college.[6]

Financial aid on the basis of need rather than merit creates some unexpected financial incentives for attending college. Scholarships big enough to compete with jobs have steered enough high-school graduates to the campus to warrant provisions in most scholarship funds against awards larger than the actual expense incurred. A former Rensselaer student stayed on campus just long enough to negotiate a student loan that would be big enough to support him for months after he dropped out.

In 1974 "educationally disadvantaged" students in California could get financial aid covering the whole cost of their education, including living expenses, up to $2,200 a year. Quite often the package, which integrates several programs, adds up to more than the student could earn or collect on welfare. Many frequently have trouble with their studies, and on a number of California campuses other students and faculty volunteers have set up tutoring centers where the disadvantaged can get the extra coaching they need to stay in school—and receive the aid. Whenever I asked how many of the tutees would drop out of school if they could get more money doing something else, I received the same blank stare, and the same chilling answer: "Why all of them, of course." These students know why they're studying—to keep their welfare checks. It is a subtle form of coercion by intellectuals who assume that everyone must go through the academic mill. The assumption should be profoundly disturbing to those who sincerely respect basic differences between equally worthy human beings.

The pay is not exactly munificent. At American River College in Sacramento where tuition is free, an eighteen-year-old black freshman drew $40 a month in

1974 as a disadvantaged student and was awarded, in addition, a college job as a file clerk at $1.60, permitting her to earn up to $75 a month more. "If she is lucky, and there are no vacations, she can earn $115 a month," a black counselor pointed out. "But, this means that she must never miss any time out of school, never take time off from work to study."

Her budget is tight. She gives her aunt on welfare $30 for room and board. Other items are books, which cost her $31.76 in one month, her student activity card for $15, and supplies, $10. The item she described to us in greatest detail was lunch: Three times a week, she said, she treated herself to a "soup-plate lunch with potato chips and apple—$1.35 or $1.40" in the college cafeteria. She added that she had nothing left over for movies or clubs on which other students spent money, and under miscellaneous she listed $5 for "extra food, thread for mending, magazine."

Her budget is a study in relative deprivation. Better off than others on welfare, she felt worse off than almost everyone she encountered during her school days. It must have been hard to resist the hot food going down that cafeteria line with fellow students who could afford to load up on anything that looked good—and very easy to lose interest in her studies when she knew that for her, at least, graduation wouldn't necessarily lead to a better job. In a loose labor market, the best that many disadvantaged students can hope to get from a degree is preference for the unskilled, dishwashing-type jobs that don't use college training.

In California students may also go to college without losing welfare rights for dependents. In 1971 the president of the student body at Mills College was a black mother of four on welfare. In 1972 a federal judge ruled that a New York City mother had the right to retain her Federal Aid to Families with Dependent Children while attending college as a full-time student, even though she already had a skill that enabled her to earn a living. The suit was brought by Fannie Jefferies, who quit her job as a typist at $125 a week and enrolled in Queensborough Community College to become a teacher. Between scholarships, loans, and the welfare for which she could qualify when she was unemployed, she was able to make it.

Every institution, from high school to graduate school, has some students who are in school because they can't get work. College graduates hang around the old alma mater, scrounging on students or faculty or merely bunking in together and supporting themselves as best they can at odd jobs. Those who hope that an extra degree will improve their job chances may take teaching assistantships. These pay so little that their dependents qualify for and often receive welfare. The communities in some university towns resemble the ominous communities of squatters attracted to cities in developing African and South American nations by the hope of employment.

Denied participation in a "real," or adult, world—participation that in our society is almost equivalent to jobholding or economic independence—young adults are forced into the subversive activities and attitudes natural to the excluded. It is natural, of course, to denigrate an activity you are denied. "Making it" has always been derided by those who cannot and especially those who are arbitrarily denied the opportunity to do so. Blacks, women, and the retired are sympathetic to the sentiments that "there is more to life than money." What is new, and alarming for the survival of the work ethic, is that an increasing number of young adults are beginning to share this feeling. I believe that the counterculture is sparked, in greater part than anyone will admit, by the conviction of young people that even with a college education many of them will never "make it."

This despair, this sense of exclusion, expresses itself in a student way of life which glorifies scrounging, tol-

erates rip-offs, and sympathizes intuitively with enemies
of the established authorities. At Wright State University in Ohio they tell a story about the experiment conducted on that campus in furloughing prisoners to college. The first group of prisoners were carefully chosen.
They were of college age and dressed in the blue
denims that are the campus uniform. In order to give
them a chance to make friends, their identity was
shielded. Fellow students, noticing the surveillance of
dormitory authorities, decided they were "narcs" (nar-
cotics agents) and would have nothing to do with them.
In self-defense the prisoners demanded that they be
allowed to surface. When their true identities were re-
vealed, they immediately became popular with their law-
abiding classmates.

Some students develop scrounging to a high art. "We
had a guy last year who had an ice cream maker," one
student recalls. "We couldn't afford cream on our
budget, but he discovered that he could fill up a milk
bottle with cream from one of the dispensers in the
dining hall of the dorm next to us when no one was
looking. Thanks to him, we had lovely ice cream when-
ever we wanted it." Students supposedly cooking for
themselves in student apartments regularly scrounge
food from dining halls and carry away the silver and
glasses they need.

Students take off for far places and even foreign
countries with little or no money in their pockets.
Travel is, of course, by hitch, a mode of transportation
so favored that it is practiced even when fares are made
available by "adults." And hitching is not confined to
highways. According to one underground newspaper, a
student looking for a plane hitch should go to the airport, find out where the private planes are kept, dress
conservatively (skirts for women), ask politely, and
wait patiently. Bring a book, the newspaper advises,
because you may have a long wait.

Food and lodging are widely available from friends,

friends of friends, friends of parents, or even parents themselves. Failing any of these resources, a student may drop in on a strange campus and simply add himself or herself to whatever housing or feeding is provided for as long as the stay suits his or her fancy. This kind of Robin Hood economy is, of course, a form of petty thievery, whether it is practiced in student America or Sherwood Forest in Merrie England.

Society pays a heavy price when it excludes any group from the mainstream, whether that group is based on race, sex, age, or social origin, but the excluded also pay, if not in prison sentences, then in self-destructive resentment and misdirected energy. College students are merely the newest "beleaguered minority" to hurt themselves at least as much as they hurt those who exclude them.

4

The Dumbest Investment You Can Make

College isn't supposed to be for the money. College catalogues never mention high earnings as a goal, and money gets a low priority when parents, students, and alumni are asked to choose among expectations of college or, indeed, among lifetime goals.

This low priority doesn't mean that college students don't care about money. Quite the reverse. They don't talk about money and college or even money and jobs in the same breath, because, as sociologist David Gottlieb reported in *Youth and the Meaning of Work*, an exhaustive investigation of student attitudes, "an adequate income is expected."[1] For many years, a majority of entering freshmen polled by the American Council on Education have agreed with the statement: "The benefit of college is monetary." Some of the first-generation college students are quite willing to come out and say so. "As far as I'm concerned, college is strictly for the money," a blue-collar student at a community college told us. But most will deny that money is their only motive for going.

It's a good thing for colleges that students think they are getting something more out of their education than increased income. For if students hoped only for money, and each student had a banker with a computer at his elbow, enrollments would drop much further below expectations than they did during the enrollment recession of the mid-1970s. I say this only because I persuaded a young banker in Poughkeepsie, New York, Stephen G. Necel, to compare college as an investment in future earnings with other investments available in the booming money market of 1974.

For the sake of argument, Steve and I invented a young man whose rich uncle undertook to give him, in cold cash, the cost of a four-year education at any college he chose—and he didn't have to spend the money on college. He could invest it, save it, or blow it—but he had to explain why. After bales of computer paper had been filled with figures, we had our mythical student write to his uncle: "Since you said I could spend the money foolishly if I wished, I am going to blow it all—on Princeton." We concluded that in strictly financial terms, college is the dumbest investment a young man can make.

In the course of our statistical workout, we discovered that an investment in potential future earnings does not compare very precisely with other forms of investment, but one figure stands out as clearly valid and significant: A Princeton graduate of 1956 could expect to earn 12.5 percent on the comparatively modest cost of four years at that institution then, but a member of the class of 1976 could expect to realize only a 9.5 percent return on his investment.[2] As human capital economists and government statisticians patiently pointed out to us, the calculations we made required heroic assumptions. We freely admit as much. But we feel that our assumptions are just as valid as those behind the calculations that have been used for more than a generation to convince taxpayers as well as students that college is worth it—"even" in money.

"A college education is among the very best investments you can make in your entire life. It will lead to an enormous payoff in increased earnings, in brighter job prospects, and in a host of intangible cultural and social benefits for which you always will be grateful."

That's what Sylvia Porter said when a 9.4 percent hike in college costs was reported by the College Scholarship Service for 1974–75.

That bit about "enormous payoff in increased earnings" was especially appealing to the class of 1976 bracing for a senior year that was going to cost an unexpected 36 percent more than their freshman year. Sylvia Porter is one of the most widely read and most credible of American economists, and when she talks about "enormous payoff in increased earnings" she ought to know whereof she speaks.

Newsmen had been equally encouraging a few weeks earlier, when the Census Bureau reported that as of 1972 a man who completed four years of college could expect to earn $199,000 *more* between the ages of twenty-two and sixty-four than a man who had only a high-school diploma.[3] Of course, everyone was earning more money, in dollars, than ever before, and headlines applauded the big numbers: COLLEGE MAN CAN EXPECT LIFETIME EARNINGS OF $601,000.

Headlines scream the conventional wisdom because their writers have time for little else. But an enterprising desk man who took a sharp pencil and a compound interest table to these two reports, issued little more than a week apart, could have supported a headline which would have attracted much wider attention:

PRINCETON DOESN'T PAY OFF IN EARNINGS
1972 High School Graduate Ahead
If He Banks the Cost of College
and Goes Right to Work

If a male Princeton-bound high-school graduate of 1972 had put the $34,181[4] his diploma would eventually cost him into a savings bank at 7.5 percent interest compounded daily, he would have at the retirement age of sixty-four a total of $1,129,200 or $528,200 more than the earnings of a male college graduate and more than five times as much as the $199,000 extra he could expect to earn between twenty-two and sixty-four because he was a college, rather than merely a high-school, graduate.[5]

Okay, you say. That's Princeton—just about the most expensive college in the 1974–75 list put out by the College Scholarship Service of the College Entrance Examination Board. How about a state-supported college?

The payoff on the lower investment in a public college education is, of course, higher to the student because other people—in this case the taxpayers—are putting up part of the capital for him. Even so, the return is not as much higher as it sounds, because the biggest part of the investment in college is the earnings a student foregoes to attend. These costs he bears himself.[6]

Preserving his college money as capital isn't much fun for the frugal high-school graduate. He can't spend more than he earns as a high-school graduate, while the college graduate with whom we are comparing him gets to live it up with the extra money he earns. And the difference—particularly as both grow older—is considerable. If the college graduate banks the yearly difference, at the 7.5 percent savings bank rate, that difference alone would grow to $1,222,965 at age sixty-four, which amounts to $93,765 more than the high-school graduate of 1972 would accumulate by banking the cost of a Princeton education. Figured this way, a Princeton degree is worth $93,765. The joker is that the Princeton graduate has to wait until he's sixty years old before his bank account pulls ahead. The advantage of his college education comes at the very end of his earning life.

When the Princeton graduate is young, the difference between his earnings and that of a high-school graduate is less than the interest on the money he has spent for college would earn in the savings bank. As of 1972, a male college graduate earned only $96 more than a high-school graduate of the same age during his first year out of college—this is nowhere near the $3,423 in interest that the high-school graduate could draw out if he had invested the cost of college in the savings bank. During his second year out of college, the college graduate, now twenty-three, earns $558 more than the twenty-three-year-old high-school graduate. He doesn't reach the "average" advantage in earnings of college graduates over high-school graduates—a difference of $4,823—until he is thirty-five years old.[7]

The big advantage of getting your college money in cash now is that you can invest it in something that has a higher return than a diploma. The options are enticing. A Princeton-bound high-school graduate of 1972 who likes fooling around with cars better than immersing himself in books could have banked his $34,181 and gone to work at the local garage at close to $1,000 a year more than the average earnings reported by the Census for high-school graduates eighteen years old, and the chances are that he could have moved up in income faster than the average high-school graduate, too. Meanwhile, as he was learning to be an expert auto mechanic, his money would be ticking away, compounding itself at the bank. When he gets to be twenty-eight, he will have earned $7,199 less, from age twenty-two, than if he had graduated from college, but he will have $73,113 in his passbook—enough to buy out his boss, go into the used-car business, or acquire a new-car dealership. As an enterpriser, he could thenceforth expect to take home more than he could have expected as a college graduate, and if he had the wit to get into Princeton, and a genuine interest in cars, he should be more likely to succeed than the average man in the business.

Supposing, on the other hand, he has the money, but neither the wit nor the interest for Princeton. After all,

about a third of the high-school graduates from families
with incomes of $15,000 or more *don't* go to college.[8]
Suppose he banks his Princeton money and travels
around, supporting himself at odd jobs, as so many
privileged young people like to do. At twenty-eight,
when he's tired of pickup jobs, he can take out his
$73,113 and buy a liquor store, which will return him
well over 20 percent on his investment as long as he's
willing to mind the store.[9] (He might, of course, get
fidgety sitting there, but he has to be extraordinarily
dim-witted to *lose* money on a liquor store, and for the
moment we are talking only about dollars.)

But suppose at twenty-eight he still isn't sure what he
wants to do and is willing to go on living on a high-
school graduate's income. At thirty-eight, he has
$156,391 in the bank and he's still ahead of the college
graduate, who at age thirty-eight has made and very
probably spent $48,166 more than his noncollege
counterpart. If he wants to quit working and loaf full
time, he can probably find a place to invest his
$156,391 for a return sufficient to keep him in the
modest circumstances to which he has become accus-
tomed.

If all this forbearance sounds inhuman, consider a
more likely comparison. Suppose that neither the high-
school graduate nor the Princeton graduate saves anything before attaining annual earnings of $12,000. The
high-school graduate will not be able to start saving
until he is forty-five, the age at which his income rises
to $12,000. The college graduate will have started sav-
ings at the age of thirty, but he will never be able to
catch up with the bank account of the high-school
graduate who started his college money earning interest
when he was eighteen.

Any fair comparison between the return on investing
in college and investing in a savings bank requires un-
naturally long-headed calculations of future gains. Most

people, and especially young people, aren't willing to
sacrifice much now for uncertain prospects in the remote future.

Bankers are different. They bet every day on the
chance that tomorrow will come, and they bet with
numbers. They regularly calculate how much they are
willing to give you today for your promise to pay in the
future. A classic tool of the banking trade is a table that
gives the present value of money due in the future, a
specific instance of which is the merchant's "discount
for cash." This discount rate depends on the interest
the money could earn if you had it now.

Discounting for net present value shrinks those impressive lifetime earnings to thinkable sums. In 1972,
for instance, the $601,000 a twenty-two-year-old col-
lege graduate was projected to earn was worth only
$165,000 when discounted at 7 percent. And because
so much of the lifetime earnings of a college graduate
come late in life, the net *present* value of his lifetime
earnings shrinks faster than the net present value of
money compounding in a savings account. In 1972, for
instance, the $416,000 a high-school graduate could
expect to earn was worth $104,000 when discounted at
7 percent. That means that the difference—$61,000—
is all a college degree was worth in dollars to an
eighteen-year-old on the day he received his high-
school diploma in 1972. This may sound technical, but
collegebound high-school graduates have to be bankers
or specialists in judging investment to prefer a bird in
hand to a bigger bird in a faraway bush.

How you come out, of course, depends on how you
figure. If you count the extra dollars a college graduate
earns in toto and compare it with the amount that ac-
cumulates if he invests in a savings bank instead of in
his education, the savings bank wins. If the college
graduate puts the extra he makes every year into a
savings account as he makes it, college wins, at the very
end. If you take the value of all these future piles at the

age of eighteen by discounting them for the wait involved, the way a banker would do, college loses to the savings bank.

What about inflation? Earnings follow the price level, while money in the savings bank does not. Those who advise a young man to invest in education almost always talk about the bright future ahead for those who are prepared to take advantage of an expanding economy. But what if it isn't going to expand? What if roller coaster inflation-depression is ahead? In 1974 some of the most sophisticated investors were advising their clients to keep their money in cash—or in the near cash of treasury bills and other money-market instruments—rather than locking it in to *any* investment. Money in the savings bank keeps options open in a time of troubles or change.

What's ahead, after all, is anyone's guess. Inflation may increase everyone's dollar earnings, but an over-supply of college graduates could narrow the advantage they have in income, too. The fifty-three-year-olds who in 1972 were earning $7,044 more than high-school graduates were twenty-two-year-olds in 1941 when a diploma was something exceptional in the job market and therefore worth more.

The decline in return for a college degree within the last generation has been substantial. In the 1950s a Princeton student could pay all his expenses for the school year—eating club and all—on less than $3,000. When he graduated, he entered a job market which provided a comfortable margin over the earnings of age mates who had not gone to college. Everything that the Sylvia Porters of the day said about the dollar value of a college education was true.

There are several reasons why the return on the investment in college may continue to decline in the future.

The number of college graduates has increased to the point where many of them are doing jobs that simply do not produce the added value that would lead to higher salaries. The gap between the income of the college educated and noncollege educated will surely begin to narrow very soon.

The return on investment in education has to be less in the future because growth rates are slower than they were, reducing the proportion of jobs for which higher education is needed. All through the 1950s and 1960s great organizations like IBM were expanding. They needed to take in lots of people with potential for advancement. But by 1974 these organizations were no longer recruiting future managers in the numbers anticipated at a time when they thought they would continue to expand.

Rates of return and dollar signs on education are a fascinating brain teaser, but it should be obvious by now that there is a certain unreality to the game.[10] Quite aside from the noneconomic benefits of college— and these should loom larger once the dollars are cleared away—there are grave difficulties in assigning a dollar value to college at all. The economists who developed the concept are the first to state its limitations.

First, there is no real evidence that the higher income of college graduates is due to college at all. As we shall see in greater detail later, college may simply attract people who are slated to earn more money anyway— those with higher I.Q.'s, better family backgrounds, and a more enterprising temperament. Statisticians try to disentangle I.Q. test scores, educational background of parents, income of parents, and other characteristics of the collegebound from the influence of their education itself by formidable mathematical maneuvers called "regression analyses." They differ among themselves about the specific results. But no one who has wrestled with the problem is prepared to attribute all of the higher income of college graduates to the impact of college itself.

Dael Wolfle, one of the first economists to calculate

the dollar value of college, thought that college itself accounted for about three-fourths of the difference in lifetime income between college and high-school graduates. Harvard professor Christopher Jencks, in his report *Inequality: A Reassessment of the Effect of Family and Schooling in America*, finds that education in general accounts for less than half of the difference in income in the American population. "The biggest single source of income differences seems to be the fact that men from high-status families have higher incomes than men from low-status families even when they enter the same occupations, have the same amount of education, and have the same test scores."

It looks as if a substantial proportion of the advantage of the college educated is due not to any benefit that college confers, but to plain, old-fashioned class distinction: the upper-class intonation, acquired in the nursery, associated with Harvard graduates at a time when most Harvard graduates had upper-class parents; the "background" rather than the schooling of the new vice-president at the bank. Jencks estimates that "an extra year of schooling seems to do about twice as much for a student from the middle-class background as for a student from a working-class background."

Does it matter what kind of college you attend? Early studies relied on the incomes reported by alumni and noted that the prestigious colleges seemed to have a higher proportion of high earners, but the recent consensus seems to be that it doesn't matter. And there is now very serious doubt that if good colleges do give you a better chance of high income, the credit goes to the quality of education you get there. If Harvard men do, in fact, earn more—and maybe they don't—it may be because employers have been unduly impressed with a Harvard degree.

One thing that is quite obvious and easy to document is that the money a college graduate earns depends a great deal on the courses he takes. Since engineers earn more than teachers, an engineering degree is going to be worth more in future earnings than a degree in education. The charges to the student are the same, so the return on an engineering degree has to be higher. (Maybe it shouldn't be, though, since the cost to the college of providing an engineering education is higher than the cost of educating a teacher.)

How much college is worth in future earnings depends on who you are and, particularly, what you look like. Blacks pay the same tuition as whites, but since they earn less, they enjoy a lower return on their investment in college. In 1969 blacks still earned only about three-fourths of the pay of whites with the same amount of schooling, and since blacks are out of work more frequently and longer than whites at every level, their lifetime earnings would be only half as much as that of their white counterparts on the basis of 1960 statistics. This doesn't mean, of course, that it isn't worthwhile for a black to go on in school. College improves the earnings expectancy of blacks by about the same percentage that it improves the earnings expectancy of whites, but since tuition, room and board, and books cost both races the same, the investment is worth less to blacks than to whites. Blacks often make a bigger sacrifice to go and get less out of it in money. One of the factors making blacks bitter is increasing educational attainment which increases their income *expectancy* faster than employers upgrade them in jobs. College hardly affects the gap between the earnings of black and white men. In 1969 black male high-school graduates averaged 79 percent of the pay of their white counterparts, compared with 78 percent for graduates with four years of college. College did a little better by black women, narrowing the race differential from 91 percent of white pay for high-school graduates to 97 percent for four-year college graduates.

Sex makes so much difference on the whole that the

return on the education of all females simply hasn't been published by the Census Bureau. They would have to calculate the lifetime income of women who work full-time year round, and have always worked, and compare it with the return of similarly employed males.

The Census Bureau didn't make this comparison on the basis of 1972 data, on the assumption that there would be little demand for this data because it affected so few. The male statisticians accept the general premise that women do not invest in college in the hope of higher full-time, year-round, lifelong earnings, but in the hope, perhaps, of performing more adequately as mothers and attracting higher-earning if not otherwise "better" fathers for their legitimate children. Data is available for 1966 and shows that four years of college boosted the lifetime earnings of women by 31 percent, compared with a boost of 49 percent for men.

Collegebound students can draw one very practical conclusion from these calculations. Averages may fascinate economists and social scientists. Averages may persuade legislators to spend on colleges. But the average income advantage of college graduates does not represent a bankable investment for any individual. The dean of the economists studying human capital is Jacob Mincer of the National Bureau of Economic Research and Columbia University. He states flatly that "for, say, 20 to 30 percent of students at any level, the additional schooling has been a waste, at least in terms of earnings." For one reason or another, whether it's I.Q. or race or sex or ambition, or temperament, or charm, or social class, or home environment, or some inextricable combination of everything that could conceivably bear on success, college fails to work its income-raising magic for almost a third of those who go. An even higher proportion of those who earned $15,000 or more in 1972—58 percent to be precise—reached that comfortable bracket without the benefit of a college diploma, 30 percent made it with just a high-school diploma, and another 12 percent had even less education. Christopher Jencks says that financial success in the United States depends a good deal on luck, and the most sophisticated regression analyses have yet to demonstrate otherwise.

PART III

THE
PAYOFFS

5

College and the Job Market

College students are sincere when they say they don't really want money. On many campuses they've revived the cardinal sin of greed, and the percentage of the young who "would welcome less emphasis on money" rose steadily from 65 percent in 1968, when Daniel Yankelovich made his first nationwide survey and jobs were easy to get, to 80 percent in 1973 when jobs were hard to get.

The young are not alone. High and low, wage and salary earner, college and noncollege, young and old—all, in varying degrees, look less to the pay of a job than to the work itself. They want "interesting" work that permits them "to make a contribution," "express themselves," and "use their special abilities," and they think college will help them find it.

Jerry Darring of Indianapolis knows what it is to make a dollar. He worked with his father in the family plumbing business, on the line at Chevrolet, and in the Chrysler foundry. He quit these jobs to enter Wright State University in Dayton, Ohio, because "in a job like that a person only has time to work, and after that he's so tired that he can't do anything else but come home and go to sleep. I'm used to hard work—don't get me wrong. But I just couldn't take that type of job."

Jerry came to college to find work "helping people." He is not at all unusual. "Helping" was checked as an important value by more entering freshmen on the American Council on Education survey than any other goal except "developing a philosophy of life." At first Jerry thought he would like to be a doctor, but when advisors "cooled him out" of this arduous ambition, he settled for a paramedical occupation. He knows he won't earn more as a paramedic than he could earn as a plumber, so he is realistically worried about going into debt to acquire this "helping" career. At the end of his freshman year he was going in with a friend on a house-painting business, because it's a way "to make a lot of money fast." When he has enough money in hand, he'll go back to college. Jerry is nothing if not pragmatic, but he is perfectly willing to spend dollars he earns at dull, well-paid work to prepare for lower-paid work which offers the reward of service to others.

Jerry's case is dramatic, but not unusual. No one really works for money alone. In order to deal with the many nonmonetary rewards of work, economists have coined the concept of "psychic income." According to the *McGraw-Hill Dictionary of Modern Economics* psychic income is "income that is reckoned in terms of pleasure, satisfaction, or general feelings of euphoria. It is to be distinguished from income that is received in money or in the form of goods and services. Psychic income is commonly said to accrue to professional persons and creative artists who take pride in their accomplishments or gain satisfaction from their prestige and status. It may also frequently accrue to workingmen and housewives who enjoy their work surroundings and the company of their fellow workers and find pleasure in a job well done. There is no standard measurement of psychic income."

Psychic income is primarily what college students mean when they talk about getting a good job. During the most affluent years of the late 1960s and early 1970s, college students told their placement officers that they wanted to be researchers, college professors, artists, city planners, social workers, poets, songwriters, consumer advocates, book publishers, archaeologists, ballet dancers, government consultants, foreign-service officers, or—God help them—authors.

The psychic income of these and other occupations popular with students is so high that they can be filled without offering high salaries. According to one study, 93 percent of urban university professors would re-choose their vocation if they had it to do over again, compared with only 16 percent of unskilled auto workers.[1] Colleges have always been able to "buy" scholars and scientists away from higher-paying business and government jobs, but automobile manufacturers have sometimes had to shut the assembly line down for lack of workers on Monday morning in spite of the steadily rising wages unions have been able to negotiate.

The monetary gap between college professor and auto worker is now surprisingly small, but the difference in psychic income is enormous. Professors enjoy the ultimate in self-expression; they are actually paid for sounding off to a captive audience of students or, through research, to an audience of their peers. And college professors enjoy bountiful quantities of all the other components in the dictionary definition of psychic income.

They gain "general feelings of euphoria" from their "prestige and status" as well as their "pride in accomplishment." They work in pleasant surroundings, enjoying the company of congenial fellow workers, and they work for the most part without any supervision whatsoever. On a more pedestrian level, they have short hours, long vacations, and considerable control over their schedules. They are seldom exposed to physical danger or exertion, and they don't have to get up the same early hour every morning, stay out in all kinds of weather, eat a cold lunch, tire themselves out, or get dirty. They have generous pensions and fringes, and,

once tenured, they run about as much risk of losing pay
as a Supreme Court judge. But the crowning attraction
is that, like missionaries, they enjoy the satisfaction of
"helping others."

COLLEGE AND CAREER CHOICE

Colleges do not officially accept the responsibility of
helping students choose a career that will lead to a job.
There's no real place in the academic system for it, and
what is now called "vocational guidance" is a relatively
undeveloped discipline. The whole idea that a person
can or must *choose* a lifework is quite new. Until very
recently, privileged and underprivileged alike grew up
knowing what would be expected of them as adults, and
even in the 1970s, *most* high-school graduates drift into
whatever jobs are open when they need to earn a living
or into the local community college if nothing better
offers. They think of their future jobs the way high-
school girls think of their future husbands as something
that will happen to them without any particular initia-
tive on their part.

The idea that a person can and indeed must choose
assumes that each person is born with a "potential"
which it is his or her duty to realize. If you are better at
numbers than at words, for instance, you should do
better at engineering than at journalism. Although colleges do not offer explicit help in making these self-
discoveries, the catalogues imply as much with general
talk about "broadening horizons" and "maximizing options." And as one student put it, "College is the only
place where you can take different courses and explore
different fields without being called a drifter or a bum."

But sometimes the exploration doesn't lead anywhere. One graduate told us that even after she transferred from one school to another, nothing ever seemed
to click. "The main thing I got out of college is that I

thought I wanted to be a social worker, and I did social work for a month and I realized I didn't want to do that. After college was all over, I knew more what I didn't want to do than what I *did* want to do."

The proportion of freshmen who could not think of any career ambition to declare on the American Council on Education Freshman Norm questionnaire crested in the early 1970s along with the proportion of high-school graduates entering college. Many left as undecided as they were when they entered. At Wright State, a working-class, vocationally oriented college, the placement officer estimates that 60 percent entered and 40 percent were graduated without vocational plans. Nor did the Ivier campuses inspire eagerness to set foot on the beginning rung of a career ladder. In 1972 nearly half of the Princeton seniors had no immediate plans for graduate school or a permanent job. What they wanted, many were frank to admit, was some respectable way to postpone career commitment.

It used to be the Peace Corps. About a third of the Stanford graduating class of 1965 wanted to go. According to Joseph Katz, the educator who studied them, they saw the Peace Corps as a legitimate way to take more time for "further development and the sorting out of motives."[2] In 1974, when the Peace Corps had few openings and less prestige than formerly, liberal arts graduates talked about helping people at home by teaching school for a few years.

"I may want to go to law school eventually, but not right away," Larry Wingert, a Hamilton senior, told us. "Maybe I'll get a Masters of Arts in Teaching degree next year and spend a year or two teaching while I'm thinking things out. Right now, though, I don't think I would want to teach for the rest of my life unless I became an administrator or something." *Ultimately* he's going to be some sort of big wheel, but not now.

Graduate school has always been the classic solution for those who avoid commitment. It has also been the

classic prescription of the education establishment.
"When I didn't know what I wanted to be in grammar
school, they told me I'd know when I got into high
school," one woman recalls.[3] "When I didn't know in
high school, I thought I'd find out in college. When
college didn't turn up any career, they told me to get an
M.A. Now I've got it, the only thing I can think of
doing is to go back for a Ph.D., but I fear the outcome
will be the same."

For those who like it, college becomes a way of life,
raising expectations of psychic income which rule out
more and more of the available jobs until the only job
that will satisfy them is the job of college professor,
which as we have seen heads the list in psychic pay.
Like old-fashioned girls who turned down one suitor
after another, many uncommitted Ivy League graduates
do not realize that as they are becoming choosier and
choosier, they are also becoming less and less desirable
because they look more and more "overqualified" for
actual work. Students who postpone commitment because they like being students run the risk of becoming
vocational old maids.

But not everyone, of course, has the talent or the
money for academic bummery, and many of the reluctant students are often reluctant job hunters as well.
Placement officers report that they are often explicit
only about what they do *not* want. They don't want to
work on a regular schedule. They don't want money or
prestige, they announce, sometimes defiantly. And they
don't want a job that forecloses their options.

What they *do* want, placement officers agree, comes
out only under probing. They want to work with people, and what they want to do with people is to help
them, particularly if they are poor people. They want
work over which they have a lot of control ("make my
own decisions"). They want to be "creative" and "express themselves." They want work that allows them
freedom to dress as they please, to come and go as they

please (no nine-to-five hours!). Sometimes they don't really care what they do, just so it is in Boston or San Diego.

Mostly, however, they want work that really matters, and since most of their life experience has been academic, it is not surprising that their definition of meaningful work grows out of the courses they've taken: cleaning up the environment, helping the poor, promoting international understanding, writing and researching, practicing the arts.

But the numbers are stacked against them. Not only are there not enough jobs in the fields that they want, but in the moderate slowdown of economic growth in the 1970s, it became evident that there never were, and probably never will be, enough jobs requiring higher education to go around for everyone. A little browsing in the *Occupational Outlook Handbook* of the Department of Labor shows why.

WHERE THE JOBS ARE

Students who told their advisors they wanted to help people were often directed to psychology. In 1975, for instance, a year during which the Department of Labor estimated there would be 4,300 new jobs for psychologists, colleges were expected to turn out 58,430 B.A.'s in psychology, about 10 percent of whom would go on for the master's degree.[4]

What happens to the rest? Of thirty psych majors who reported back to Vassar what they were doing a year after graduation in 1972, only five had jobs that could possibly use their courses in psychology, and of these, two were working for Vassar College in counseling, and the others were trainees in hospitals. Among the rest were a delivery driver, diet technician, claims adjuster, branch loan officer, secretaries, typists, teachers, and waitresses. A similar spot check at the

University of Wisconsin disclosed much the same dismal picture: an occasional psychology graduate found work as a "juvenile advocate," a mental health trainee, or a Teen Tween supervisor, but the rest were waitresses, typists, delivery men, with a few odd occupations such as "soil counter." In 1974 a twenty-two-year-old graduate in psychology was training with the New England Telephone Company for a job as a wire splicer because she couldn't find anything else.

Sociology was a favorite major on the socially conscious campuses of the late 1960s and early 1970s, but graduates found that social reform was hardly a paying occupation. Among male sociologists gainfully employed a year after graduation from the University of Wisconsin, there were a legal assistant, sports editor, truck unloader, Peace Corps worker, publications director, a stockboy—but no sociologist per se. None of the men graduated in social work that year was in any profession, and the highest paid worked for the post office. A few of the women sociologists were in youth work, but among the rest were a claims adjuster, a swimming instructor, a library aide, a utility worker, a camping instructor and the usual scattering of factory workers, waitresses, and secretaries.

For liberal arts graduates, future prospects are not much better. Publishing, writing, and journalism are presumably the vocational goal of a large proportion of the 104,000 majors in Communications and Letters expected to graduate in 1975. Considering the sea of printed and spoken words washing over the American public, you'd think there would be work for all of them and more.

Not so. People outside publishing do not realize how very few editorial workers are needed to produce and package the steady stream of words that keeps newsstands, mailboxes, and garbage cans lined with printed paper. A few dozen editorial workers and free-lancers are all that it takes to put on an extremely respectable issue of a national magazine. Even fewer are needed to "create" all the music, drama, and art propagated by the mass media.

So what's the outlook for these 104,000 graduates? For replacements and growth, the country's daily newspapers this year are expected to hire 2,600 reporters. Radio and television stations may add 500 announcers, most of them in local radio stations. Nonpublishing organizations will need 1,100 technical writers, and public relations activities another 4,400. Even if the new graduates get all these jobs (and of course they won't), more than 90,000 of them will have to find something less glamorous to do.

Or take museums. They have been a great favorite recently, but how many aspiring curators know that there are little more than 7,000 museums of all kinds in the whole country, most of them so small that they employ no more than three persons. In the "real world," museums are run by curators who have no need, thank you, of any but the most pedestrian kind of assistance, much of which they can get free from volunteers. They couldn't hire very many of the 40,000 graduates in fine and applied arts, or the 5,000 anthropology graduates, to mention only a few of the museum-oriented disciplines.

Is there any other work for the fine arts graduates except for a few teaching jobs? According to the Department of Labor, there'll be openings every year of the 1970s for 3,400 commercial artists. As for *pure* creative artists, the possibilities are so dismal that Newell Brown, Princeton's career services director, warns the artist to proceed at his own risk.

As for the anthropologists, only 400 will be needed every year in the 1970s to take care of all the college courses, public health research, community surveys, museums, and all the digs on every continent, and all of these, of course, will need graduate work in anthropology to qualify. Jane Brandfon is not untypical of those

who do go on. After she got her M.A. in anthropology
from the University of North Carolina, she dropped out
of the Ph.D. program, which would have prepared her
only to teach at the college level, which she did not
want to do. She went to work in her family's car business while waiting to get into law school.

A lot of the jobs that attract the liberally educated
come under the heading of nice work for the few who
can get it. Like being an interpreter. The idea has probably occurred to all of the 22,000 expected to earn a
B.A. in a foreign language in 1975, but Newell Brown
doesn't think that more than 1,000 men and women in
the entire country earn a living at it, and just about all
of them learned the languages somewhere else than in
an American college.

Some of the most popular fields are pathetically
small. Only 900 foresters a year will be needed during the 1970s, although schools of forestry are expected
to continue graduating twice that many. Some will get
sub-professional jobs as forestry aides. Schools of architecture are expected to turn out twice as many as will
be needed, and while all sorts of people want to design
things, the Department of Labor forecasts that there
will be jobs for only 400 new industrial designers a
year. Landscape architecture attracts students who are
turning away from protest and activism to a private
concern with nature and the outdoors, but only 1,100 a
year are expected to find jobs.

The most popular occupations may be growing fast
without necessarily offering employment to very many.
A company can double its demand for recreation
workers by deciding that the one person employed in
that capacity needs an assistant. Recreation work is
always cited as an expanding field, but it will need relatively few workers who require more special training
than life guards. "Urban planning" exploded not only
in the media, but in college catalogues and the plans of
undergraduates. And the U.S. Department of Labor has

doubled its estimate of the number of jobs to be filled every year in the 1970s—to a big, fat 800. Oceanography was everyone's love, but a mere 200 oceanographers a year will be able to do all the exploring of "inner space" and all the exciting underwater diving demonstrated on television for the whole decade of the 1970s. Like the urban planners, the oceanographers will all need graduate training.

Graduates in the vocationally nonspecific fields invade each other's disciplines for jobs. The 127,000 education majors graduating in 1975 will be competing for scarce elementary and secondary teaching jobs with much larger numbers of liberal arts graduates who qualified themselves to teach by taking a few courses in education.

Teaching, at all levels, is a growing fallback for all liberal arts graduates who don't get their first choice of law or publishing or the Foreign Service. More than 279,550 were expected to graduate in the social sciences in 1975. What else can you do except teach, when there are no jobs for those with a degree in anthropology, economics, geography, history, international relations, political science, public administration, or sociology? Colleges were expected to hire only 24,000 new teachers in all fields. The rest would have to peddle their undergraduate majors as general background for work in government and business. And here's where the game of revolving door begins.

Liberal arts graduates in the social sciences will have to share the 17,500 social work openings with the 7,760 graduates of professional schools of social work.

Market research for the social scientists? Only 2,600 job openings.

Personnel work? Only 9,100 openings, not nearly enough to go around for the 58,430 majors in psychology with a prime claim on the personnel jobs.

So it goes for just about every sizeable occupation open to the generally educated B.A. Whatever college

graduates *want* to do, most of them are going to wind
up doing what there *is* to do. During the 1970s, according to the U.S. Department of Labor, the biggest demand will be for stenographers and secretaries
(411,000 annual openings), followed by retail trade
salesworkers, hospital attendants, bookkeepers, building custodians, registered nurses, waiters and waitresses, cashiers, typists, licensed practical nurses, foremen, kindergarten and elementary school teachers,
receptionists, cooks, cosmetologists, private household
workers, manufacturing inspectors, and industrial machinery repairmen. These are the jobs which will eventually absorb the surplus archeologists, urban planners,
oceanographers, curators, editors, and college professors. The Department of Labor reports that three-
fourths of the social science and two-thirds of the humanities majors who came out of college in the early
1970s have had to take jobs that are not directly related to their majors.[5] The men tended to become
salesmen; the women, clerks.

Trends in the economy make a great deal of difference in the ease with which majors in different fields are
able to get work for which they have been prepared. In
1971, before the teacher surplus became acute, 78
percent of education majors got jobs which the Office
of Education said were "directly related" to their major
field of study, compared with 51 percent of the majors
in business and commerce, 44 percent of humanities
majors, and 35 percent of social science majors.

Majors in the social sciences and humanities have a
harder time getting jobs not only in their fields, but in
any field, than majors in business, engineering, or even
in education. The pure scientists majoring in biology,
chemistry, physics, math, and botany have always fared
better in both employment and pay, because there have
never been very many of them no matter how great the
demand and because more of them head directly for

graduate or medical school and so take themselves out of the job market.

If college does not find students jobs, it does find them their tongues. News of the job market feeds back swiftly to the campus. One of the most popular documentaries produced by WEWS-TV in Cleveland followed up Kent State graduates. It filmed an education major serving in a cocktail lounge, a psychology major repairing hearing aids, and a geography major sweeping out schoolrooms. Most of them said they wished they had majored in something else.

The lesson is not lost on undergraduates and their parents. A mother of two elite college graduates, one working in a hamburger house and the other as an unpaid volunteer, wonders, rather timidly, whether they might not have been happier "if they hadn't had such a broad spectrum of studies and maybe more or less specialized." She was relieved that her third was headed for a major in music. Music might not lead to a job, but at least it was something definite.

Liberal arts professors are genuinely sorry for students who have to go out into the dull world of business but they don't see what they can do about it. "Our students know they can't get jobs in Spanish," a professor of Spanish at the University of North Carolina told me. "They take Spanish because they like the stuff, and college is their only chance to study the humanities."

"What I teach is absolutely useless," a professor of Russian declared proudly, "but the kids eat it up."

Placement officers don't find this uselessness so glorious. They wish seniors were more realistic. "Yesterday one student just frankly told me that he thought a job came with the diploma," a counselor at a large California campus told an associate. "When I explained how you go about planning a job campaign he just looked at me and said, 'I thought I could just come in and you would tell me where to go for a job.' "

Many placement officers blame the faculty for encouraging these unrealistic attitudes. John Shingleton, director of placement at Michigan State University, accuses the academic community of outright hypocrisy. "Educators have never said, 'Go to college and get a good job,' but this has been implied, and now students expect it," he told an administrative group at that institution. "If this is not the case, we need to tell students as emphatically as we can that they are being educated for other than career purposes."

Shingleton and his less outspoken counterparts in other colleges feel that the academic community disdains their function as "vocational." Professors staunchly refuse to consider the job prospects for students in their fields, the placement officers say, but some of them aren't above recruiting majors to their departments under false pretenses. At a midwestern university, for instance, a student who said he wanted to travel after graduating was encouraged to major in geography so that he could qualify for a job in a travel agency. When he started job hunting he discovered that travel agencies don't favor geography majors.

"Okay," he told the placement officer. "So what kind of a job can you get with a geography major?"

After some hemming and hawing, the placement officer thought he might find work somewhere as a cartographer. On further examination, however, it turned out that cartography wasn't taught in the geography department. He'd have to go to a trade school to learn it. Any jobs at the end of this road? No one knew. The would-be travel agent is now selling shoes.

"If we care what happens to students after college, then let's get 'involved' with what should be one of the basic purposes of education—career preparation," Shingleton urged the Michigan State faculty. "I see increasing numbers of students graduating who don't know where they've been, don't know where they are, and don't know where they're going in terms of the world of work. This is 'detachment' to the point of diminishing returns."

Most professors violently resist the suggestion that they should consider the needs of employers in planning curriculum. "We've never asked employers to hire our graduates," a professor of English said. "If they do, that's their lookout, not ours."

In the 1970s, however, some of the more practical nontenured professors began to see that jobs for graduates meant jobs for professors, too. At Oneonta College in New York State, a history professor wants the placement office to list schools of public administration which would favor history majors. There may not be jobs teaching history, but why can't the history department develop courses that would prepare students for jobs in government? "It makes sense to me," she says. "But there are members of my own department who think I'm a heretic." Can language departments be saved? One way might be to put on courses leading to career work in "the international field" so attractive to travel-minded students. None of these proposals is particularly realistic, but they have at least the virtue of trying to respond to student needs.

THE NEW VOCATIONALISM

There have always been students who have come to college with specific career goals in mind, but in 1973, after a year or so of political apathy, career commitment emerged, with almost explosive suddenness, as the new look on campus. Courses in business, nursing, agriculture, health sciences, and training for the handicapped were oversubscribed. At the Ivy League colleges, followed instantly by everywhere else, undergraduates declared, in droves, for law and medicine. By the end of 1973 reporters were calling the "New Vocationalism" a welcome return to the ethic of achievements and service. Students were still idealistic, the reporters wrote, but they now saw that they could best make the world better by healing the sick as physicians or righting individual wrongs as lawyers. Students were everywhere reported to be studying, reading the assignments, hanging around the library, behaving with unaccustomed decorum, and even listening to the advice of their elders. Many professors were delighted. "It's almost fun to teach again," one of them said. "Students are actually *polite*."

But the big difference was not in students themselves —in spite of what they said, they had always expected college to insure a better job. Now, when jobs were hard to get, they had to face the truth about themselves, and many were appalled. The new interest in "making it" drew more sneers on campus than anywhere else. Some flaunted their new hard noses. "Once you give up wanting to be a fireman or a cowboy, you're only in it for the money," Larry Peobles, a student at City University of New York, told a reporter in 1973.

In the fall of 1973 the proportion of freshmen who thought that it was very important to be well off financially rose to 55 percent from 41 percent the year before. That, of course, was in the privacy of the Freshman Norm Survey. In public, and especially when talking to reporters, students deplored the crass materialism of their fellows. When we asked whether they thought that more or less than half of the students on campus would quit if convinced that a diploma wouldn't raise their earnings, a substantial number protested that while they themselves would stay, more than half of the other students were in school primarily for the money, and they made no secret of their contempt for them.

Toward the end of 1973, students at an Ivy League school complained that premedical students were actually sabotaging each other's laboratory experiments in order to cut down the numbers credentialed to apply.

"What kind of compassion," students asked, "can you expect from a doctor who would do a thing like that?" In March 1974 I heard the same story from students in California. Shortly afterward, it was repeated on the "Today" show, along with reports that students were cutting pages out of texts in the library and passing out misinformation to fellow students to keep as many as possible out of the running. In May a recent graduate who was retiring from the "rat race" to live on an organic farm in Vermont told me about a case of sabotage that had happened to a friend of his.

Whether true or not, the sabotage of laboratory experiments spoke to the real fear of the New Vocationalism—the fear of competition for the limited number of places in medical school. The sheer numbers were frightening in themselves. At the University of California at Davis, more than 1,000 students were enrolled in the introductory course in genetics. It had to be taught by tapes available around the clock in specially designated carrels, and laboratory experiments couldn't have been sabotaged because there simply wasn't room or equipment for students to do them. They watched demonstrations on television instead.[6]

Conditions like these carried their own message. The competitive would-be physicians realized that all the premedical undergraduates couldn't make it to the M.D. and wouldn't be needed if they could. Medical statisticians agree. In 1971 the American Enterprise Institute estimated that there would be more than the target ratio of 100 doctors for every 100,000 population by 1980.[7] This ratio would develop, they predicted, even without subsidizing medical students because "there is a surplus of qualified applicants to medical schools willing and able to pay the price." In 1974 the new Mt. Sinai School of Medicine in New York City had 3,152 applicants for its 65 first-year places.

Whether access to medicine should be limited to

those with the capital to pay for a medical education is aside from the problem of numbers. The fact is that we would have ten times the target ratio of doctors if every entering freshman who checked "doctor" succeeded in becoming one.[8]

The odds were little better for the would-be lawyers. Harvard Law School gets 8,000 applicants for its 500 places annually, and while law schools are easier to start and expand than medical schools, they were already graduating twice as many new lawyers every year as the Department of Labor thinks will be needed, and the oversupply was growing every year.

Doctors and, particularly, lawyers can make work for themselves by treating ailments and undertaking lawsuits formerly ignored, but there is a limit to which any society can be "medicalized" and "legalized" in this fashion. If the profession-bent entering freshmen seem to smile infrequently, it may be that they know that the numbers are against them.

If it was medicine and law at Harvard and Yale, it was engineering, business, nursing, agriculture, accounting, and the health care technologies at the state schools, and welding, auto mechanics, business machine operation, printing, medical record technology, dental hygiene, television repair, and a long list of specific skills at the community colleges that have seldom been taught in classrooms. Community colleges continue to grow, but they have been attracting students who want jobs, not a transfer to a four-year bachelor's program elsewhere.

The new vocationally oriented students were responding to the easy putoff the graduates ahead of them had encountered at employment offices: "Too bad you didn't specialize in a marketable skill." From the employer's point of view, this was the sensible thing to say to the generally educated applicant. When asked what colleges and students could do to improve the job outlook, employers queried by the annual Northwestern

Endicott Report said, "Offer more business-related courses."[9]

Phil McKee is one who took this sensible advice literally. His father is a barber, his mother a seamstress. At twenty Phil had worked as a tutor, a busboy, a factory worker, a road construction worker, and a blackberry picker. He went to a midwestern university to learn engineering so that he could get a good job in a field which was beginning to expand again. Phil's interest was straightforward. "If I could have found an easier way to get ahead, I would have taken it," he told us.

In the 1970s enrollments were everywhere shifting from the liberal arts to courses bearing the names of occupations. The shift pinched colleges financially. It costs almost three times more, for instance, to educate an engineer than it does to produce a Chaucer scholar who pays the same tuition, and some of the vocational courses required heavy investment in equipment for a very few students. In 1967 the Bronx Community College set up a formidable battery of industrial machines for a two-year course in plastics technology. In seven years only twenty-six students had completed the course, and in 1974 no one was enrolled in the program.

Matching vocational courses to job markets hasn't been easy for colleges or their students. Second-guessing next year's job market is rough, and the more specialized the vocation, the more hazardous the investment. Community colleges try to work closely with local employers, but they are perpetually overshooting or undershooting limited specialities. In 1970, for instance, Pittsburgh hospitals needed inhalation therapy specialists; news reports of the shortage attracted so many students to the courses at local colleges that by 1973 the program had to be "adjusted" to accommodate slower expansion and replacement needs. Meanwhile, Modesto Junior College had a big run on Hospital Driving, an occupation glamorized by a television show depicting the excitement of emergency medical service.

Manpower matching by publicity is inevitably wasteful. In the 1950s, when computers were new and glamorous, so many people trained to be programmers that there has frequently been an oversupply of trained applicants. The classic "yoyo" effect is in the demand and supply of engineers, an occupation which attracts square young men who aim to succeed. Because demand is volatile and training takes at least four years, today's shortage is apt to produce a big crop of engineering graduates after the need for them has crested. Defense cutbacks at the end of the Vietnam War discouraged students from engineering, so that by the mid-1970s, employers were bidding against each other for the thin graduating classes, and the more thoughtful personnel specialists were admitting to each other that cheaper nonprofessionals could be trained to do many of the jobs into which engineering graduates were "stockpiled" when their employers planned to expand.[10]

PROFESSIONAL TRAINING

It is reasonable for students in professional fields to expect that when they are graduated they will get a job in the field they've studied in preference to someone who hasn't studied it, and, barring catastrophe or an unusual mismatch such as we have had in education, they usually do. This seems only right and proper. A profession is a "learned" profession because it requires higher education. People who doubt the job value of a liberal education are quick to except professional schooling—both graduate and undergraduate—from their criticism.

"College doesn't really help you on the job unless, of

course, you want to be a doctor or a lawyer or an engineer."

I hadn't really been thinking of professional training when I started this inquiry, but the frequent exception piqued my curiosity. How necessary are these supposedly most necessary of all college and postcollege courses?

Not as necessary, I discovered, as everyone assumes. Teachers, engineers, and other professional workers are always surprised, when they turn up for work, to discover that their elaborate schooling hasn't prepared them for what they are asked to do. They discover that 1) Students in professional schools learn a lot of things they never use; 2) Professional workers have to learn a lot of things that are never taught in schools; and 3) Most of what professional schools teach is less likely to "come in handy later" than it is to fade from memory and relevance.

Professional schools are adding practice to their curriculums, but they still have a long way to go. If you doubt this, ask a young doctor, lawyer, architect, engineer, librarian, journalist, or nurse to tell you a single thing he did in the past week that he or she learned to do in school. Chances are you'll draw an awkward blank, followed by a rather defensive account of the value of professional training peppered with slippery words like "basic," "fundamental," "principles," "theories," "approaches," "attitude," and very frequent use of the adjective "general."

Professionals on their first jobs complain that their education isn't used at all. Employers demand a degree in engineering or science and then put the graduate to work at jobs that would not tax a mathematically inclined high-school student. Manpower specialists say that this talent stockpiling creates an artificial "shortage" of scientists and engineers and erodes morale. In order to see how well college prepared engineers and scientists for actual paid work in their fields, Carnegie

Commission researchers got permission to query all the employees with degrees in science or engineering of two firms. Only one in five said the work they were doing bore a "very close relationship" to their college studies, while almost a third saw "very little relationship at all," and an overwhelming majority could think of people doing their work who had majored in a different field.

Majors in nontechnical fields reported even less relationship between their studies and their work. Communications majors who make good can be blunt. "College is phoney," Charles Lawrence, the producer of "Kennedy & Co.," the Chicago morning television show, says. "You have to learn all that stuff and you never use it again. I learned my job by doing it. If I went back to college, I'd study government." Bob Kennedy majored in communications at Fordham University, but he credits his success as a talk show host to the logic the Jesuits taught him. "If you are going to keep conversation on the track, you have to make sure you have a door before you talk about what color to paint it."

Formal courses may handicap a natural-born learner, even when the subject is highly technical. Amy Van Doren dropped out of architecture school, she says, because she "got fed up" with designing restaurants "in the Frank Lloyd Wright style" and segregated housing for the elderly, whom she believed might prefer to live with younger people. At nineteen she plunged right in to building real buildings. Working with community groups in Pittsburgh and New Haven, she helped fix up slum buildings, made a church basement over into a medical clinic, and turned a two-story warehouse into an office building. She and other young architecture students learned the hard way—with a hammer in hand.

Didn't all that building take more theoretical book learning than she had stayed long enough in architecture school to get?

"No," says Amy. "It's much easier to learn by doing than it is to learn by thinking about doing. As for calculating beams and weights so that a house won't fall down, well, there are tables for that sort of thing you can get in a library. You don't have to go to school to find them. All you need is to have someone point them out to you." But in 1974 she was back in school, getting her degree at George Washington University. "You have to have a degree to get anything, though it doesn't seem to matter how you get it," she concluded grimly. The credential, not the knowledge, was what she needed.

If job-hunting liberal arts graduates often wish they had a definite skill to offer, technicians who have pursued a specialty for four years frequently complain that they have spent precious college time in meaningless jargonland. A browse through college catalogues discloses what they mean. Consider, for instance, the first course listed in the nursing department of Georgetown University's *Bulletin* for undergraduate schools:

> *Personal and Social Dimensions of Nursing.* An introduction to nursing as a practice discipline, a profession and an occupation. The course focuses on the forces which structure nursing from within and outside the profession, making it operational in society. Emphasis is placed upon the development of a dynamic concept of nursing and an understanding of the essential behaviors of student members of the profession.

For the sake of their future patients, one can only hope that the student nurses don't get the idea that nursing is primarily a verbal exercise.

Or take a look at a course that purportedly addresses itself to the facts of sickness.

> *Introduction to Basics of Medical Science.* An introduction to the basic and applied sciences the

focus of which is primarily disease related. Introduction to medicine is given, indicating relationships of the elements of pathogenesis, pathology,
physiology, and diagnostic and therapeutic metho-
dologies. The broad content elements of the disciplines of pharmacology and nutrition are provided.

This covers a lot of ground, at least semantically, and
while nurses may need special training in the private
language of physicians, the "methodology" that under-
takes to cure sickness by words is not called medicine,
but magic.

Business administration attracts young people and
their parents who hope that the schooling will help
them rise in a good company or maybe add something
to one of the very large number of family-operated
small firms. Their bent is practical or they wouldn't
enroll. What awaits them? At the State University of
New York at Albany, a businessbound student interested also in "people" might consider

341. *Behavioral Science for Business.* An intellectual foundation for constructive executive leadership is developed through improved understanding
of group dynamics, superior–subordinate interac-
tion, and worker performance, motivation and
satisfaction under defined conditions of industrial
organizations, operation, technological change and
macro-societal influence. . . .

No, this isn't for doctoral candidates in sociology. It's
an undergraduate course in *business.*

If this is good, more has, until quite recently, been
held much better. During the late 1960s big companies
snapped up Masters of Business Administration at
starting salaries much higher than they were paying
men and women of the same age who had been working
for the firm instead of attending college. Shiniest of all
the M.B.A.'s were those from the Harvard Graduate

School of Business. In addition to the patina of scholarship enjoyed by anything with the name Harvard in it, the "B" School (so dubbed, perhaps, because in Cambridge the very word "business" is too shameful to say outright) offered not mouth-filling theory, but vicarious experience in solving actual business problems—the famous Harvard-designed "case method."

For a generation, the brightest sons of the richest businessmen have gone to Harvard to grapple with each other over the way to deal with a specific business decision faced in the past by some manager.[11] Big companies latch on to the graduates when they are planning expansion, but most medium-sized enterprises—the size most favored by business graduates in the 1970s—think they are "too high powered" for the work available, especially when no mind-blowing new ventures are planned. A Harvard Business School graduate who is now president of a department store won't hire "B" School graduates because "they are trained only for my job—but not for any job I have to fill."

Maybe it takes one Harvard man to catch another. Most critical of formal business schooling in general, Harvard's included, is J. Sterling Livingston, professor of business administration at the Harvard Business School. "Formal management education programs typically emphasize the development of problem-solving and decision-making skills, but give little attention to the development of skills required to find the problems that need to be solved, to plan for the attainment of desired results, or to carry out operating plans once they are made," he writes in, of all places, the *Harvard Business Review*. Analysis, he goes on to say, may be fine for professors but it isn't what makes money, which is what business is all about. A fine analysis, professor, and right to the point.[12]

The only art that can really be demonstrated in a classroom is the art of teaching. Unfortunately, however, very little of *that* art is transmitted that way. In order to qualify as a teacher, you have to sit for hours and hours in classes not to watch *how* teaching is done but to take notes on how the teacher thinks it *ought* to be done.

The literature of education is luxuriant, or more properly speaking, rampant. Schools of education are among the biggest on campus, to say nothing of the hours and classrooms filled with short courses, conferences, and training sessions. Formal instruction in teaching is regarded as so important for teachers already on the job that schoolchildren are regularly sent home early—or kept home all day long—so that their teachers can ply each other with the theory of what they are supposed to be doing.

Does it help? Incredible as it seems, no one has ever attempted to find out. Back in 1950, two educators searched through 673 articles on teacher competence without finding a single study which reported any relationship between competence and the amount of training.[13] A later attempt failed also. But the problem is even worse than it sounds. The competence of a business manager might be crudely measured by the corporate income account. The competence of a teacher might be measured by the grades his students make on an objective examination. However, executives and teachers resist these practical measures in favor of evaluations based on mastery of theories about their work taught in schools of business and education. Millions of teachers and thousands of executives have won raises solely on the basis of taking courses.

And what courses! A kindergarten teacher with more than twenty years of experience got her M.A. because the salary increase would permanently increase her pension. One of the courses she took at a major university was called "The Psychology of Hazard Control"— which meant discussions of accidents that could happen on school playgrounds. Not only did it require no books, no work, and no examination, but no attendance was taken. The grading system was simplicity itself and designed to maintain the professor's enrollments: all former students of the professor got A, all new students, B. During the course, the new students had time to discover that it was possible to take three other courses with the same professor, all variants of Hazard Control offering the same commonsensical material.

Unfortunately, Hazard Control is not exceptional. The story is sure to stimulate the informed reader to think of a topper. The irrelevance of the professional education offered in nontechnical occupations and the number of students enrolled in them are both so enormous that an editor of *Fortune* once proposed writing an article about what would happen to the economy if all the schools of education, business administration, and yes, even journalism, were wiped off the map in a single night. His conclusion: nothing would be lost except the jobs of their faculties.

The plain fact is that what doctors, nurses, lawyers, journalists, social workers, broadcasters, librarians, and executives do all day long isn't taught in classrooms. Doctors are the most responsible and most highly trained professional workers, but they spend their days bandaging, suturing, and trying to give injections without hitting a nerve ending. Even specialists spend most of their time on the common illnesses and minor complaints which the barefoot doctors of China learn in a three-month cram course *after* being chosen by their neighbors and patients. On a visit to China in 1971, Dr. Victor W. Sidel, chief of social medicine at Montefiore Hospital, couldn't believe they could learn enough to do it in so short a time until he had watched them. "At every level, people are trained just enough for the work they must do," his wife added. "In our country, doctors are overtrained for most of the work they do."[14]

No one is suggesting that we stop teaching sophisticated medical techniques simply because they are seldom used. What we do suggest is that the expensive overeducation of physicians in the United States is not an innocent, public-spirited attempt to provide superior medical care, but a device to line the pockets of doctors by limiting their numbers. An immediate remedy would be to utilize the paramedics who were trained and seasoned in the Vietnam War to do many of the simpler medical chores which command high fees because it is presently illegal for anyone but a doctor to do them.

Proof that medicine as practiced is considerably less complicated than medical school catalogues indicate is the survival of scores or perhaps hundreds of fake M.D.'s who have learned their medicine the way it always used to be learned—by hanging around hospitals and doing like the doctors do.[15] The wonder is not that these fakes, when exposed, have killed so few, but that they have been able to do so well. The reason of course is that medicine as it is actually practiced is empirical and that for all the medical jargon, the antibiotics, appendectomies, and other procedures that really cure are likely to be rather simple and straightforward.

Psychiatrists are the medical mystificators par excellence. According to David Viscott, a psychiatrist himself, most practitioners operate on the basis of some quirk of their own personality, and the theories they learn in school have very little to do with their ability to help patients. What does help, he writes, is "common sense from someone who cares," and he readily admits that a good psychiatrist does no more than what a good friend can do.

Most learned professions are really a little bag of tricks which professional schools often disdain to transmit. Journalism schools don't tell you how to get the street addresses of a phone subscriber in another city. Law schools don't tell you where to look for a public record or that Blumberg's law blanks, available to anyone at the stationery store, will cover 90 percent of the documents any lawyer will have to draw in a long and lucrative career—or even that such blanks exist. Engineers don't learn how to test a batch of concrete or inspect a steel girder until they get out in the field and confront a construction crew which knows they don't know. Perhaps because of their artistic orientation, architects are even more disadvantaged by the all-too-concrete nuts and bolts of their media: no one learns how to build a stud wall in school, let alone how to get someone who can build one to do it the way the plans specify. The medium of architecture is not words, but intractable material that cannot be hauled into classrooms.

Like the real nakedness of the emperor in the folk tale, the ineffectiveness of professional training is nothing a polite adult will admit in public. Professional training is, after all, limited to a few privileged individuals who are expected to learn how to deal with patients or clients or even how to build actual bridges and buildings from seniors on the job and, very frequently, from lower-rated, job-educated specialists such as foremen, nurses, and the sergeants from whom newly graduated second lieutenants have traditionally learned how the army works.

The learned professionals, like almost everyone else, spend their days on the job doing work that is never taught in any classroom. But when students complain that their courses are irrelevant, everyone tells them that the mismatch between work and study doesn't really matter, because the best preparation for life or work is a broad general education in the liberal arts.

6

The Liberal Arts Religion

The academic dean of a famous old college lowered her voice, glanced apprehensively around her office, and confessed: "I just wish I had the guts to tell parents that when you get out of this place you aren't prepared to *do anything.*"

Actually, it did not take much guts. The "best" colleges are the liberal arts schools which are the most "academic"—they don't teach students anything useful in particular. Even after they have to face the world, alumni expect no more. In a study intended to probe what graduates seven years out of college thought their colleges should have given them, the Carnegie Commission found overwhelming preference for "liberal" over "vocational" goals.[1]

What does anyone mean by "a liberal education"? People shift their ground when they try to explain what it is and why it is so important. It's hard to tell whether they're talking about *subjects* that can be studied in school, such as philosophy and literature; a *process* of learning or thinking; or a *personal transformation* ("college opened my eyes"); or a *value system* to which the wise and honest can repair.

The *subject matter* of the liberal arts used to be the classics. If not the ancients, then newer books on history, sociology, economics, science, and other products of the minds of men. As we near the twenty-first century, however, most educators have given up the attempt to pass on the "great tradition of Western man" in a four-year core curriculum. It's not *what* you study, they say, it's *how* you study it.

"A liberal education is an experience that is philosophical in the broadest sense," David Truman, dean of Columbia and later president of Mount Holyoke, has said. "The particular subjects do not so much contain this quality as provide jointly a possible means of approaching it. The liberal arts, then, include those subjects that can most readily be taught so as to produce an understanding of the modes of thought, the grounds of knowledge, and their interrelations, established and to be discovered."

In plainer language alumni say, "College taught me how to think for myself." If you ask people what they mean by thinking and how college teaches it, they recoil from the implication that the kind of thinking they mean is a specific skill, such as the art of rhetoric, but start talking about a "whole new way of looking at the world"—a personal transformation.

Personal transformation, not only in how one's mind works but in how one views the world and oneself, is the most cherished expectation—and sometimes it is achieved. "College changed me inside," one alumnus told us. Some wax poetic. "The liberal arts education aspires to expand the imaginative space and time in which a person lives." Others talk about the "broadening" that occurs when a young woman from a Midwest farming town encounters adults who don't regret the fact that MacArthur was not elected President, or when the son of a city plumber learns that the police are not always right and that some people on welfare aren't cheating. Discoveries like this are valuable, alumni say, because they force students to "formulate the values and goals of my life," as the Carnegie Commission puts it.

And this turns out to be the hidden agenda of a

liberal arts education. A value system, a standard, a set of ideals to keep you pointed in the right direction, even if you can't get there. "Like Christianity, the liberal arts are seldom practiced and would probably be hated by the majority of the populace if they were," said one defender.

The analogy is apt. The fact is, of course, that the liberal arts are a religion in every sense of that term. When people talk about them, their language becomes elevated, metaphorical, extravagant, theoretical, and reverent.

In answering a black student who charged the Kirkland College curriculum with "irrelevance," President Samuel F. Babbitt remonstrated that her liberal arts education aimed to expose her "to the values, the successes, the failures of great minds, great men and women engaged in every conceivable endeavor through the study of history and literature and art and the other disciplines that man has formed in order to understand where he has been and how to order his world."

"The purpose of the liberal arts is not to teach businessmen business," Alfred Whitney Griswold, former president of Yale told an alumni gathering. Rather, he went on, it is to "awaken and develop the intellectual and spiritual powers in the individual before he enters upon his chosen career, so that he may bring to that career the greatest possible assets of intelligence, resourcefulness, judgment, and character."

These thickets of verbal foliage are embarrassing to the more sensitive spokesmen for higher education. John T. Retalliata, president of the Illinois Institute of Technology, told an audience of parents in 1973, "I suppose a generalized goal is to have your sons and daughters, somehow, become 'educated' and, with that education, become well-employed and happy." Clark Kerr, notable as the embattled president of the University of California during the 1960s, told a 1972 television audience that "generally, the studies show that people who've been to college, oh, enjoy life more, they have more varied interests, they participate more in community activities." On another occasion, he told Alan Pifer, president of the Carnegie Corporation, that "with all that has happened in the world of knowledge in recent years, it is really impossible for people in higher education to come to agreement on what constitutes a liberal education."

Intellectuals have trouble describing the benefits of a liberal education because the liberal arts are a religion, the established religion of the ruling class. The exalted language, the universal setting, the ultimate value, the inability to define, the appeal to personal witness, the indirectness, the aphorisms—these are all the familiar modes of religious discourse.

As with religion, no proof is required, only faith. You don't have to prove the existence of God. You don't have to understand the Virgin Birth. You don't have to prove that Camus is better than Jacqueline Susann. Camus is sacred, so Camus is better and so are the people who dig him. If you don't dig Camus, the trouble is not with Camus, but with you.

Faith in personal salvation by the liberal arts is professed in a creed intoned on ceremonial occasions such as commencements. It is blasphemy to take the promises literally, and if you don't understand what the words mean, you are only admitting your lack of grace.

Take, for instance, the goal of college most fervently sought by the alumni queried by the Carnegie Commission, "development of my abilities to think and express myself." Only the captious dare to ask, "What do you mean by your ability to think?" If you inquire, it very quickly develops that those who value this objective aren't talking about what the Swiss educator Jean Piaget, the semanticist Noam Chomsky, or the Harvard psychologist Jerome Bruner mean when they talk about "thinking."[2] The kind of "thinking" the cognitive psychologists are talking about has to be acquired long before you are old enough to go to college, and if Piaget is right, most of it has to be learned before a child is old enough to go to school. What the alumni and employers expect college to teach is the habit of logical analysis and the conventions of rhetoric that make it possible to resolve differences of view on human affairs by debate and discussion. Colleges with very small classes try to give their students practice in the art of dialogue, but the students who speak up in class are usually the ones who have already learned how at the dinner table at home and in bull sessions with friends.

If the liberal arts are a religious faith, the professors are its priests. Professors are not accountable to the laity they serve. They themselves define the boundaries of their authority and choose their own successors. Their authority is unassailable, because by definition they know best. As such, they are invulnerable to lay criticism. One of the educators with whom I talked dismissed the doubts of students out of hand. "I am not convinced that eighteen-year-olds can or should be expected to know what college will ultimately do for them."

The professors disclaim arbitrary personal power. They go by rules. They contend that right is not what they think but what the sacred scriptures or the ecclesiastical courts decree. Professors say that truth is what comes out when you subject data to a process called the scientific method, and it is this process, rather than its product, that is written in the stars. But the process itself, this very scientific method, is also a product of the mind of man, and it may not be the only process the mind of man can devise. Other processes may produce other kinds of truth. No one, for instance, would suggest that the visions of William Blake could be "disproved" by the scientific method.

Colleges govern themselves by their own rules and sometimes confront civil authority. Only during the 1960s, when the students were out of control, did college administrators admit the right of the local police to "invade" the campus. And, like the church, American colleges have used their credibility to exercise political, economic, and social power in an irresponsible way. Along with access to heaven, they don't mind controlling access to the good things of this world. So long as the diploma is a credential for good jobs, giving or withholding it determines the fate of students here on earth. The colleges do not claim that they are preparing candidates for executive work, for instance, but they do not renounce their role as gatekeeper of the best jobs. As one professor told us, "We can't help it that the big companies like to hire our graduates."

To be blunt, the colleges have been as willing as the church to grab the power the faithful thrust upon them. Through their power to issue the diploma, they decide the fate of individuals. Through their power to determine who shall be admitted to college, they select as "naturally better" those who manipulate abstract symbols and unwittingly consign to the damnation of dead-end, second-class roles, those whose intelligence is manual, visual, or artistic. The power we allow them to have makes our society more vulnerable to words and abstractions than it would otherwise be, and it is not necessary to have a settled opinion on whether this is good or bad to recognize the danger of subjecting young people during their formative years to control by authorities who are pursuing objectives that leave most of the population cold. We think they are benign, therefore we accept their rule over our young. Imagine the outcry at the very idea of turning our surplus young people over to the military for safekeeping!

Americans have always been sensitive to the attempts of their armed forces to use military competence as a basis for exercising political power. But we do not distrust the same kind of bid when it comes from the professoriate. Through their control of research, they decide what frontiers of knowledge shall be pushed back. Through their interpretation of the scientific method, if not the sacred writings of "the great Western tradition," they decide what shall be accepted as good, or true, or even beautiful.

But just as technical progress threatened the various monopolies of the church at the end of the Middle Ages, so the informaton explosion today threatens the monopoly of college over knowledge.

Of all the forms in which ideas are disseminated, the college professor lecturing his class is the slowest and the most expensive. The culturally deprived for whom college is supposedly so broadening are in the best position to see this. "I can read a book just as good as the man can talk," a black woman student told us. "Nine chances out of ten that's all you get—a professor who's just reading out of the book."

A better college experience would, no doubt, have provided more stimulation than students encountered in the overloaded colleges of the 1960s. But this begs the issue.

Today you don't have to go to college to read the great books. You don't have to go to college to learn about the great ideas of Western man. If you want to learn about Milton, or Camus, or even Margaret Mead, you can find them. In paperbacks. In the public library. In museum talks. In the public lectures most colleges offer for free. In adult education courses given by local high schools. People don't storm these sources because they aren't interested, and there's no particular reason why they should be. Forcing people to "learn" about them by all sorts of social and economic carrots and sticks implies that those who have had contact with "high culture" are somehow better than other people.

And if you do want to learn, it isn't always necessary to go to the original source. I say this knowing that I am stamping myself as an academic heretic. But the culture consumer should be able to decide for himself exactly why, when, how much, and in what form he

would like to partake of Daniel Defoe's *Robinson
Crusoe*, or Milton's *Areopagitica*, or Simone de Beau-
voir's *The Second Sex*. When I was in high school during the 1920s, the whole English class took a month to
read *Ivanhoe*, Sir Walter Scott's novel about the cru-
sades. In 1969 my eight-year-old son zipped through a
Classic Comic version in fifteen minutes, and I don't
think the original warranted the extra time it would
have taken him. If you are not interested in the development of the English novel, *Robinson Crusoe* can
be an exasperating, slow-moving yarn, significant only
because the name has become a symbol of lone adventure and one of the passwords recognized by all men
who consider themselves educated. Milton's *Aréopa-
gitica* is another password, important for what it says
and when it was said. There's a benefit in knowing
about these works, but the benefit to any particular
person at a particular time may not justify the cost of
taking them raw. For many people, and many purposes,
it makes more sense to read a summary, an abstract, or
even listen to a television critic.

The problem is no longer how to provide access to
the broadening ideas of the great cultural tradition, nor
even how to liberate young people so that they can
adopt a different lifestyle than the one in which they
were reared. The problem is the other way around:
how to choose among the many courses of action proposed to us, how to edit the stimulations that pour into
our eyes and ears every waking hour. A college experience that piles option on option and stimulation on
stimulation merely adds to the contemporary night-
mare. Increasingly, overloaded undergraduates give up
the attempt to reason and flirt, half seriously, with the
occult, which leaves vexing decisions to fate.

In order to deal with options, you need values. When
Morris Keeton and Conrad Hilberry attempted to de-
fine a liberal education in their book *Struggle and
Promise: A Future for Colleges*, they found that one of

the recurrent themes was that it provides "an integrated view of the world which can serve as an inner guide,"[3] and more than four-fifths of the alumni queried by the Carnegie Commission said they expected that their college should have "helped me to formulate values and goals of my life." The formation of values may not be the first goal mentioned in discussions of a liberal education, but it tends to be the final ground on which hard-pressed defenders take their stand.

How does a student acquire a standard of values? The liberally educated are forbidden, by their own creed, from any procedure so simple as telling students what is right and good. In theory a student is taught how to decide for himself, but in practice it doesn't work quite that way. All but the wayward and the saints take their values of the good, the true, and the beautiful from the people around them. When we speak of students acquiring "values" in college, we often mean that they will acquire the values—and sometimes we mean only the tastes—of their professors.

The values of professors may well be "higher" than many students can expect to encounter elsewhere, but often those values aren't relevant to the situations in which students find themselves in college or later. Too many academics systematically overvalue symbols and abstractions. Historians will recall that it was a professor of history, President Woodrow Wilson, who sent American soldiers abroad to "make the world safe for democracy."

In addition to a distressing confusion of symbol and thing, professors are sometimes painfully ignorant of many essential facts of life. A lot of them know very little about the economic structure of the United States, and their notions of what goes on inside major corporations are based on books written forty years ago about conditions prevailing fifty years ago. And they may also be partially responsible for some of the "alienation" of the young because they have encouraged the belief that transactions of power and money are to be avoided as a dirty business.

In so doing, of course, they are intuitively defending the legitimacy of their own power. A poor boy who wanted to make good in the Middle Ages had to become a priest and at least profess to see the world in spiritual terms. A poor boy who wants to make good in twentieth-century America has to get a liberal education and at least profess to see the world in intellectual terms.

The academic elite are the self-proclaimed guardians of what's right. Who's to tell them when they are wrong? Academics pride themselves on introducing students to a free marketplace of ideas, but they are the ones who make the rules, and the rules themselves can perpetuate dangerous distortions of reality. Not so long ago, for instance, no painter who drew pubic hair on a nude figure could expect to be taken seriously as an artist. It would have been vulgar to see it. The oversight is amusing now, but it was not trivial. Victorian prudery was hard to combat because it was a convention of the "best people." It's easy to laugh, but harder to be sure that we are not overlooking some other facts of life today.

A liberal arts education does, of course, transmit standards of value, and those in charge assume, almost as self-confidently as that great Victorian, Matthew Arnold, that "the best that has been known and thought in the world" is what they say it is. Intellectual leaders today worry about sounding snobbish, but they are just as sure as the great eighteenth-century English essayist Richard Steele that "it is the great aim of education to raise ourselves above the vulgar." And those who have been so educated are happy to accept the distinction. At Harvard commencements there is an audible sigh of emotion when the president, as he has done for 300 years, welcomes the new graduates into "the fellowship of educated men." (Since 1970, it has been "the fellowship of educated men and women.")

7

The Diploma: America's Class Distinction

"The fellowship of educated men" is an informal organization, but the piece of paper that attests membership in that company is a reliable passport to jobs, power, and, as one older Ivy League graduate put it, "instant prestige."

The reason is embarrassing. In our supposedly classless society, the diploma is our class distinction. By giving it to everyone, egalitarians hope somehow to make everyone upper class.

This is plain speaking. The proponents of college for all, the employers who prefer college graduates, and the mothers who "want the best" for their children don't like to think of themselves as snobs. That's why the language in which they discuss college is murky and the reasoning strays.

"He might be handicapped some time in some way if he didn't have a college degree," a mother will say. "He can go. He can get in. We have the money. And since there's nothing better for him to do right now anyway —well, why shouldn't he go?"

And then comes the father with the vocational clincher: "Maybe he won't need college to do the kind of job he'll probably want, but he'll need a degree to *get* it in the first place."

Professional people cheerfully agree. Thomas Putalik

is now a business systems manager for AT&T. In retrospect, he isn't really sure why he went to Manhattan College fifteen years ago to get a degree in electrical engineering, but he remembers thinking that it would give him a "leg up, so to speak, in the organizational climb that I was going to get into. A union piece of paper to a slightly better job from a starting point."

Personnel analysts say about the same thing. One of the most thoughtful is Glenn Bassett, a specialist on the staff of General Electric. "In some parts of GE, a college degree appears completely irrelevant to selection to, say, a manager's job. In most, however, it is a ticket of admission."

Pressed for specific advantages a liberal arts education confers, employers often say that the college man "gets along with all kinds of people" and "communicates better." Listen to Glenn Bassett again: "An education which *takes* . . . permits its possessor access to the experience of a wider range of people over limitless distance, and even backward into recorded time. There are jobs in the upper reaches of an organization where effective long-distance communication, without direct personal experience to carry you, is essential."

A telephone company engineer says that the course that helped him the most was one in English composition which has made it easier for him to write effective interoffice memos. "College prepares a person to operate in the culture of management," Dominick Carbone, a personnel supervisor for New York Telephone told us.

The college educated are especially important in contacts with customers and outsiders, the so-called "front" jobs. Stanley Marcus, the Harvard-educated head of the famous Dallas specialty shop, has taken advertising space to proclaim that "a liberal arts education is the best qualification for future Neiman-Marcus executives."

Neiman-Marcus caters to the affluent and the sophisticated who either are or respect college graduates for their status.

What these people are saying, in a very polite and often oblique way, is that the tone of voice and language of an educated man implies a superiority that commands attention. The "educated" man "communicates" better not so much because he speaks more articulately or even because he has something more relevant to say, but because people—subordinates, associates, customers—listen to him more respectfully.

Instant operational prestige with strangers, the words and accents that make traffic cops believe your side of the story. This is one of the practical benefits of sounding educated, and it has very little to do with what is learned in expensively equipped classrooms or libraries. Very frequently it's what employers and parents are really buying for the price of a college education, and some are frank to admit it. One parent we interviewed hoped, rather vaguely, that a college education would be a "business and social asset" to his son for the rest of his life. A woman student hoped that college would enable her to "carry on a conversation with her husband's boss when he came to dinner."

The more secure of the old-fashioned college professors are often daring enough to admit that their renowned liberal arts is "really" a "finishing school" to "hone the sensibilities" of gentlemen who can afford to pay the high price of these intangible and largely ornamental benefits. Some of them think it's a joke that employers set such store by the right accents. Although it's good form, these days, to sound apologetic about it, they are quick to admit that they aren't teaching students anything practical. They are teaching "attitudes" and "approaches" and providing "broad, general background" for "making decisions." Their graduates have no specific skills. They are being trained not to do the dirty work but to get other people to do it.

The notion of the executive as "gentleman" has been incorporated into management science. He gets other people to do things. He knows how to motivate, how to lead, how to get others to do what he wants them to do. If he pitches in and works with the "men" he's a confessed failure.

The "gentleman" of an earlier era led by virtue of his birth. In the nineteenth century power was open to those with "personal magnetism," like Napoleon. In a supposedly egalitarian society like ours, there must be another route, one open to all.

We have said that higher education is the legitimate road to power and have enshrined in its curriculum and its environment the diversions and tastes of the powerful. College has taught large numbers of people to read books, buy art, attend concerts, go to Europe, visit museums, play tennis, savor wine, and cope with menus written in French. It costs a great deal of time and money to acquire these amenities, and, though many are happy with the bargain, real power remains as closely held as ever. Very few of the new art collectors, for instance, have anything to say about zoning regulations, interest rates, income tax provisions, nominations of candidates for elective office, the acquisition policies of museums, and the Ford Foundation's choice of research projects, to name a few examples of real power. The people who make these ground rules are the same old people who were born to do it.

No one likes to say it out loud, but in America we have cruelly deluded the lower middle class into thinking that they can gain access to power by studying, in formal classes, the arts, amusements, concerns, sentiments, and conventions of the "gentlemen" who are the successors if not the descendants of the "gentlemen" who inherited power along with their land.

The respect for the "gentleman" as leader is founded on an ancient fallacy. The Greeks invented the idea of rule by the best, "aristocracy." In ancient Greece, all of the dirty work (and some of the intellectual work, too) was done by slaves. Philosophers didn't have to get their hands dirty so they didn't. Hand and head were separate departments, and heads had political and economic power over hands.

The dichotomy between hand and head continued through the Middle Ages. Nobles ruled and serfs plowed. Knowledge advanced slowly when scholars thought it was beneath them to use their senses for experimental verification. It was not until physicians began actually looking at the human body that medicine moved beyond Hippocrates, and it is instructive that the first professors of anatomy who used actual models still felt it would sully their dignity to touch the organs themselves.

Scientific research, even when it dirties the hands, had now become prestigious, but an invidious distinction between "pure" and "applied" research still divides the scientific and intellectual communities. The prestige of pure researchers can be measured by the extra salary commercial companies have to pay to lure them away from universities where they supposedly deal in universal and eternal generalities, rather than in specifically useful truths. The same reasoning holds a liberal education "better" because it makes you a "better person" in general, rather than for any specific purpose.

The inference that college makes a person "better" has become credible because college graduates do better on almost every measurable test that can be devised. It's hard to name anything desirable enough to test for that isn't more apt to go to those who check "sixteen plus" years of schooling on surveys. The college educated are healthier, wealthier, happier, wiser, and morally superior in every way to those who haven't been to college.

As for health, they live longer, and, although they go to the doctor more often, they are out sick less. They are less apt to have nervous breakdowns, and less apt to report symptoms of psychological distress, such as dizziness and headaches, but more apt to consult a psychiatrist if they feel they need one and more apt to profit by psychotherapy once they undertake it.

As for wealth, they have more assets and are better paid both in dollars and in psychic income. Not only do they like their work more than the less educated, but they are more apt to value it for intrinsic interest or social value rather than pay or prestige. It's nicer work, too: safer, cleaner, steadier, physically easier, with longer vacations, more fringe benefits, and more chance for advancement.

They are happier. They have fewer divorces. They have fewer babies. Although more introspective and concerned about their relations with others, they get more pleasure from them and have a greater sense of well-being and satisfaction. They are more confident and optimistic about their own outlook and the national economy, too.

They are wiser in all things both great and small. They test out more "open, flexible, critical, objective, and nonjudgmental."

They are more internationalist, more opposed to war, military spending, and the personal possession of firearms. They are more liberal on social issues, more apt to blame society than the criminal, to favor abortion and male sterilization, and to accept marriages between blacks and whites, Protestants and Catholics, or Jews and non-Jews. They are more inclined to support lowering the voting age and giving birth control pills to teen-age girls. They are more likely to vote for higher school taxes, even when they are paying private school tuition for their own children.

The list is long, but could easily be extended. Some of the items were collected by Stephen Withey for the Carnegie Commission on Higher Education, and, although he was careful not to claim too much for them, the message is unmistakable: send everyone to college and everyone and everything is bound to get better.[1]

During the 1960s we doubled the number of young people attending college, and everyone and everything seemed to get worse. The most charitable conclusion is probably correct: College has very little, if any, effect on people and things at all. Now, in the 1970s, the false premises are easier to see:

1) College doesn't make people intelligent, ambitious, happy, liberal, or quick to learn new things. It's the other way around. Intelligent, ambitious, happy, liberal, quick-learning people are attracted to college in the first place. Going to college in hopes of being like them, if you are not, is like playing tennis to look like the tennis-playing rich. It doesn't work.

2) Colleges can't claim much credit for the learning experiences that really change students while they are there. Jobs, friends, history, and most of all the sheer passage of time have as big an impact as anything even indirectly related to the campus. Something that happened during a summer is so frequently the most significant learning experience a student can cite that it is tempting to wonder whether the best thing colleges do is to provide young people with unstructured time off.

3) Colleges have changed so radically that a freshman entering in the fall of 1974 can't be sure to gain even the limited value added reported in studies made during the middle 1960s. While we don't know what the new impact will be, all indications are that it will be considerably less than in the past.

For whatever "academics" have ever been worth in the impact of college, the sheer size of undergraduate campuses of the 1970s makes them even less than they ever were like the log which supported Mark Hopkins on one end and a lone student on the other end. We found many motivated students who were disappointed with their courses and professors. They had expected an intellectual orgasm that did not come off. Not only do bigger classes dilute faculty–student dialogue, but the shortage of college teachers during the years of expansion and the big rise in academic pay attracted the mediocre and the less-than-dedicated. And as we will see later, most college students do not live in the plush, comfortable surroundings that their parents envisage or even remember.

But the first proposition is the most important. College graduates are superior and desirable because they were superior and desirable to begin with. College presidents know that the best place to improve an institution is in the admissions office. Gifted students ought to ask themselves why personal phone calls, entertainment, and lavish printing is being spent to sell them on the virtues of going to Good Old Siwash or Great Harvard. The answer should be obvious: gifted students can do at least as much for Podunk (or Harvard) as Podunk or Harvard can do for gifted students.

It seems highly unlikely that we can credit all the stellar virtues and stunning privileges of college graduates to anything that happened during their postadolescent college years. It seems more likely that college attracts the privileged and the intellectually predisposed and cools the less favored out before diploma day.

In the first place, "everybody" does not go to college. College graduates who have been out of school long enough to establish any kind of track record are a far more highly selected group than is generally appreciated. In 1940, 5.8 percent of the twenty-five to twenty-nine-year-olds were college graduates; in 1950, 7.7 percent. Thanks to the great tuition-free, state-supported system of higher education built after 1950, 16.4 percent of the twenty-five- to twenty-nine-year-olds had completed four or more years of college in 1970.

We know a lot about how earlier graduates differed from the common people. They started out richer and brainier, and, as educators building the state colleges constantly reminded legislators. money talked louder than brains in deciding who got to go to college. During the 1960s, for instance, a male who was lucky enough to fall into the upper quarter in mental ability and family socioeconomic status (SES) had an 85 percent chance of entering college, but this chance dropped to 73 percent if his family happened to be in the second SES quartile, to 70 percent if they were in the third quartile, and to 48 percent if they were in the lower. SES is, of course, mostly money.[2]

It was primarily for the poor bright boys that legislators voted the money for state colleges, but as more and more were enabled to go, it became obvious that sizeable sectors of the American population wouldn't go to college even if they were paid to go. We now know this is true because we have tried it. Veterans of the Korean and Vietnam wars enjoy even more extensive and flexible education benefits than the famous G.I. Bill of Rights conferred on World War II veterans, yet fewer of them have taken advantage of the opportunity. A Congressional committee suggested even higher payments "to motivate the black veterans to enter training," but we can't be sure that even more money will do it. There seems to be some other determinant in the decision to go to college, some X factor strongly associated with, but not identical to, SES and brains.

The best evidence on what the X factor might be still comes from an extensive study of a big random sample of high-school graduates of 1959 and 1961 made by James W. Trent and Leland Medsker, and it found, predictably, that "a very large proportion of able youth either did not attend college or withdrew before graduation."[3] Just as the educators had been saying, those who did go to college were those whose parents were better off financially, educationally, and occupationally, good old socioeconomic status (SES). The more able academically were more apt to go, of course, but ability counted less than SES. But Trent and Medsker turned up some "other factors" as well.

They administered a battery of psychological tests to their thousands of subjects and found some interesting similarities among those who went to college. On the Omnibus Personality Inventory, the collegebound perceived their parents as "emotionally supportive, alert, and interested in their progress." They were more apt to view education as "worthwhile in itself rather than as utilitarian vocational training." They differed significantly from the non-collegebound in academic motivation, personal autonomy, and in deciding to go to college at an early age.

"Academic interest and motivation *instilled early in life* were related to college entrance and persistence, together with and independent of ability and socioeconomic status," Trent and Medsker reported. (Italics ours.)

What is "instilled early in life" is usually instilled by *parents*. When asked "Why are you here?" college students most often say, quite simply, "because my parents wanted me to go." This suggests that poor boys with no more than average intelligence can get through college if their parents want them to go badly enough, and we know that some do enter. Trent and Medsker found that family encouragement to go to college was more important than mental ability in determining whether a high-school graduate went. They also found that the schooling of parents made more difference than their money. Schooling seems to beget itself. The Vietnam and Korean veterans most likely to take up their educational benefits were those with more schooling to begin with, according to the Congressional report.[4]

Where does this bring us? College seems to attract and hold those who like school, and those who like school are those brought up to like it. If half the high-school students enter college and half of those who enter graduate, then the graduates are highly selected for liking school. So what else is new about them?

Two things, and both significant. One is that the

school likers were more "flexible, tolerant, and intellectually disposed" all along the line; that means those who tested nonauthoritarian in high school were more likely to enter college, and, of those who went to college, the nonauthoritarian were more likely to persist in college.

Second, and most interesting of all, when the same students were tested four years later, the school likers were those who improved their personality scores the most. They gained most in social maturity, self-expression, interest in people, and they scored lower on anxiety. "The longer students attended college, the more they showed a gain in autonomous, intellectual disposition," Trent and Medsker concluded. "Young people not in college showed little and sometimes no discernible personality development, as measured by the instruments used. The least flexible, tolerant, and intellectually disposed individuals were found among high-school graduates who never attended college, followed by college withdrawals." Some actually scored lower four years later on these scales. Chief among those who slid backwards personally were women who married right out of high school and became full-time homemakers and mothers.

Trent and Medsker thought they had proved that more ought to go. "Large numbers of society's ablest youths place little or no value on higher education and demonstrate few signs of intellectual or innovative behavior," they lamented. They concluded that it was up to educators to motivate those whose parents fail to inculcate a love of schooling. But another conclusion seems equally valid today. It may well be that college attracts large numbers of those who are predisposed to change and learn—and that they would score high on all the tests whether they go to college or not. If this is so, if college selects rather than creates ability, the diploma has become what Christopher Jencks of Harvard calls "a hell of an expensive aptitude test."[5] A

Harvard colleague and collaborator of Jencks, David Riesman, points out in a footnote that the very word "diploma" (folded-over paper) means a recommendation.[6]

If that folded-over piece of paper serves only to identify those who were talented to begin with, it is not only outrageously expensive but inefficient and unfair to candidates and employers. It is unfair to the candidates because they themselves must bear the total cost of selection—the cost of college. Candidates without the funds, the academic temperament, or the patience for the four-year obstacle race are ruled out, no matter how well they might perform on the job. Employers who rely on the diploma may be paying higher wages than the job requires and avoiding analysis of what it actually takes to do the job.

This is the case against "credentialism," a newly coined word for an ancient anomaly. It has been officially defined as "the imposition by employers of educational requirements that are not clearly indicated by the requirements of particular jobs." The definition comes from Margaret S. Gordon, associate director of both the Carnegie Commission on Higher Education *and* the Institute of Industrial Relations at Berkeley, and with that definition both the education and industry establishments have to be against it.[7]

No one denies that the diploma is worth more on the job market than anything learned in winning it. The most elegant proof is the finding cited by Ivar Berg in *Education and Jobs: The Great Training Robbery* that the fourth year of college, when capped by a degree, adds much more to the salary a graduate can command than the third year adds to the salary available to a dropout with only two years of college. It's not the fourth year that employers are "buying" when they offer so much more money for it. It's the degree.

The purest example of empty credentialing is probably the extra salary routinely offered to teachers who get a master's degree, even though there is no evidence whatsoever that what they learn has any effect on their pupils. Many organizations, notably the civil service, accept higher education as an alternative to years of job experience. The notion that a college education enables anyone to do anything better is so well accepted that graduates feel aggrieved when they don't get more money than those with lesser education who are doing the same work.

During the expansion of the 1950s and 1960s, college training was justified for entry jobs on the ground that progress was changing the tasks to be done so fast that most employees would spend a large part of their working lives learning new methods. College graduates were cheaper, the economists specializing in "human capital" maintained, because they learned faster and could become productive with less training. Prosperity generated a heady rhetoric of rapid and rosy progress. Automation was going to relegate the dull work to machines. And if human beings were to be left with nothing to do but "human work," what better preparation than the humanities? Daniel Bell, the Harvard sociologist, forecast a "post-industrial society" run by autonomous and highly specialized "knowledge workers."

Vocational advisors and employers readily accepted this reasoning. "Employers are seeking people who have higher levels of education because many jobs are more complex and require greater skill," the *Occupational Outlook Handbook* of the Department of Labor declared. "Furthermore, employment growth generally will be fastest in those occupations requiring the most education and training."

Young people and their parents read the message loud and clear: The world is becoming so complicated that you're not going to be able to make a decent living in the future without a college degree.

Well, maybe. The *world* may be more complicated than it used to be, but it is singularly difficult to prove that the *jobs* most people do are more complicated. Many ancient craft skills have been simplified or eliminated by mechanization. Ivar Berg reported on studies that concluded that most common jobs did not require more skill in 1965 than they did in 1940.[8]

V. Lane Rawlins and Lloyd Ulman were even more emphatic about the constancy of skill levels in their study which they described in a chapter of the Carnegie Commission report entitled *Higher Education and the Labor Market*. They found that in many cases, the more highly educated workers don't do the job any better than it was formerly done by those with less schooling. And while the education level and/or pay of many occupations has measurably risen, the two have not invariably been related. During the years of the teacher shortage, when less experienced teachers had to be hired, their average educational level dropped while their pay rose. Some of the most dramatic increases in average educational level occurred for manual occupations such as oyster fisherman or truck driver in which efficiency does not depend on academic achievement.[9]

The fact is, of course, that most of the work for which employers now expect college training is now or has been capably done in the past by people without higher education. The most dramatic examples are in the top-level jobs of large-scale enterprises which command the highest pay of all jobs. A majority of the management of Bethlehem Steel made it, and some to the very top, without diploma,[10] while many other executive suites bristle with academic types and resemble lavishly redecorated faculty clubs. The variation is almost a matter of taste, organizational tradition, and geography. Jobs which are routinely filled by people with some college training in the United States, for instance, do not require college training in Germany.[11]

The educational requirement for many common jobs is ambiguous and inconsistent. Hotel clerks, orderlies, bank tellers, and cashiers may be high-school dropouts or they may be college graduates. The same is true, a Department of Labor study found, of typical craft workers such as welders, press feeders, production machine operators, and wire workers.[12] Not only do the educational "requirements" set by employers for these jobs vary arbitrarily from region to region and firm to firm, but educational level has nothing to do with how well the jobs are done, how well they are liked, or how long workers stay with them. Differences seem arbitrary or depend on availability: some employers prefer college graduates and can get them, while others don't care or can't get them.

Educational requirements go up and down with the supply and demand of applicants. In some communities the phone company can require a college degree for service representatives, while in other communities high-school graduates are hired. When the navy was hunting for men during the manpower pinch of World War II, men with two years of college were accepted for flight training. When fewer were needed and civilian jobs dried up they were able to get college graduates.

Since the end of the draft, the armed forces have had a hard time enlisting enough men to keep the force up to strength. Educational requirements have been lowered, but not fast enough to fill quotas. In 1973 army recruiters illegally took more high-school dropouts than the law allowed, and by June, 100 recruiters had been charged with falsifying I.Q. tests upward to meet the quotas set for them.[13]

Supply and demand have always made it possible to require higher educational qualifications for those applicants who are selected on the basis of a formal or informal quota. The Coast Guard has accepted male recruits with less than a high-school diploma, but when they first began taking women, so many applied that they were able to demand high-school graduation for the limited number of women that they intended to accept. When I complained to the commanding officer that this constituted discrimination against women, I received an explanation that is an explicit and official statement of the deliberate manipulation of educational requirements. Higher requirements for women, the Coast Guard officer in charge of civil rights wrote, were not intended to make it harder for females to enter the Coast Guard, but were "based on the assumption that we would have a surplus of applicants for the limited number of openings for women and that we would therefore be in a position to select the best qualified applicants. In the case of male applicants, we have not been achieving quotas and have therefore not been requiring that they be high-school graduates. We have recently increased the number of openings for women in the Coast Guard and no longer have an excess of female applicants. Accordingly, we are amending our enlistment requirements so that neither women nor men will be required to have a high-school diploma or certificate."[14]

In Russia they tell people where to work. We shunt them into the work where candidates are needed by manipulating educational requirements. Hundreds of occupations get state and local governments to protect their wages by licensing regulations which stipulate longer training than is really necessary to "protect" the public. When doctors or electricians or barbers are needed, "standards" of training may come down to admit more. When "destructive competition" threatens the livelihood of those already in the field, state boards are urged to raise "standards."

In California, dental hygienists are licensed by the state. To get the license, they must attend at least two years of special schooling. They then command $10 an hour. Dental assistants do everything that the dental hygienist does except clean the patient's teeth. They are not licensed and get their training directly from their employers. They start at $400 a month. Requirements for nurses of various kinds reflect the job market.

Nurses associations have long favored requiring a B.A. degree or at least some college for entry into nursing school. They want the training to be as long and as difficult as possible and they argue persuasively that higher "standards" are in the interest of patients. Now there is evidence that the main impact of this expensive training is to limit the number of nurses so that their wages price nursing care out of the reach of all but the richest patients. A demonstration at Bakersfield College, California, has shown that a two-year nursing course can train nurses as well as the four-year courses.[15]

We pay in many different coins for the apparent ease with which we balance the supply and demand of manpower by switching the educational signals. The total cost of the market operation is borne by the applicant. He or she takes all the risk and assumes all the expense of investing in schooling which may or may not be needed. Second, the increasing arbitrariness of the requirement erodes the credibility of schooling. A student nurse cannot be expected to take her training seriously if she suspects that it is not based solely on the needs of patients.

Finally, the system is unintentionally cruel. In a dictatorship individuals may be badly treated, but they know there is nothing personal about it. Our system is less honest. We don't come out and tell applicants that they are turned down because they aren't needed. We convince them that they aren't bright enough or qualified enough to do the work to which they aspire. According to Colin Greer, a critic of American education, the real function of universal public education in the United States has not been to upgrade the poor but to teach the poor to accept a lesser place. In *The Great School Legend* he points out that since 1890 more children have failed in school than succeeded—they dropped out of the competition for better jobs. As demand for unskilled workers dwindled, more children stayed on in school and it took longer to "cool them out."[16] It used to be that you could get a good job if you stayed in school through high school. Then when employers could hire high-school graduates to deliver groceries, everyone had to go to high school to be sure of a job in the grocery store, and the ambitious went to college. Now that everyone has to go to college, college no longer serves to cool the surplus applicants out.

The next step in the inflationary spiral is inevitable, and in the 1970s, it was already under way. In spite of a disastrous decline in demand for college professors, which forced the dismissal of some tenured faculty, graduate schools enrolled 2 percent more students in 1973 than in 1972. Most of those who "go on" for a graduate degree imagine that their own superior qualifications or perhaps a stroke of luck will land them one of the few openings available. If they fail, they will blame themselves rather than the system.

It is easy, perhaps inevitable, for placement officers to concur. They are, after all, part of the system. One state university placement officer cited, as an example of the "unreality" of graduates, a senior who couldn't understand why his diploma did not entitle him to a job. "Do you mean that this piece of paper is no good at all?" he finally asked.

The student felt gypped. Maybe it was naive of him to feel this way, but those who propelled him to more and more schooling had some part in misleading him. What they had gypped him out of, of course, was his most precious possession—time. In his slender but elegant book entitled *Diplomaism*, David Hapgood, a contributing editor to the *Washington Monthly*, makes a devastating comparison: "The years in school are growing faster than our life expectancy."

Saddling the candidate with the total expense as well as the total responsibility for the system invites another and better recognized form of cruelty. Jews and women have always had to have better grades or present more years of schooling to get desirable jobs, but they have welcomed educational credentialing because it was an objective criterion which allowed them to compete. "Graduate school may be irrelevant as you say," one young faculty woman told me, "but for a woman, it's the only game in town." Blacks who make it tend to be more supportive of the system than whites, because it has served some of them better than any other leg up they could get. But unlike Jews and women, blacks often have a harder time with the academic work needed for educational credentials than the male WASPS who bar them, because of their frequently inadequate preparation for advanced schooling. Arbitrary educational criteria are in fact *racially* discriminatory. In the 1970s rising applications for police work have enabled more than a score of police departments to demand a college diploma for admission to the force. In New York and other big cities, minority applicants who are educationally disadvantaged have challenged the requirements as irrelevant and discriminatory *in intent*.

This perception may ultimately collapse the credentialing system and force a new, fairer, and more efficient system of allocating desirable work. In 1971 the Supreme Court of the United States decided in *Griggs v. Duke Power Company* that it is illegal for an employer to demand a qualification which systematically excludes a class of applicants unless it reliably predicts success on the job.[17]

Like many southern employers, the Duke Power Company had kept black applicants out of the office by requiring a high-school diploma for all office jobs. The civil rights lawyers who represented Griggs were able to show that the company had no proof whatsoever that a high-school diploma improved performance of the messenger work for which Griggs applied, and the rule was upset.

In 1974 the full implications of the Griggs doctrine

were still unresolved, but personnel authorities in major corporations were frankly worried. "Griggs is a sleeper," said an executive of AT&T.

"The embarrassing thing about the Griggs decision," said a personnel specialist in testing at the University of Minnesota, "is that we simply do not know how to predict competence in any job really worth having."

If the Griggs doctrine should ever be widely applied, it could force employers to investigate, for the first time, what it really takes to do the jobs they have to fill. When they take that unaccustomed look, they may have to admit what they intuitively know and deny: that the only way to "prepare" anyone for a job is to tell him he can do it, throw him into it, and make him want to succeed badly enough to learn how to do it.

8

A Place to Grow Up —Or Not

Many students and graduates are not deterred by the evidence that college will not necessarily insure them more money or a better job. It's worth it, they say, because it helps you grow up. Even students who aren't getting anything out of their studies told us they would go again "because of the people I met."

"As you come out of high school, you're not looking for a straight academic education," Charles Verrill, a senior at Hamilton, said. "What you are looking for is to get in private touch with people your own age."

"Self-assurance," said another senior when we asked him what college had given him. "I feel more confident about myself than I did when I was eighteen. Just having been in various situations and having experienced a lot more than I would have if I had stayed home and gotten a job." The "various situations" did not sound as if they referred to professors or classes.

Employers, parents, and in their more candid, unofficial conversations, even the professors agree that the chief benefit of the four-year investment is not intellectual but social.

"I thought that most of the learning would probably be through books and in the classroom," a political science major told us. "But most of it came through experiences I had with other people. Learning to accept different people and different people's ideas."

"I made friends with people who grew up in places like China I'd only read about before I came," said another.

A history major, both of whose parents are in academic pursuits, didn't find Augsburg College, a Lutheran-affiliated school in Minnesota, "intellectually fulfilling," but "I've made some very close friendships from college, which I think now is more important than what I actually learned in courses."

Predictably, several women students told us that the big thing they got out of college was learning to get along with men. For a lot of women, and even more of their parents, college is still the best place to find a husband. But mate hunting is not a one-way street. A Hamilton man endeared himself to our woman interviewer by telling her that college had been worthwhile for him because it had found him "a woman I can love."

"College changes people inside," said a woman who returned to college after dropping out because she felt she needed it for a decent job. The theme turned up at all ages and all kinds of schools. A woman graduating from an Ivy League school was disappointed with the education she received, "but I'm glad I went—it scares me to think of the kind of person I'd have been if I hadn't gone."

College is a time to try out new and different parts of a person. "I am still trying out different ways of relating to people—trying shyness and astounding bluntness, not caring about what I step on as well as watching carefully before making any sort of move," wrote a Russell Sage student.

"College definitely paid off," reported a midwestern graduate. "It was four years of living in and being involved in a community that I enjoyed and learned from. It was sharing a bathroom with thirty-five girls and fighting for washing machines on Saturday. It was discovering friendships—all of the 'social' discoveries that make you aware of yourself and others. College was also a time of assessing yourself."

The evidence is overwhelming. For college-age undergraduates, personal development, a chance to practice social skills, and "sort out my head" is the real value of college, and it has nothing to do with the curriculum. Classes serve primarily to bring students into contact with each other.

College professors know this, and they don't always like it. Some actively disdain the "people orientation" of undergraduates. "None of my students is interested in what I'm doing," a professor of social statistics told me. "They want to interview people. I want to design interview *schedules*. Classes are a struggle."

Another professor suggested, only half facetiously, that every campus ought to have two divisions yielding the identical degree: an intellectual division offering courses and a social division offering only opportunities to mingle with other students. And a faculty member of a southern school said that college is a place for adolescents "to cure, like hams."

"Growing up," "finding myself," "maturing"—what the psychologists now call "adult socialization" has become the primary function not only of the four-year liberal arts college, but of community colleges and trade schools as well. Personal growth ranks well ahead of vocational or intellectual growth as a goal on the 1973 Carnegie Commission Survey of Faculty and Student Opinion.[1] A whopping 83 percent of students queried agree "strongly" or "with reservations" that undergraduate education would be improved if more attention were paid to the "emotional growth" of students.

What kind of "emotional growth" does an eighteen-year-old need? The psychologists and educators are just beginning to ask the question. "Adult socialization" of the glandularly mature "postadolescent" emerged as a field for research in the late 1960s and 1970s. It didn't even occur to Harvard Professor Talcott Parsons, the great social systems theorist, that "post-adolescents" were going through any special stage of life until the middle 1960s, when "postsecondary" education, with its economic dependence, became the norm for all eighteen-year-olds.[2]

"Modern society is entering a period when a college education is becoming a requirement for maximal societal and occupational participation," Parsons wrote in a long essay triggered by the student revolts of the 1960s. "Since a new stage is emerging, a new name for it may be appropriate: we have entitled it the 'studentry' phase."

In the Parsonian world the first stage of life is infancy, during which you are socialized by the family. Then comes Oedipal childhood and latency, a stage that caused strain during the historical period when fathers began to leave home to work and children were sent to school to learn "capacities suitable for participation in industrialized society." Eight grades sufficed to prepare a boy to work in a factory, and a boy of fourteen automatically became an "adult."

Adolescence did not become a stage, a word, or a problem until we began pushing all young people into high school fifty years ago. The stress of adjusting to this new stage brought on adolescent "turbulence," a phenomenon that presumably did not exist or was not recognized before. In the past decade the whole thing happened all over again at the college level. When we pushed every high-school graduate to go to college, we created the new stage of life Parsons named studentry. Inauguration of this new stage helped to provoke the campus unrest of the 1960s.

And just as the nineteenth-century grade school, with its bolted-down seats, conditioned little children to sit still in the factory, and high school, with its clerical regimentation, conditioned "adolescents" for office paperwork, so college, says Parsons, conditions postadolescents for a contemporary world characterized, in his phrase, by "greater differentiation, pluralization, and complexity."

Parsonian theory is quite neat, but it isn't much practical help to college administrators or to students who want to know exactly what they can expect for their four-year investment. College teaches students to accept "authority rationally required by coordinated effort" and to develop "capacity to participate in and accept a more differentiated environment together with extensively pluralized courses of action" through exposure to the "value of cognitive rationality." With apologies to Professor Parsons, this sounds a little like "learning to get along with all kinds of people," "making my own decisions," and even "sorting out my head."

Students may agree with Parsons about what college ought to be doing for them, but they don't give their own institutions very high marks for succeeding, and they don't really see themselves quite as Parsons sees them. After reading his extended analysis (I made it their final examination), Russell Sage and R.P.I. students in my seminar agreed that college was a convenient place to go when the time came to get away from home, but opinion differed on whether it was the *best* place to mature, and while almost everyone thought college was, in some respects at least, a *nice* place, very few were willing to argue that it was the *only* place to grow up properly. Quite a few said college could be a *bad* place to mature.

The best thing about college was also, in other aspects, the worst thing: you could get away from home and live on your own without having to support yourself financially.

Some found semi-independence maturing. "It is not until you are living away from home that you can decide for yourself when you are going to study, when you're going to go out or cut a class or leave for a weekend of skiing," one student wrote. "Gradually more and more decisions are left up to you. You begin to control your life. While in this 'suspended' status of studentry, people do a tremendous amount of learning and maturing."

"The freedom that one feels while a student is what enables him to devote time to investigating and experimenting with various lifestyles," another pointed out. "As it is termed often on college campuses, one is able 'to find himself.' "

Others found the status of studentry ambiguous. "For four years I have lived in a sheltered life—away from parents, yes, but under a different type of restriction. My education has been paid for, my meals are made for me, my entertainment is abundant, my peers close by. I have few responsibilities other than to read, take tests, write papers, be in by curfew, respect my elders, do my laundry, etc. It is a very strange situation —one I frequently complain over, yet am dubious to relinquish. Life, at the moment, could not be better or easier for me."

Time—a "moratorium on commitment" is the campus term—rated second only to "freedom" as a maturing aspect of the college experience.

"A student can afford to 'flounder around' for these years until he formulates his own opinions and adopts a lifestyle for himself," one student wrote.

The very word time keeps cropping up. "Learning how to act with people and how people act takes *time*," one student wrote (italics ours). To another, studentry is "a *time* to learn not only to get along, but also understand people better, a chance to learn to live with your own values before bringing them into the many-valued society or adulthood." To still another, studentry seems "an opportune *time* (for those who wish) to learn more about the world and to pursue other cultural and intellectual activities." While waiting to grow up, one might as well take in an art gallery or two.

The most revealing comment came from a student who was driving me to the airport from Lafayette College in Pennsylvania. "College isn't the only place you can grow up. It's just the only place you can do it without holding down a job."

In their several tongues, students, graduates, employers, faculty, and Talcott Parsons seem to be saying the same thing: College is being used to get kids who look grown up out of the parental nest and into making their own decisions in a wider community more tolerable, egalitarian, and rational than the "cold hard world" without making them earn their own living in it.

It's a great idea. A sheltered way station between the ideal and the real world is so badly needed—and not by kids only—that in the twentieth century we would have to invent one if we didn't have colleges to convert to the purpose. The only trouble is that the reconversion is wasteful; colleges were designed to teach subjects to students in classes and laboratories and support research on the side. As maturing parks, they are saddled with the hideously rising expense of an academic apparatus that for all but a handful of students may serve only—if we listen to what everyone is really saying—as an excuse for keeping students out of the rat race for a few years.

And that's not all. Colleges are withdrawing from responsibility for feeding, housing, policing, or even protecting students just at the time when the *environment* of colleges has become the most important service it renders. College officials are refusing to "intervene" in the personal lives of students. They won't take over from biological parents, but are insisting that students take full adult responsibility for their plans, achievements, and behavior.

The fact is that college in the 1970s is no longer the pleasant place to be that parents of contemporary college students recall. The campus itself is less sheltered. College "life" is less rewarding, both physically and socially.

For most students, entering college doesn't even mean getting away from home. At the Census of 1970, a majority of freshmen of both sexes were domiciled "in household of parents," attending local or community colleges. A growing proportion of the big new enrollments—more than two million in 1973—were having to work for at least part of their support. Many were married or taking on emotional, if not financial, responsibility for a mate. And wherever they could, students were deserting college dormitories to find their own quarters in the "cold hard world" surrounding the campus.

Living off campus became popular as a way of escaping the parietal rules which reminded students of parental authority. At the height of the college building programs of the early 1960s, some colleges had to require freshmen to live on campus in order to pay off the bonds on their new dormitories. "Do you really like to keep house all that much?" I asked women students when I saw them lugging groceries up two or three flights of rickety stairs to cook on a hot plate in an overpriced furnished room. "We like the freedom," they would answer. "This way we can eat when we please. The dorms are zoos."

The rules are gone now, but there are other problems. Open dorms, particularly when they are coeducational, are noisy, and shy students are helpless to protect their privacy. What, for instance, is a student to do when his/her roommate brings in a sex partner? Open dormitories invite campus crime. The rules which once locked students *in* their dormitories after ten o'clock at night also served the purpose of locking burglars and rapists *out*.

The new dormitories built in the 1960s are not only

coldly institutional—resembling prisons—but many have the same cracks in the picture window that flawed the housing projects thrown up on G.I. mortgage money after World War II.

On some campuses, plumbing, roaches, and mice have replaced the immoral war in Vietnam as a political issue that expresses discontent with the ambiguous status of studentry. In the fall of 1973 Roberta Spagnola, dean of residence at Columbia University, spent a week in Furnald Hall to find out firsthand whether students rooms were really as "small and depressing," and the roaches and mice really as formidable as students complained. She concluded that the complaints were a symptom of loneliness: in open dormitories, men and women students have too little contact with each other, rather than too much.

Once upon a time all students had to gather at stated hours for breakfast, lunch, and dinner on pain of going hungry. Who sat next to whom was an issue. Now students are fed in continuously operating cafeterias, or they wolf snacks while studying. Quite aside from its disastrous impact on health, the new eating patterns make it possible for students to escape that contact with people different from themselves which they rate as one of the benefits of college.

The college environment of the 1970s may be more "relevant"—meaning more like the outside world—but the huge impersonal campuses look less than they ever did like the lush country club playgrounds glorified in Hollywood movies. Bulletin boards are littered with notices of apartments to share, cars to sell, books to buy, and the drift of conversations in the grimy, automatically vended food stations from which students derive most of their nourishment suggests that a lot of energy is dissipated arranging for food and shelter and scrounging enough cash to survive. Living conditions on and off campus recall the discomforts of immigrant ships of old which were endured because they were temporary vehicles to freedom and the hope of a better future.

Colleges have become less collegiate. Loyalties are national, the faculty to their specialties, the student to the status of studentry. The faculty no longer thinks of itself as a community of colleagues singing *gaudeamus igitur*. With rare exceptions, college spirit is as suspect as the American flag. The exceptions are mostly in the South. Mizzou, the University of Missouri, is still a "collegiate" campus, big on football and Greek-letter societies, and so is Vanderbilt at Nashville. But elsewhere extracurricular activities have all but disappeared. Yearbooks have frequently been dropped for lack of interest, student newspapers blink out for lack of student help, and there is little competition for class offices. Cars and jobs have transformed some campuses into "suitcase colleges," deserted not only on weekends, but increasingly during the week itself, as students elect to take courses in neighboring colleges or retreat from classes to independent study projects that take them into the "real world."

"Alumnae come back, they say, to sing Wellesley songs," an undergraduate on that campus observed contemptuously. "I don't know any Wellesley songs." So many graduates skip their own graduation exercises that in order to muster an audience for the event some colleges now charge absentees $25 to $50 for diplomas claimed afterward and find that many don't think the document worth the fee. In 1972 a senior speaking at her own graduation attacked the whole exercise as "false" because the graduating class was composed of individuals who had "no real reason to get together for anything."

"The idea of community, at least in the current situation, cannot be revived," concluded Clark Kerr, chairman of the Carnegie Commission on Higher Education. "Students generally are limiting their contacts to a small number of very compatible people. Even Swarthmore, with its traditions and its small size, has broken down into a series of subcommunities or 'families,' little friendship groups."

It is no news that students lost interest in politics, national or campus, after the Vietnam War. What, then, *do* they care about?

"Making soup," an administrator at Syracuse University answered unexpectedly. She was serious. In 1972 small groups of friends made a totally absorbing three-day project out of soup. They shopped for greens and soup meat. They kept watch together over the long, slow hours of cooking, and when it was done they brought in other friends to help eat it. Making the soup can be taken as a symbolic protest against the industrial efficiency of canned soup, but it is also a vote, and maybe a plea, for cooperative involvement in a common task.

Sensitive college administrators—particularly the student life officers who have replaced the wardens and deans who policed parietal rules—know that personal growth is what students need and want, and they are exploring ways to provide more of it. On many campuses, for instance, student-operated "hot lines" provide continuous service for students who need help, a friendly ear, with profit to those who give the help as well as those who receive it. New flexible curriculum arrangements make it possible for a student to do virtually anything he needs to do anywhere and get credit for it.

But no matter how imaginative the experiments, they all have a fatal defect: they are still *college* exercises in reality rather than the real thing. To become a soldier, you have to train under live ammunition. To be "really" grown up, you have to take real risks. Students who disagreed with Talcott Parsons argued that college actually keeps students from growing up.

"Maturity involves responsibility, decision-making and adult attitudes," a student engineer from R.P.I.

wrote. "It seems that the culmination of these traits is delayed when an individual spends several years in a college environment."

Some of his elders would say that students are not the best judge of what college can do for them and won't know until later on in life exactly how much they have benefited. But there is no proof except the retrospective, subjective feelings of some graduates who have to find something good to justify an experience that cost them so much time and money. The weight of the evidence is actually on the other side. In 1974 Theodore Newcomb, an educator who has specialized in psychological studies of the impact of college, said that all the evidence points to the conclusion that college does not change people very much. A disenchanted Russell Sage student felt this intuitively: "It is a rare eighteen-year-old whose values, beliefs, and behavior are so set that they do not undergo a transformation as he grows older. Change would probably occur more rapidly if the individual did not attend college." Maybe, for this particular student. If we don't really know, we have to rely on a student's own perceptions about whether or not college is doing anything for him.

Some think that college is helping them grow up, others feel that it is actually retarding their maturity. Some like what college has to offer in the way of personal development, just as some like the courses—and others don't. Some like the chance to meet people their own age; others think the campus is a youth ghetto. "It's nice to talk to an adult," said a senior when I thanked him for driving me to a speaking engagement.

"As far as education goes, I feel it's really been a total waste," an English major at Ohio University in Athens told us. "I can learn more by reading *Time* every week than I do by going to classes. And there's nothing here but kids—18,000 of them." The redeeming feature of the experience was meeting some natives of Appalachia "who live a pretty hard life."

Again and again, disenchanted students described college as a limbo or a hothouse protecting them from the maturing experiences of full participation in adult responsibilities.

"College delays maturation instead of acting as a supernutrient of it," a Russell Sage student wrote. "Students are merely tucked away temporarily in a sheltered cove before the whirlwinds of the world dash them off to their destinations. Today, in the U.S.A., college temporarily places people whom our society has no immediate place for."

"Studentry may be just the thing for an unstable-type person who is not sure what he is going to do with his life," another volunteered.

As we have seen, the word "adult" on campus has a technical meaning. It is used to distinguished the financially self-supporting from those in the status of studentry. Again and again, students viewed this status not as an aid to maturity, but as the major bar to it. "The majority of students share similar backgrounds and goals and are relieved of at least full financial responsibility by kin or society," one student wrote in definition of Talcott Parson's new stage of life. "In my opinion, a person cannot be considered mature until he is independent and accepts full responsibility for himself."

Students are more egalitarian than Talcott Parsons. They were unwilling to deny full participation in contemporary life to those who didn't go to collége. "From my own experience with friends who never attended college, it appears that they seem, for the most part, equally as mature as the average college student and often more mature," one student protested.

"Students are not yet faced with the responsibilities of holding down a job, raising a family, or even supporting themselves financially." "I just cannot say that the past four years have given me anything in the sense of maturity or feelings of self-worth that a job would not have," wrote another.

For many students college is a letdown. The same studies that show that college doesn't really change them find that many entering freshmen tend to expect a personal transformation, and when it does not happen, college itself can lose its reason for being. And for some unhappy students, the letdown can be fatal.

THE RISING SUICIDE RATE

The freedoms won by the rebellious students of the 1960s have unloaded on the students of the 1970s responsibility for establishing their own identities at a time when careers are uncertain and the familiar guidelines to status and behavior are giving way. Not all postadolescents can bear the crushing burden of themselves.

As we have seen, a big campus with high-rise dormitories and no parietal rules is not a halfway house. It can be cold and cruel, and the open dorms that the inhabitants call "zoos" are often depressing and physically unsafe. Students who act out their discontent face not the proctor or the old dean of students, but the reluctant local police. Those who used to get "BAND-AID" help for psychic hurts informally from faculty residents in their dormitories increasingly have nowhere to go but the college psychiatrist, who now sees upward of 10 percent of the campus undergraduates. But it's more expensive to treat troubled students with psychiatry than it is to police them, and the shift from policing and counseling has occurred at a time when college budgets are in crisis. Only 10 percent of all colleges have their own mental health services.[3]

The unhappiest students of all try suicide. College students are 50 percent more apt to kill themselves than people their age in general, so it is no surprise that the suicide rate rose among the young along with the rate enrolled in college. In California, where the enrollment rise has been the fastest and the proportion of young people who go to college the highest, the suicide rate of people fifteen to twenty-four doubled between 1960 and 1970.[4]

These rates add up to an appalling total of young lives. According to the best estimates, about 1,000 college students do away with themselves every year—and that's not counting the many "accidental" deaths that are probably also suicides. But the actual deaths are only the beginning. Observers estimate that 100,000 students threaten suicide every year, and 10,000 of these actually try it. Sometimes campus suicides are almost epidemic. On one New England campus, authorities coped with five attempted suicides during an examination period.

In the 1970s death, dying, and the ethics of suicide have become fashionable. Students talk about death to their counselors, to each other, and to their professors. On some campuses, courses in death and dying were attracting students the way sex and civil rights attracted them when these topics were shocking.

Suicide is mysterious. We know a lot more about who commits suicide and when than we know about why they do it. The classic explanation is isolation, or "anomie," the term Emile Durkheim, the pioneer French sociologist, coined in the nineteenth century to describe the rootlessness of city dwellers. Durkheim was also the first scientific student of suicide, and he all but proved his diagnosis by comparing the suicide rates of groups most vulnerable to his anomie (singles, males, city dwellers) with those presumed to enjoy a more stable "place in the social order" (the married people, country dwellers).

Suicides are loners. This is the most important finding of all the studies of campus suicide mounted when the rising rate caused concern in the 1960s. Many people think that drugs and sex problems cause suicides, but according to a California State Public Health study, drugs and sex problems are merely other symptoms of the social isolation and withdrawal which lead to suicide.

The typical suicide is outside of the student culture. "Who was he?" fellow students often ask when grilled by investigators about the habits of the deceased. "I noticed him," others will say, "but I never really knew him." One Berkeley student killed himself in his college room and wasn't missed or even discovered for eighteen days.

Students who commit suicide are not as apt to be victims of the going student culture as completely outside of it. They frequently set Olympian standards of academic achievement for themselves. "She took her work seriously, and she set high standards for herself—perhaps too high," the academic advisor of a Barnard suicide told newspaper reporters. Found dead in her dormitory in 1974, the twenty-year-old senior was described by a fellow student as "a very straight self-disciplined kind of person who didn't partake of the sort of ruling vices of the student subculture." "I'd say hello when I saw her, but that was about all," a student in her dorm recalled. Nobody seemed to know her.

THE DROPOUTS

The loneliness which leads to suicide is one of the many reasons why some students drop out of college. "I was overcome with a huge desire to be among a great number of people rather than a mere 800 or 900 in which I felt isolated," a Bennington freshman said in explaining her decision to go to New York to work. Like the suicides, the dropouts have few or no close friends, and dropout rates are higher on the big, anomic campuses low in "cohesiveness"—or "college spirit."

Friends figure prominently in what students think they are getting out of college, and they may well be the number one reason for leaving, too. The "maturing" contact with people "different from myself" can be overwhelming for youngsters who have not learned how to be "open" while still protecting themselves from devastating relationships, sexual and otherwise. A black student who first told us she had left her Seven Sister college because the work was too hard confessed, after we got to know her better, that she left to escape a black woman roommate who demanded almost continuous attention to her personal problems.

A Barnard premedical student quit at the end of her junior year to get away from classmates whom she found so competitive that "they'd kill you to get half a point on a grade." Dropping out meant earning her own living, because, like many parents, hers would support her only if she remained in college. She earned money as a bookkeeper, saved it, and then went abroad. "If you want to change yourself, you have to get away from the people who know you the way you are," she explained.

Like the ultimate withdrawal of suicide, withdrawal from college is rising. After forty years during which about half of the entering freshmen dropped out, and only 40 percent graduated on schedule, the proportion who quit began to increase in the 1960s.[5]

Maybe most of them will come back and finish later. Many already do. Older students have become so common on modern campuses that they no longer feel out of place. But whatever they do later, the fact remains that more of those who try college are now leaving because they find the campus as alienating and disappointing as the outside world.

We know that students don't drop out because they can't do the work or don't have the money, although they may, at first, say so. As a matter of fact, the reasons students give for stopping out, staying out, or dropping out sound remarkably like the reasons they give for coming to college in the first place: "To get my head together"; "to find out what I want to do." Those who go to college to get away from home may find, a year later, that maturing requires that they get away from college, too.

A liberal arts college is supposedly designed for helping students figure out their values, what they want to do. They are surrounded by potential counselors, relieved of direct responsibility for earning a living. They are exposed to a barrage of the great minds and the great books and a wide array of peers with whom to interact. If ever there was a place designed to think things through, this should be it. Yet every year, on every campus, some students quit to find a better place to "think."

What's better about someplace else? "I just felt too deadened, or involved, to get a perspective on what college really means," said a Kirkland graduate. "My mother will probably admit that she sent me to college to get my MRS. Taking time off was probably the best thing I've done in the last four years. I spent the semester working in a state institution doing music therapy with retarded kids. I did a lot of reading and thinking. I just put things in place in a way that I had never been able to do here."

Many students drop out in pursuit of the very intellectual development the catalogue promised them. One student spent her sophomore year working in a kibbutz because she found that "too much academics interferes with your education." College didn't leave her enough time for herself or enough time to read. "College can drain you of your energy for learning," another complained.

Paul Chernick dropped out of M.I.T. after his sophomore year and many changes of vocational interest because he expected an intense intellectual involvement, "something different from high school." When he didn't find it, he quit and tried founding a magazine and living in a commune. Finally, he just tagged along to help his mother start a new math course in the high school where she taught and discovered almost by accident his real vocation. "I didn't realize that I wanted to be a teacher because at M.I.T. everyone looks down on teaching," he explains.

Again and again the internal dialogue recurred. Different faces, different voices, different campuses, but the same search for direction "somewhere else," the same rejection of the academic treadmill. And always it was some of the most adventurous, some of those with the most self-confidence and some of those with the highest ideals for themselves who dropped out in order, as one of them put it, "to find something I'm really enthusiastic about." Like many other students, this one added that she feels she would have been better off if she had done her searching in the outside world before getting into academics at all. "Then I would have known better what courses to take."

Baptism in real world water may illuminate vocational goals. "One month with a social work agency convinced me that doing good was not my dish of tea and that sociology was for the birds," a former sociology major told us. "It's a good thing I found out in time." How do young people find out what kind of work they really want to do? The process is as mysterious as falling in love; you know when the right choice comes along, and it may take a novelist rather than an analyst to tell what clicked. Those who have experienced the "click" are almost as incoherent about the experience as lovers. For some the light dawned in the classroom, in a conversation with a professor or a friend, but it is just as apt to happen somewhere else.

Take, for instance, a Vassar student who wishes to be known only as Cathy. She was propelled to college, like many other students, without any definite purpose, and she selected a good liberal arts major—American Studies. In 1970 the Vassar scene fell in on her. She quarreled with her parents over the student strikes, and she could not see where her studies were leading. Was it all worth the money? The campus didn't seem the best place to decide, so Cathy made a practical move. She left college and went to work in an electronics company in Boston. At the end of the year, she worked with Puerto Rican children from the inner city. The experience was exciting, and it recalled the occupational therapy that vocational advisors at college had suggested. It sounded interesting, but Cathy wasn't sure about it. Then she went to Germany to visit her sister and to travel. The change of scene helped her decide to go back to school. She went back to work to earn some money first, and finally began to study occupational therapy.

This sounds roundabout. Couldn't she have saved time and made the decision earlier? Cathy had plenty of vocational guidance. The tests she took in high school suggested an aptitude for artist, forest ranger, or car mechanic, none of which appealed to her at the time. Tests she took in college suggested a psychology-related career, but she wasn't ready to consider any career at the time, in spite of considerable pressure to choose a major.

It would seem, offhand, that a year spent doing routine office work would be less promising an environment for decision-making than a liberal arts campus replete with all kinds of intellectual and social stimulation, including batteries of sympathetic and skilled advisors.

But if the time is not right, the time is not right. Cathy refuses to regard the year of office work as a waste. "I learned how to work with older people," she says. "I learned how to deal with the customers who phoned in with complaints and questions. I learned how to use office equipment efficiently. I knew that I didn't want to do office work in the electronics industry indefinitely, but the job was in some ways better for thinking than college. I could work from eight to five and then forget the job, and there weren't all the diversions of the campus which fill up the time you might otherwise be devoting to serious thought. Some people can do their thinking over a summer's vacation, but I needed longer. And it was a great relief to have money coming in, rather than going out, while I was thinking!" You'd never know, from Cathy anyway, that college was a place to think.

What emerges from the testimony is that the availability of *time itself* is more important in the education of young adults than where they spend it. What they need may be just what they say they need: the opportunity to mull in reasonable peace and quiet.

Paul Coleman, the eighteen-year-old son of the iconoclastic president of Haverford College, thinks everyone would profit by taking a year off before college. "You need some time to be able to think about what kinds of things you want to do and why, and whether you *do* want to go to school." He worked as a mechanic during the summer and in 1974 was considering whether he wanted to know more about forestry and ecology as well as "more about everything" urgently enough to go to college in the fall.

"I would have been the last person to think of not going to college," Melissa Drier told us. "I think if someone had come up to me my senior year and said, 'why don't you take a year off,' I would have fainted. I just wouldn't have known what to do with myself." But after two years at college, she felt she needed a break. "I felt I wasn't using my faculty, myself, the facilities; I was just going through the motions. I was writing papers because I had to write papers. I wasn't involved, and I couldn't stand not being involved. It was torture. I was petrified that I was nothing more than a student and that outside of my books I didn't exist. So I 'split' and went to Europe. I was terribly committed to school when I left, which is maybe why I left. It was difficult and it was hard, but it was good. It gave me a bit more confidence in myself. I knew that I could not continue to look to my work to give me my sense of self."

Some of the ablest students seem to look up from their books some bright morning and decide that the books are not for real. After trying Case Western Reserve and Bennington, Max Kirsch decided that no one should go to college before the age of twenty-five, so he dropped out and got himself a job taking care of the rats on a research project in the Museum of Natural History in New York, the place students of anthropology would most like to be.

A black girl who talked to us was so discomfited by the "unreality" of the campus that she took to escaping from Columbia by subway to view "other scenes" downtown. As for the "books," she thinks she learned as much working in a bookstore in the Times Square area of Manhattan as she did in any of her courses. While escaping, she wangled a job on a research project funded by Cornell University. She applied through a black employment agency and just told the interviewer she had her degree already.

Not all the dropouts will find rewarding academic alternatives to college, but even those who fared badly in the "outside world" say they learned from the foray. The overwhelming majority of all Harvard and Radcliffe students who took from one to five semesters off between 1963 and 1972 thought they were better off for the experience whatever it had been. Why? Because they were on their own. Most wished they had known more about what to do, but only a few wanted more guidance from Harvard. Whether it was, as one student put it, "a breeze or an agony," making the decision and planning for the time out was the most important benefit of the experience.[6]

"Please, Mother, I'd rather do it myself." This line from a television commercial of the 1960s vividly portrays a state of mind the most sensitive guidance counselors have long appreciated. Even in the 1950s, when overcrowded colleges threatened stopouts with lock out, sensitive guidance counselors ganged up with students to persuade both parents and school authorities to make exceptions for students who quite obviously needed to "do it themselves." In the 1970s it is the exceptional guidance counselor or college administrator who would try to argue a potential student into "sticking it out" in the classroom against his wishes—even though students dropping in and out make planning difficult both financially and residentially.

In spite of the scramble to recruit able students, most colleges no longer penalize students for taking a year out and many will accept a freshman for the following year under a formal "deferred admissions" plan. In the past a sizeable proportion of freshmen entered a year after high school simply because they had to earn enough money to go. What's new is official sanction for time out for those who need it for other than monetary reasons.

Who needs it? "It's hard to put your finger on," says Jean Aldrich, admissions officer of Bennington. "They are the ones who are hesitant about college, who don't know why they want to come. Sometimes you can see, by a precipitous drop in their grades during their senior year in high school, that they are simply tired of studying and need a rest."

BREAKING THE LOCKSTEP

The "best" or at least the most scholarly colleges have led the way in sympathizing with the revolt against academic force-feeding. Princeton's director of University health services made the case for the hiatus between school and college in 1967, when the draft made this positively dangerous. "The adolescent has a need for time which we ought to respect, but don't," he wrote on the basis of extensive experience with the problems of post-adolescent Princeton undergraduates. He obviously felt that many were not prepared for the pressures of Princeton life and needed "prestressing," like the concrete around steel bars, by a period of seasoning.

As far back as 1964 President Kingman Brewster of Yale was urging experiment with a "fifth year" of "interruption between the first two and the last two years of college" to be spent living in a foreign culture. In 1970 he warned against the "assumption that formal education is best received in continuous doses," and he went on to say flatly that "education takes too long." The term "stopout" is credited to Clark Kerr, president (1958 to 1967) of the University of California at Berkeley.

Psychologically oriented students of higher education have always favored what Erik Erikson, the psychoanalyst, called a "moratorium" on learning. He linked time out with the postadolescent search for identity. "The four-year college cycle may come as a random intrusion upon a cycle of personal development that is completely unrelated to it," wrote Joseph Katz, the educational psychologist who studied the class of 1965 at Berkeley and Stanford. And in 1971 the Carnegie Commission on Higher Education proposed "not only that all colleges should encourage prospective and continuing students to obtain service and work experiences, but also that some colleges may wish to *require* it before admission or at some point during matriculation."

Historian Oscar Handlin put it straight to the graduating class of Brooklyn College in 1972. "Prolonged detachment from life deprives many of you of the opportunity for experience. Nothing real happens to those lapped in comfortable dependence and shielded by beneficent institutions against exposure to the elements. As a historian I cannot but contrast your lot with that of your ancestors, who were men and women at thirteen or fourteen and had tested their powers well before they were out of their teens." According to the *New York Times*, the graduates fidgeted.

Employers may overvalue the *degree* but they have nothing against a stopout who returns, especially if he uses his time out to get job experience and a clear idea of what he wants to do. "The temporary dropping out of the formal educational process can be enormously beneficial for many students," Stewart S. Cort, chairman of Bethlehem Steel wrote in 1973. "A job applicant who dropped out for a while to work and do some soul-searching, then returned to campus with a strong sense of purpose, is a good candidate for my book."

Many go back with a renewed interest in their studies. "I have a hunch that if I worked and saw just what goes on in the real world when people don't go to college and get stuck in jobs that they don't like, I'd work harder when I was here," one student confessed in discussing whether she should drop out for her own good. "I have a hunch that I'd come back. I know I would." It's a mistake to fault college students for self-indulgence. Most of them are much too hard on themselves.

Young people who embark on a program of hand-to-mouth travel and work are proving themselves in a world which gives sheltered young adults few opportunities for the thrill of betting on themselves and the satisfaction of winning once in a while.

Knowing you can manage by yourself, make a living, get around the country on your own—these are the gains the returning dropouts mention. A dropout who worked on the *Clearwater*, an old-fashioned sailing vessel plying the Hudson River with an ecological message, discovered that "I was smarter than I thought I was. When you are in an academic setup surrounded by bright people, you don't realize that you are competent, too."

Real-life experience may be the only way to develop that tolerance for ambiguity which is the hallmark of effective maturity. A student who dropped out of college to do volunteer work with the United Farm Workers in Keene, California, discovered that she could function with all kinds of people, including illiterate chicanos, but she also "found out a lot of things about myself. I found I could stand up for myself and demand a change of assignment. And I learned that a social movement isn't going to make all the farm workers happy."

"One of the virtues of dropping out is that you sort of loosen up and let things happen to you," said Armand Henault, a twenty-year-old involved in the founding administration of the Campus Free College, a nationwide nonresidential college which draws its faculty from many different colleges around the country. "You can't do it when your time is programmed by formal classes."

Students have always dropped out, but they used to be made to feel that they were psychological, if not academic or financial, failures. A few educational radicals demurred, but the prevailing view was that anyone who voluntarily chose to drop out of a place like Harvard ought to have his head examined.

Head examiners agreed. Psychiatrist Armand Nicholi found "psychiatric reasons" for more than 43 percent of the students who dropped out of Harvard between 1955 and 1960, and he classified reasons under such dubious rubrics as "motivation," "emotional," "immaturity"—labels that classify in what way "you're crazy if you choose not to go."[7]

More recent studies of dropouts rehabilitate the mental health of dropouts and fault the institution instead. Dropouts may, for instance, be choosier. A study of 151 nonstudents of college age living in the Berkeley academic community found that their career choices (or their refusal to opt for a traditional career) were more consonant with their "creative and intellectual dispositions" than those of regular students.[8] This is, of course, a politically charged view—but its bias on the other side makes it easier to see the social coercion implied in the view of the dropout as a "maladjusted" failure.

The political and economic, not to say social, basis for condemning dropouts who "put themselves" first is evident in the controversy over the appalling dropout rate at the Air Force Academy, an institution symbolic of the regimentation imposed by war. Neither poverty nor grades caused the 42 percent dropout of the Air Force Academy class of 1974. The Academy is free to students, so the taxpayers paid the whole bill, something like $10,000 a year per student and more than a third of the dropouts ranked in the top half of their class in academic and military performance. "The people who run the Academy think something is wrong with the cadets," Dr. Louis Mutschler, a former Academy staff psychiatrist told reporters. "That's not it. It's the Academy." He ascribes the high dropout rate not only to a residue of feeling against the war in Vietnam but to "the absurd system."

Dropping out is still a litmus paper which brings out the beholder's attitude towards traditional values. The practice is dismaying to uninvolved bystanders who prefer a tidy world in which people do "what they ought" to do instead of pursuing "their own thing." Opposition still comes as well from those who make a living out of college and the parents and taxpayers who have to pay for uncompleted or extended educations.

Dropouts and stopouts are a nuisance and a worry to college administrators. The study that reported the favorable experience of Harvard dropouts warned of "fiscal and housing" problems in estimating enrollments, particularly when students are allowed to change their minds at the last moment. Less selective institutions frankly can't afford to lose the tuition money.

Dropouts are a reproach to college professors.

"Maybe I'm a bad salesman," wrote president John Coleman of Haverford about his unsuccessful attempt to sell his faculty on a mandatory year off for all students. "Maybe I'm a bad politician, but the hard scientists want their majors to stick close to the laboratory, and the whole idea may strike more fear into academicians than I realized. At a time when some faculty members are already profoundly uncertain as to how to work with today's students, the leave idea seems to downgrade the faculty member's role in education."[9]

Parents approve only out of high liberal principles—and even then the strain is evident. Their interest is straightforwardly financial. Families which have budgeted for four years of college are hard put to meet the rising costs, let alone stretch the years of dependency out for an indefinite period, and they have ways of putting pressure on their children. ("Is that. what you *really* want to do?")

The convention that makes parents responsible for four years of college—and that's all—has been recognized in law. Social Security benefits to dependent children of a retired or dead parent, end at eighteen *unless* and only so long as the dependent child continues as a full-time student.

Finally, we have opposition from students, most of them from limited backgrounds, who are torn between what they perceive to be their economic and their developmental best interest. A farm-bred student at Hamilton trying to decide in 1974 whether to become a psychologist or a minister recalls that he was tempted to take a year off to "travel around to see if I could find what I wanted to do, but I heard of kids who had done that and still didn't know what they wanted, so I decided to give college a try."

High-school students with whom I've talked echo this fear. "Once I got out of the habit of school," one senior told me, "I might never get myself to go back."

These students and their parents are aware that the

biggest cost of college is the income a student foregoes, and those from homes with modest incomes simply do not trust themselves to give up earnings of their own once they have had them. And from a macroeconomic point of view, of course, it's cheaper for the economy as a whole to support students during their younger and least productive years. Whether taxpayers, parents, or students themselves, those who pay the bill have an interest in "getting education over" rather than stretching it out indefinitely.

Stopping out, trying alternative ways of growing up, has always been a practice of the affluent, who not only can better afford it, but some of whom also have an intuitive confidence that they can probably make out in the world whether they collect credentials or not.

PART IV

THE ALTERNATIVES

9

The Anatomy of Success

Malcolm Bricklin doesn't quite know how he managed to make a million dollars before he turned twenty-five, but he is half-serious when he suggests, "Maybe it was because I quit college before I learned why I couldn't do it."

Ten years later, he was producing the "Bricklin," a car embodying safety and antipollution features turned down as impractical by major car manufacturers.[1] No newcomer had challenged the Big Three of Detroit since Henry Kaiser tried it unsuccessfully just after World War II, but Malcolm Bricklin had managed to attract $20 million of outside funding for his car of the future.

Bricklin makes his first million sound easy. After two years at the University of Florida at Gainesville, where he says he majored "in time and space," he quit to start up a building-supply business similar to the one his father had just sold. With his father's name and old employees he made a go of it at once, sold it at a profit, and opened the first of what soon became a chain of "Handyman" stores which stay open evenings to cater to employed do-it-yourselfers.

How did he learn about the retail business? "Well, I had a lot of experience buying things in stores myself," he answers. "I go by me. If I like it, other people will like it."

Bricklin has nothing against learning. Learning things can be fun. But he wants to learn things he can use, and he picks them up anywhere. "I learn a lot from cheap paperback novels I pick up in airports," he says. "It's fiction and the stories are all alike, but that's because people are all alike, and they are all like me."

Bricklin is, of course, wrong when he assumes he's like everybody else. But he's very much like other people who make it really big in money, power, or prestige. Like Bricklin, the successes very frequently get a head-start from a father's connections. Like Bricklin, they hit upon an original idea and go with it for broke. To outside observers and associates they seem "ambitious," "motivated," "opportunistic," "practical," "quick," "energetic," "indefatigable," "hard-working." They "understand what people want." On top of everything else, they're just plain lucky. And a great many of them, young and old, do not have a college degree.

If you define success in monetary terms, the fact is that a majority of men earning $15,000 or more in 1970 did not have a college degree, and a majority of college graduates did not earn $15,000 or more. This is true even of young college graduates. In 1972, for instance, only 46.3 percent of men twenty-five to thirty-four reporting incomes of $15,000 were college graduates. No matter which way you look at the charts and statistics, high earners and college graduates are not the same people most of the time.[2]

One exception helps explain the figures. Many of the highest incomes are earned by talents which have to be developed full time during college years. Baseball players, singers, musicians, actors, ballet dancers, and entertainers have a short career span and they simply cannot take time out, at least during their early twenties, to "broaden" themselves. They know what they want to do already, and the speed with which they develop shows what can be accomplished during the high-energy years when that energy is targeted.

Younger singers, dancers, musicians, and actresses sometimes wish they could go to college with their age-mates, but they don't need it vocationally.

But for those without talent to develop, we have seen that college is important primarily as a credential that certifies the graduate is a better bet for his first employer. It insures a place on the starting line, and it certifies to the probability that a beginner has a higher I.Q., a better home background as measured by the income and education of his parents, and a bigger capacity to learn and change than a candidate without the credential of the degree.

Graduates cheerfully agree that the diploma is valuable largely as a credential, but they hate to think that the four years they spent acquiring it was no other help in getting ahead: maybe the academic program didn't teach them how to "think" in the technical sense cognitive psychologists use the word "think," but they feel it stands to reason that all those classes, books, papers, and discussions must have made them smarter. At the very least, they argue, college courses gave them practice in marshalling evidence, making decisions, expressing themselves, and in other arts essential to business and professional success. They have to believe that all that studying did something for them.

Unfortunately, the faith in the value of college as a learning experience cannot be corroborated. The evidence is indirect, but suggestive.

First, if academics paid off, students who got good grades in college would be more successful—no matter how you measure success, than students who just squeaked by to the credential of the degree. It's easy to think of reasons why this should be so. If exposure to the great minds of the past makes you able to do everything better, as liberal arts apologists claim, then college grades ought to predict occupational success. If liberal arts courses actually teach you to think, then those who get good grades in liberal arts courses ought to think straighter than those who get poor grades. If college courses teach you how to learn, then those who get good grades should be the fastest and the best learners of how to learn. If these qualities of thinking and learning really lead to occupational success, then students with good grades should hold better jobs in later life than classmates who made poor grades.

Well, they don't. In spite of the initial boost honor students enjoy in getting into professional schools and management training squads, there is no proof that successful men were better-than-average students in college or that better-than-average students climb higher on the career ladder.

If proof fails, it is not for lack of trying. The grades of men eminent enough to be listed in *Who's Who* have been sampled.[3] The scientific achievements of research scientists as measured by patents, publications, and the opinion of their peers have been correlated with their undergraduate grades. The achievements of lawyers, doctors, and teachers have been studied in the same way. AT&T, the nation's biggest private employer, studied the undergraduate records of large samples of its own management ranks in 1930 and again in 1963.

In 1965 the American College Testing Program, a nonprofit organization, reviewed all the attempts to date.[4] It found the studies of differing value and beset with all kinds of technical difficulties, but the preponderance of evidence supported an unequivocal conclusion: "College grades bear little or no relationship to any measures of adult accomplishment." The only scientifically respectable study that showed a substantial correlation was the investigation undertaken by R. W. Walters and Douglas W. Bray for AT&T.[5] The results were so different from every other study that the ACT reviewers wondered whether the phone company might be more likely to hire and promote on basis of grades than other employers.

Why don't grades pay off? If intellectual ability is

important in getting ahead, maybe college grades don't measure it. Educators aren't sure just what high college grades mean. Psychologists aren't sure just what I.Q. tests mean. We have, however, enough I.Q. scores and college grades going back years to say with some assurance that a high I.Q. predicts high college grades much more reliably than it predicts high income. If I.Q. tests and college grades measure the same thing, what they measure isn't what it takes to make it big.

Army I.Q. tests on millions of men over a half-century show that a surprisingly modest level of mental acuity suffices for most occupations.[6] Doctors and lawyers and accountants average higher I.Q. scores than truck drivers and lumberjacks, but some of them seem to get by on quite average scores. Accountants head the I.Q. list for men recruited to the Air Force, followed by lawyers, engineers, public relations men, auditors, chemists, reporters, chief clerks, and teachers, on down to the teamsters, who bring up the rear.

But the averages are nowhere near as interesting as the ranges. Teamsters average an I.Q. of only 57.7, but the lowest teamster managed to make a living with an I.Q. of 46, and the brightest teamster tested out at 145, which makes him brighter than 99 percent of the population. The accountants were the brightest, averaging an I.Q. of 128, and the brightest accountant, like the brightest lawyer, hit the top score of 157. But one of the accountants had managed in that exacting profession with an I.Q. of 94, and the lowest scoring lawyer tested only 96.

If all the lawyers were brighter than some now are, half the population could function as lawyers, while if all the teamsters had to be as bright as some are, there simply wouldn't be enough teamsters to keep the nation's supermarkets supplied with groceries. Some of the more anomalous occupations—those which are slated to be "educationally upgraded" in the 1970s— had the widest ranges. Clerk typists, for instance, ranged from 68 to 155, stock clerks from 54 to 151, auto mechanics from 48 to 151, and farm hands from 24 to 141.

Intellectual ability, then, is important primarily as a floor. You can't be an accountant if you are an innumerate dumbbell, but you can wind up running an adding machine if you are the world's most spectacular mathematical genius. This is no figure of speech. It was the last occupation of William James Sidis (1898–1944), the Harvard prodigy who at five invented a method for calculating the day of the week on which any date for the past 10,000 years had fallen and who was ready for college at nine.[7]

The best example of the difference between being smart and being smart in school is the story my father used to tell about two boys who graduated at the bottom of his college class from the University of Wisconsin in 1894. Everything was hard for these two, but they wouldn't give up. When the other boys were out having fun, they could be seen swotting away late into the night at the courses they feared they would fail. They made it—and they made the most of it. After graduation, they founded a correspondence school designed for students who had as much trouble understanding ordinary textbooks as they had had. And, as my father used to deliver the punch line with a chuckle, because they were smart enough to see that most students were like them, they ended up making more money than anyone else in the class.

The anatomy of success is the same now as it has always been. People who make it big in money, power, prestige, or achievement have always educated themselves in what they need to know, and they are still doing it today, whether they go to college or not. Now, as in former times, innovators draw on their own resources rather than formal training. Of the eighteen case examples by Lawrence A. Armour in his 1973 book *The Young Millionaires*, only nine were college graduates—you can make it without a college degree even today.[8]

Successful people are cut from the same cloth. They follow a pattern easily recognized by journalists who routinely interview newsmakers, psychologists who study them, and recruiters paid to spot them on the way up.

The recurring elements are a new idea, the simpler the better, that solves a problem for a great many people; a burning ambition to put that idea over; extraordinary physical energy; and extraordinary good luck. It's better, of course, if all the ingredients occur together, and they did in the success of Malcolm Bricklin. His Handyman stores were new to Florida hardware retailing. They served the growing proportion of do-it-yourselfers who ran out of supplies after store hours. Bricklin is highly motivated, and he had the extraordinary good luck to be born the son of a successful businessman whose departure from his industry created a unique opportunity for his son to start a similar business.

If you think about it for a moment, it is obvious that college cannot teach any of these conditions of success.

First, college doesn't teach how to come up with a new idea. Colleges teach old ideas. Academics encourage analysis and criticism. They reward students for seeing why things won't work. Back in the 1920s, for instance, a leading electronics authority had proven mathematically that a radio tuning coil had to be two and a quarter inches wide to work. William Powell Lear didn't know about this "law," so he went ahead and built one that was only two inches wide—small enough to make the first car radio. Bill Lear credits his originality to his lack of schooling.[9]

Neither colleges nor anyone else knows how to make new ideas emerge. They seem to arise in a spontaneous flash of analogy that puts disparate things together in a way that opens up new possibilities. A good example is

the way Joe Resnick, a television installer, thought of
the preassembled television antenna. The first television
antennas came in pieces which had to be hauled up to
the roof and bolted together in all kinds of weather.
While struggling with the awkward task one day, Joe
Resnick thought how nice it would be if all those rods
were hooked together at the factory so that they could
be brought up to the roof in one piece and opened up
like an umbrella. A high-school dropout, Joe Resnick
learned radio in the Merchant Marine, but he managed
to follow a television manual well enough to make a
working model of his simple idea which made life easier
for television installers and made a million dollars for
Joe Resnick.[10] We don't know much about how these
fruitful analogies occur, but we know that they occur
much more often to some people than to others. If you
watch these people, you notice they are constantly
scanning their environment and processing their experience, turning impressions around to see how they look
upside down, putting two and two together. They are
curious. And they are always looking for patterns or
making patterns of the things that happen to them.

Academics claim that a liberal arts education can
help people react creatively by stimulating their curiosity and helping them to see more aspects of experience
than those with less knowledge. In defending a liberal
arts education on national television, Freda Rebelsky,
professor of psychology at Boston University, gave an
example out of her own experience. While walking on
the beach at Martha's Vineyard, she noticed a stone
that she recognized, from her college course in geology
twenty-two years earlier, to be a manmade artifact, and
this led to the discovery of an Indian colony. "A liberal
arts education makes you notice things you wouldn't
notice." Maybe, but most students promptly forget
what they've learned in class. People remember what
has meaning for them. My guess is that Freda Rebelsky
remembered the signs of an artifact because she is an

observant and a creative thinker who has always been interested in archeology.

The archetype of this kind of creative person is the fine artist, and one of the things that we know about fine artists is that they do not have to be intellectuals and they don't develop their talents in colleges. Colleges wish that they did. Academics admire "pure" creativity. They invite artists and poets to live on campus in hope that their example will inspire undergraduates. They offer courses in writing novels and painting pictures, but the kindest verdict on these "creative" courses is that they succeed in teaching appreciation of existing works of art.

At best the usual academic program is no help to creative people. At worst, it can actually damage them. Nevitt Sanford, a critic of higher education, warns that creativity can actually be impaired by "premature or obsessive book learning." A study of college students identified as creative by the University of California Center for Research and Development in Higher Education showed that a high proportion dropped out of college to pursue their own artistic development and seemed the better for it. Academically, they were found to be erratic performers who found institutional arrangements irksome.

Scientists need more academic grounding than artists, but the creators and inventors operate the same way as artists. Edward Land, inventor of the Polaroid Land camera, dropped out of Harvard to market his first important development, a plastic that eliminated glare by polarizing light. He made his fortune on a simple idea that occurred to him while turning an everyday experience around in his mind to solve a minor problem vexing many other people as well. When one of his daughters complained of the delay in seeing vacation snapshots, Land thought of a solution: Why not develop the picture right in the camera? Ole Evinrude conceived the idea of putting a motor on a rowboat while rowing two miles to bring his fiancée some ice cream. The ice cream melted, but the very next day he started working on the outboard motor. Richard G. Drew fixed up the first Scotch Tape for a car painter whose masking tape had stripped away the paint he was trying to protect with it. Evinrude quit school after the third grade, Drew after a year and a half of college.[11] The inventions of tomorrow that will make great fortunes will undoubtedly be the same kind of simple, innovative response to little problems that most people grin and bear.

And the problems are far too trivial to engage a learned professor. Academics pride themselves on the complexity of their thought, and their speciality is the "academic" idea that is of no immediate practical use. Like the folding television antenna, the ideas that make fortunes are often so simple that you can't imagine why anyone had to invent them at all.

Intentionally or not, colleges often tend to make students look down on the burning ambition to win money, power, prestige that is indispensable to success. A management consultant who had spent years watching the successful puts it brutally: "If you want to make a million dollars, the first thing you need is to want to make a million dollars more than you want anything else." Politicians respect the chances of the candidate who wants office so bad he can taste it. The book title *How to Succeed in Business Without Really Trying* is funny because everyone knows it's impossible.

Tillie Lewis never stopped trying. Though she left school at twelve, she eventually founded and developed a multi-million-dollar tomato-canning business because she refused to believe the experts who assured her that the Italian pear-shaped pomodoro tomatoes, preferred for sauces and pastes, could not be grown in this country. She read books on tomatoes, consulted with agricultural experts, and wrote to universities around the world. During the Depression, when a 50 percent tariff was placed on imported pomodoros, she learned some Italian from the Berlitz textbook, sailed second class to Naples, and persuaded a leading exporter of tomatoes to back her in a growing and canning operation in the United States, even though she had never been in a cannery or worked on a farm. She came home with a check for $10,000 and sacks of pomodoro seedlings, and then induced reluctant farmers in California's San Joaquin Valley to plant them. The tomatoes grew, and the cannery flourished. In 1966, Tillie Lewis Foods, Inc., was sold to the Ogden Corporation for $9 million, and Tillie became Ogden's only woman director.[12]

Colleges discourage the single-mindedness that makes for success. On the contrary, they aim to make students "well rounded," and they sometimes succeed. Graduates frequently mention the cultivation of "other interests" as a benefit of college, and seniors are more likely than freshmen to seek other aims than making money.

Academics are poor role models for any kind of success. They urge students to be cool and objective, but in order to succeed at anything, including the purest public service, you have to be hot and committed. Vocationally, as well as intellectually, academics play it safe.

"If I had a college education, I would have gone to work for some big corporation and I'd still be there," E. Joseph Cossman told Matt Dana for a chapter in *Instant Millionaires*. Instead, Cossman blew the $276 he had when he got out of the armed forces at the end of World War II to start a mail-order export business that made him a million dollars.

Cossman and Bricklin probably overestimate the danger of college when they imply that college could have stopped them. Nothing could have stopped them. If you're a real winner, you don't have time for the professors and you don't care what the wise men say. You're too busy going for broke.

David B. Chase, the author of the J. K. Lasser income tax manual, survived both college and law school. His simple idea struck him when he was a briefless young lawyer in Jersey City during the Depression of the '30s. If the Depression ever lifted, he told his father-in-law, J. K. Lasser, there would be a bright future for lawyers specializing in tax management. Like many accountants, J. K. Lasser thought of lawyers as competitors for his clients' loose dollars. He saw no place for a lawyer in his firm. But Chase offered to go to work for Lasser without pay. His insistence was the making not only of Chase and Lasser, but of one of the most active legal specialties of the 1970s.

If college doesn't stiffen the backbone, then what does? Sometimes Sammy runs all his life to overcome a youthful deprivation. Margaret Brand Smith, a Texas lawyer who made a fortune merging and developing insurance companies, was poor as a child. She recalls vowing that she'd never be cold when she grew up. She hasn't been.

As for hard work, college isn't the best place to learn that habit. Students complain they are overloaded, and they are occasionally moved to all-night bursts of intellectual labor, but employers are probably right in suspecting that some college graduates aren't willing to stick at a job they don't like. Nothing that can possibly happen on a campus disciplines the reluctant as emphatically as a tour of duty in the armed forces, membership in the kibbutz, the threat of eviction for nonpayment of rent, or the moaning of cows demanding to be milked in the morning.

"Hard work" is the single most common recipe successes give to inquiring reporters, and they do not give it as a putoff. They mean it and they do it. They start early and keep working late. Helen Gurley Brown, a college dropout, is both prototype and creator of "that *Cosmopolitan* girl." She admits to outworking and out-

lasting everyone around her, and often takes manuscripts along to read on social weekends.

C. Kemmons Wilson, a high-school dropout who
built the first Holiday Inn and eventually presided over
an empire of motels, once recommended an "eighty-
hour week" to students at the University of Alabama.
His public relations literature does not record the reac-
tion of students to this advice from a high-school dropout, but associates complain that his own week is closer
to 100 hours. On occasion he has worn out two associates, one after the other, without stopping. Those who
meet with him are advised to eat a hearty meal before
they come, because once launched, Wilson may not
break for lunch.[13]

The origin of the inexhaustible energy of the successful is mysterious. It looks at first like the gift of an
extraordinary physical constitution, but a great deal of
strenuous work has always been done by highly motivated invalids like Harry Hopkins, the architect of New
Deal relief programs who simply moved into the White
House with President Franklin Roosevelt; Florence
Nightingale, the famous "Lady with the Lamp" who
reorganized British military medicine from her sickbed
after the Crimean war; and legions of physically fragile
people who keep going on what is popularly known as
nervous energy.

Until recently, the habitual lunchers have consoled
themselves by imagining that they would attend the
funerals of work hellions like Wilson. But recent evidence suggests that the hard work that always goes with
top responsibility may not be lethal after all. According
to a Metropolitan Life study, the men who occupy the
top three executive positions in the 500 biggest U.S.
corporations live longer than men in general.[14]

It may be that success is good for you physically as
well as financially. Successful people may keep going
long after everyone else drops out because they are

doing what they like. Everyone keeps going when the going is fun. And the burning energy may be related to the burning desire to succeed and the active response to experience that are such conspicuous syndromes of success.

The successful are lucky, all of them, but colleges do not hand out rabbits' feet. Of course, the luck of meeting the right people may strike more frequently in colleges than in other places. Poor boys *do* make friends who give their careers a boost, and girls from modest homes have been known to find rich husbands at college, but most who hope for some advantage in making the right "contacts" are disappointed.

The trouble with luck is that it is as rare and unpredictable as lightning. Many people have bright ideas that would help millions and in addition squander prodigies of energy promoting them to no avail. Every single big winner owes his biggest debt to luck, and most of them readily admit it.

Of all the turns of the wheel, the most influential is the accident of birth. Kay Graham, the influential owner of the *Washington Post*, doesn't think her own success is very instructive because, as she puts it, she got there "by patrimony and matrimony." Her father owned the paper, and she took over running it following the death of her husband. This modesty underestimates the extent of her own drive, energy, and originality—daughters and widows are not as compelled to make a go of a family business as sons or sons-in-law. However, those who had the wit to select rich and well-educated parents so often enjoy the advantages of superior background, superior intelligence, and superior schooling that statisticians wrangle learnedly over whether one caused the other or which helped the most. But one fact is quite plain: the accident of birth is related to the other goodies and chronologically, at least, it came first.

When you were born can make almost as much difference as your choice of parents. Most graduates of the U.S. Military Academy expect to retire as colonels, but an unprecedented 59 of the 164 members of the West Point class of 1915 retired as generals, and one of them, General Dwight D. Eisenhower, who was sixty-first in the class at graduation, went on to become President of the United States. Was the class of 1915 brighter, braver, or brainier than other West Point classes? Not necessarily. They simply were graduated into the promotional opportunities of World War I and were still eligible for promotion when World War II came along.[15]

If stars fell on the West Point class of 1915, dollars fell on the 1949 graduates of the Harvard Business School. Because they started their business careers at the beginning of the unprecedented postwar expansion, 199 of the 621 Harvard M.B.A.'s of that year were presidents or board chairmen of their companies twenty-five years later.[16]

Birth and timing are just the beginning of luck. All along the way there are "breaks" which help or hurt: acquaintances made, trips taken, books read, and just plain freak accidents that make all the difference. Who would ever have predicted three months in advance the accession of Lyndon Johnson or Gerald Ford to the Presidency of the United States?

On balance the verdict has to be that the pattern of success is splendidly impervious to higher education, because, as Theodore Newcomb, the author of many studies on the impact of college, put it, "So much of what colleges are supposed to do is predetermined by the kinds of people who are admitted in the first place."[17]

The most spectacular learners have always taught themselves. We owe electricity, the automobile, and the airplane to four natural-born learners who had little formal education.

Thomas Alva Edison, the creator of the electric

power industry, had only three months of formal education when he was eight years old. A minister-teacher then termed him "addled" and his angry mother withdrew him from school. She taught him herself with what books she had. One of these was R. G. Parker's *School Compendium of Natural and Experimental Philosophy*, a science textbook describing experiments that could be done at home. Edison continued to experiment when he went to work at twelve as a train newsboy. Between trips he read science in the Detroit Public Library. He then became a telegraph operator and an inventor.[18]

Henry Ford, the creator of the Model T automobile, was sixteen when he left the McGuffey readers of a rural school for an apprenticeship in Detroit machine shops. He valued practical experience so much more than book learning that he virtually paid his son Edsel to go to work at Ford after high school. When Edsel was twenty-one, the age at which he would have graduated from college, Henry gave him $1 million in gold for obeying.[19] Following this noncollege tradition, no male Ford won a college degree until Edsel Bryant Ford II, son of Henry II, was graduated from Babson College in 1973.

Neither Wilbur nor Orville Wright, the brothers who built the first successful heavier-than-air flying machine, ever graduated from college. Wilbur had planned to go to college, but an ice-hockey accident disabled him. His younger brother, Orville, took special courses at high school that did not lead to a diploma. The bicycle shop in Dayton, where the two brothers developed their first invention, the "safety bicycle," was their real university. They succeeded where others failed—in part at least because they disregarded the existing untrustworthy scientific data and made their own experiments and measurements.[20]

These four were geniuses. If they were graduating from high school in the mid-1970s they would probably go on to college like everybody else, and their colleges would undoubtedly take credit for any achievements they would make, but it is hard to see how college could have helped them, and it might have discouraged them. "Discoveries," Edward Land, inventor of the Polaroid camera, once remarked, "are made by some individual who has freed himself from a way of thinking that is held by friends and associates who may be more intelligent, better educated, better disciplined, but who have not mastered the art of the fresh, clean look at the old, old knowledge."

Book learning may not help inventors, but it sounds essential for those who make their living packaging the printed word. Yet while colleges continue to graduate far too many majors in English, journalism, and the liberal arts for the beginning jobs in publishing and writing, a majority of the writers, editors, journalists, and authors reported by the Census of Occupations do this supposedly intellectual work without a college degree, some of whom are among the best known. Jessica Mitford, author of three best-selling books, never attended school a day in her life. She explains that her mother didn't believe in education for girls.

College may actually be a handicap for communicators who must speak the language of the mass market. DeWitt Wallace, the founder of *The Reader's Digest*, is said to be the most exceptional phenomenon, a really average man. Like Bricklin, he relied on his own judgment. If he liked an article, a million other people would like it too. He dropped out of college and learned his trade by doing it. Helen Gurley Brown, the tireless editor, also has absolute pitch for the voices of her readers. She admonishes contributors to *Cosmopolitan* to make everything "baby simple."

In writing, as in other fields, success goes to those who have good new ideas, the persistence to pursue them against obstacles, plus a little bit of luck. Carl Bernstein and Robert Woodward unravelled the Water-

gate conspiracy by dogged sleuthing and an unwilling-
ness to accept the factitious explanations of authority.
While Woodward is a product of the Ivy League, Bernstein is a college dropout who went to work for the
Washington Star as a copyboy. Both had the temperament for investigative reporting.

Originality and persistence paid off for Edith Hills
Coogler, the woman's editor of the *Atlanta Journal*
who has become an institution in her community. She
decided in the seventh grade that she wanted to write,
so she began her way alphabetically through the Atlanta Public Library. When she enrolled in Oglethorpe
University, she found she knew more than the teachers,
and after a few weeks she dropped out to badger the
Atlanta Journal for a job. She hung around, offering to
do editorial chores for free, until they finally hired her.
A newspaper can be a better school than the campus
for the highly motivated.

One of the paradoxes of the word business is that
the schooling of authors, writers, editors, and journalists has not increased significantly along with the educational attainment of the population in general which
has increased the market for the printed word, their
product. A study reported by the 1974 Carnegie Commission Report, *Higher Education and the Labor
Market*, finds that the years of education expected of
authors, on the basis of contemporary job descriptions,
declined from 18 to 16 between 1950 and 1960, while
the actual education of authors fell slightly from a median of 16 years in 1960 to 15.7 years in 1960. This
means that in 1950 as many authors were college graduates as not, and in 1960 a majority of authors did not
have a degree. Writers are, in any case, an unimpressive
factor in the labor force. In the 1970 Census reports,
they were lumped in with artists and entertainers, and
the educational attainment of the whole classification
was less than four years of college.

If there is any job for which the liberal arts should prepare, that job is the Presidency of the United States. The President should have the wide horizons, the broad perspective on history, the deep understanding of human potential, and the high moral purposes that the liberal arts aim to cultivate. Above all, the President should know how to listen and how to learn.

All our Presidents have been natural-born learners, but not all of them have been college graduates. Abraham Lincoln wasn't a college graduate. Neither was Andrew Jackson, an ancestor and personal hero of the most recent President to attain that office without a degree, Harry S. Truman.

Truman's self-education provides a laboratory test of the proposition that college adds little to the stature of a motivated learner. Even at the turn of the century, when few went to college, Harry Truman was considered "college material." Accounts of his childhood picture his father reading Plutarch aloud and his mother plying him with biographies of the U.S. Presidents. Young Harry read the Bible through twice before school and read everything in the local library.

Then, when he was ready for college, there was no money and he went to work instead. When World War I broke out, he qualified for officer's training, and the army provided the nearest thing to formal education Truman ever had. "They tried to give me a college education in three months," he later recalled, "and my head never recovered." What he really learned about in the army, however, was not books, but men. In France, he commanded a battery of tough, young Irishmen from Kansas City. Three former commanders had failed with them, but Truman succeeded and returned home their idol.

"He came out of the army," his daughter wrote, "convinced that if he could lead these wild men, he could lead anyone."[21] Like all the natural-born learners, Truman extracted from his overseas service the one thing it had to give: practice in personal leadership. After the war and his ill-fated venture in the men's furnishings business, he went into politics and, with one exception, won every election he entered.

We cannot split the high-school graduate Harry Truman into two identical twins and send one to college to see if the college-educated Truman would have done better than the Harry Truman who later became President of the United States. It is hard, however, to imagine that Truman's plain talk, like Abraham Lincoln's eloquence, would have been improved by a course in English composition. College training might have "refined" him, but he could not have learned more than he already knew about the value of reading. "The thing I found out from reading," he explained to his biographer, Merle Miller, "was that there is damned little information in most schoolbooks. . . . If I wanted to find out why France was against England during the Revolution, and the why and wherefore of Jefferson's being able to buy Louisiana, you had to go look it up for yourself. It didn't matter how good your teachers were. They never taught you things like that."

Truman was, of course, an exceptional learner. Young men like him regularly go to college in the 1970s, so we'll never know whether any of them would exhibit, as he did, superior judgment in public affairs without sixteen years of education. Exceptional learners extract personal development from any circumstance just as Truman learned leadership in the army. Benjamin Franklin did it also and left a detailed blueprint in his autobiography. And so, in greater or lesser degree, have all extremely successful people.

The touchstone seems to be that learners learn from anything that happens, while the nonlearners insulate themselves from the most cunningly contrived educational traps. It may be that the compulsive learners can no more stop growing—short of spectacular deprivations (and some of the world's best books have been written in prison)—than a child given minimal nourishment can help growing taller.

Compulsive learners may be exceptional, but I happen to believe that they are really not made out of a special brand of clay. If they can learn from any circumstance, a lot of unhappy college students can probably learn something from nonacademic experiences, too.

10

Student Liberation: Some Consciousness-Raising Suggestions

Sweeping changes will be needed to rescue reluctant students from the academic youth ghettoes, where their futures are controlled by a self-perpetuating and largely unaccountable professoriate, and restore them to full participation in the mainstream of American life. Attitudes won't change until institutions—and their funding —are restructured on some new premises:

1) High-school graduates have the same right as older people to take responsibility for their own lives in their own way without special privileges or "protection"; and 2) Professors should be stripped of the political, economic, and social power they now wield over young adults and stick to teaching whatever it is they actually know to anybody anywhere who really wants to learn it.

Both premises sound reasonable enough until you see where they lead. Then they sound outrageously revolutionary. When you begin to spell out specific proposals, the consequences are easier to see.[1]

1) We might fund—and so legitimize—all the ways in which a young person can get what students have told us are the real benefits of college: getting away from home, living on their own, making friends different from themselves, exploring knowledge, trying a field of work, training for a job, growing up. The most direct way to be independent, or "adult," as students say, "is

188

to pull your own weight, and the simplest way to do that in our society is to earn your own living. For that, a young person needs a job—something that needs doing for its own sake, whether or not it is paid and whether or not it is directed to a lifetime career.

This means taking money away from colleges where young people are demeaned by the "make-work" of academia and investing it in the "real" work and learning students would choose if it were available. We need—and not especially for the development of any particular group—enough people to tidy up and patrol the streets, answer all the patient bells in hospitals, coach the slow learners in grade school, talk with the troubled, the suicidal, and the drug addicted, run down all the complaints of consumers, put all the library books back on the shelves, answer all the mail Congressmen get, haul in groceries for citizens physically unable to push supermarket carts, deliver the mail, and do all those small but essential services that keep a society civil.

A lot of these activities simply don't pay and are going to have to be funded out of taxes. Let the money come right out of the appropriations now being spent by institutions of higher education, and then allocate it on a formula which takes into account not only the need for service, but how many people would like to render it. (Services which are needed but hated, such as garbage collection, should be allowed to rise to their market wage which, in a well-run economy, will be high enough to warrant radical new labor-saving systems. This is coming anyway and will need no special legislation.)

The new jobs to be created should not be specially tailored for young people or designed in any way as learning opportunities. The professoriate will have to keep its pedagogical hands off. The jobs will be open to, and attract, other members of our society now arbitrarily excluded on the basis of age, sex, or some other

irrelevant circumstance such as retirement or special-
ization in an obsolescent field. For the sake of everyone's self-respect, we must avoid creating a new age- or
sex-segregated job ghetto.

2) Some of the money withdrawn from the colleges
should, especially at the outset, be spent on pilot demonstrations and explorations of specific alternatives to
college. This is the philosophy of a report entitled
"Youth: Transition to Adulthood," made by the Panel
on Youth of the President's Science Advisory Committee chaired by James S. Coleman of Johns Hopkins
University. The committee recommended a pilot program of disbursing vouchers to students equivalent in
value to the cost of four years in college that could be
applied toward a wide range of skill-training programs
as well as higher education.

One area for exploration would be extension of the
present system of apprenticeship to many more occupations than are now covered by our state apprenticeship
regulations. We could also experiment with new, more
open and more flexible ways for beginners to learn on
the job. Instead of funneling money into vocational
schools, which have to spend a lot of money to create
the working conditions under which students can learn
to cook or repair cars or run machines, we ought to use
that money to encourage employers to hire and train
beginners on the job, and the tax rebates or subsidies
should be awarded on a system of accounting which
recognizes the high cost of supervising the inexperienced.

3) We ought to explore a national service plan that
would require or permit all young people to spend at
least a year of their lives serving their country in a
capacity over which they had some choice. This would
give them the chance to get away from home and give
them opportunities to mature, to work, and perhaps to
make a real contribution of time and labor to some of

our most pressing problems. It's not an easy solution, and it could easily cost more than college.[2]

To many people "national service" sounds as coercive as the draft it was originally intended to replace. The Task Force on the Draft and National Service of the White House Conference on Youth of 1971 recommended against a compulsory program, but a Gallup poll of 1973 showed a majority favoring one year of required military or nonmilitary service for all males.

4) Pilot projects might be funded to explore a nationally supported program for making widely available some of the alternatives invented by dropouts and stopouts. One that deserves a second look is the time-honored system of sending a young person to live and work with another family. During the Middle Ages, gently bred young people were farmed out to the castle to work as pages or ladies-in-waiting and learn "manners." In contrast to the public schools which replaced it, this informal apprenticeship did not segregate the young, did not put them under the control of a schoolteacher class, and afforded them the self-respect of self-support. At worst, they did "real" work actually needed or wanted by someone else. The practice of sending a daughter to work in a neighbor's house rather than help her own mother helped to make the domestic arts socially respectable in Scandinavian culture.

5) Present colleges and universities should be returned to the teaching and learning activities for which they were founded by shedding the power they now exercise over access to jobs and social prestige. While administrators are essentially empire builders, most good professors would welcome a system which would insure them smaller classes of students interested in learning for its own sake.

Higher education should be treated like any other consumer product. Those who enjoy studying for its own sake should get no more subsidy for this amusement than those who like to ski, nor should this choice confer on them any special fringe benefit of power or prestige.

For starters, we might follow the recommendation of the Committee for Economic Development and target financial aid directly to students rather than allow institutions of higher education to dole it out.[3] This would not only reduce the temptation to use the money to aggrandize the college or its special programs, but it would make all institutions compete with each other to meet the real needs of students—as they are perceived by the students, and not as they are defined by administrators, bureaucrats, and educational experts.

If the institutions of higher education were forced to compete with alternative development programs, they would be much smaller and need much less financial aid than they now get. The money saved could go to finance the other things that young people want to do and find both personally and socially rewarding. The change would clear up some of the inequities in financial aid policies which become troublesome when we attempt to enforce social and economic equality by forcing everyone through the academic process.

Take, for instance, student jobs. Need, not merit, is now supposed to be the basis for all financial aid, including jobs, but it is hard to enforce this egalitarian ideal so long as the aid is doled out by colleges competing with each other for the students who can enhance the institution's academic reputation. In spite of strenuous efforts to make places for the poor and underprivileged, the academically gifted, who come predominately from the middle classes, tend to receive the outright grants and the pleasant jobs that free them to study harder and get even better grades, while the less academically gifted, who are apt to come from poor families, have to take the manual jobs that leave them less time for studying.[4] It would be nice if the bright students were poor and the mediocre students rich, but the facts of life are the other way around. The present financial aid system would be fair enough if it was intended only to finance bright students through college, but it gives the academic establishment unwarranted economic power to impose their intellectual values and discriminates unfairly against the nonacademic—especially when college is used as welfare for the unemployed young.

6) In order to reduce the stranglehold of academic values, if not the professoriate, on the future of the young, we must take aggressive steps to decredentialize employment. Fairness to applicants and efficiency both require that jobs go to the candidates most competent to perform the duties actually required. The first step would be to separate the licensing of lawyers, doctors, teachers, and other professionals from the influence of the professional schools which prepare candidates for licensing examinations.

Schools could cram their students for examinations, but their graduates would not automatically be licensed, nor would a diploma be required in order to take the examination. This would keep the professional schools honest because they would have to compete with other ways of acquiring the competence tested by the licensing examinations. Competitive channels for acquiring professional competence would make the professions accountable to the public. It would, for instance, be harder for law and medical schools to perpetuate as "professional ethics" practices which result in the padding of bills, the provision of unnecessary services, and the withholding of information patients and clients have a right to know.

In the mid-1970s, a number of states were working on a system that would get better teachers into classrooms than the present system of licensing all graduates of accredited schools of education. In New York State and in Pennsylvania plans were under way to require all candidates for a teacher's license to demonstrate their competence in the actual classroom.

7) Laws forbidding discrimination in employment on the basis of race, religion, sex, and age should be amended to prohibit discrimination on the basis of educational status, too.[5] This may, in fact, be the law of the land right now, since the 1971 Griggs decision of the Supreme Court declared it unlawful to require for employment a qualification which rules out any particular group unless that qualification can be shown to predict performance on the job.

Personnel administrators shudder when they imagine what a strict application of this principle would do to their employment practices. The awful truth is that there has been very little "validation" of employment tests to see whether they do, in fact, sort out those best able to perform on the job. According to Marvin Dunnette, a personnel test specialist at the University of Minnesota, the situation is even worse: most employers don't really know how to describe competence, much less test for it.

Removal of the diploma as credential will force employers to think through how work is really done and what kinds of people are really needed to do it.

A first step towards decredentializing the diploma might be to require colleges to state what their diplomas actually mean. In the winter issue of *Daedalus 1970*, Peter Caws suggests that institutions of higher education simply fill out a standard certificate showing how long a student has attended and the competencies he has acquired as measured by standard tests. This would be more helpful to employers and it would break the arbitrary power of the professoriate to require students to take courses the students regard as irrelevant in order to get the diploma required for a job.

8) Open learning to all comers, of every age and educational status, by offering courses at times and

places convenient to anyone in the community who wants to take them. Substitute a gigantic network of adult education for the present age-segregated (and, in some cases, sex-segregated) programs which aim in part at least at sociability and personal development.

Schools would offer whatever anyone wanted to learn. This would return control of the curriculum to the students instead of forcing them to consume whatever schools think they should have. Offerings would include recreational courses, such as gourmet cooking, and professional courses, such as certified public accounting for people in mid-career who need it as well as beginners. Young and old, employed and still to be employed would learn together, each student bringing his or her own contribution and taking according to his or her own need. Teachers who have taught mixed classes say that the discussions are more meaningful when fueled by varying inputs.

9) In order to make learning available to people when they need it, we should adopt the proposal of the Carnegie Commission to guarantee all high-school graduates two years of postsecondary education they can take any time in their lives.

10) To break the lockstep which incarcerates so many nonacademic young people in school, the National Commission on the Reform of Secondary Education has proposed lowering the school-leaving age from sixteen to fourteen. This would free younger teen-agers for alternative forms of learning or job training, much of which, of course, would have to be provided by new programs.

11) The personal development and social experience provided by residential schooling should be extended to students of all ages as well as both sexes in order to provide a more diverse, more natural, and more rewarding experience for all. Teen-agers are not the only citizens who can profit by the shelter of a campus environment. Older people, particularly those

in mid-career, frequently need "time to think" in an uncommitting but stimulating setting. For maximum benefit, both old and young would stay on campus only as long as they continued to feel that the campus experience was rewarding. Consequently, colleges would not be able to count on controlling their students for an arbitrary period of four years and they would have to adapt financially, intellectually, and logistically to consumer preferences.

12) Stop making young people carry the burden of social reform. We have assumed for so long that education can solve social ills ranging from race prejudice to poverty that we unwittingly saddle our children with the burdens adults won't shoulder themselves. Busing school children is less threatening to adults than desegregating housing. And as Christopher Jencks points out in his book *Inequality,* universal higher education is a clumsy and expensive way to help the poor. If we want to redistribute wealth, it would be simpler, cheaper, and fairer to tax the rich and give money to the poor, rather than do it hypocritically and indirectly by offering "equal opportunity" to win credentials in a loaded academic setting which serves to legitimize class distinctions.

11

Student Liberation:
Available Alternatives

Tomorrow's utopias aren't much help to today's college-age young and their parents, but with goodwill and ingenuity it ought to be possible to rescue the reluctant students who are in college only because they can't get any other kind of "job." At the very least parents don't have to coerce a nonacademic child into staying in college by refusing to support him anywhere else.

How long should parents support a high-school graduate who will neither go to college nor to work? The issue is not academic. One counterculture high-school graduate we know is simply parking at home on principle. "Existing" is more important, he tells his embarrassed parents, than doing anything in particular. Others his age are asking for money to travel or for support while they pursue a dream or wait for the ideal job.

To explore the current state of thinking, we put a hypothetical question to as many parents of teen-agers as we could find: "One of your two children is headed for college and is talking about going to graduate school. The other has been unhappy even in high school and wants to travel around the country making new friends. You have set up a college fund for each child. Would you give the nonacademic 'his' college money to do with as he pleased? Or would you feel justified in turning his college money over to finance graduate school for the scholar of the family?"

Parents thought it a hard question and most protested that it wasn't *their* problem, thank heaven. *Their*
children wanted to go. A number of parents were impressed, however, by the equity of giving each child the
same stake and agreed, with varying degrees of enthusiasm, that they might finance alternatives to college.

Some are actually doing it. One is Dr. Ernest L.
Boyer, chancellor of SUNY who presides over seventy-
two educational institutions in the state of New York
and an annual budget that would run governments like
Syria, the Philippines, Trinidad, and Tobago. In
1973–74, Boyer's son spent the money his family had
budgeted for his second year at Potsdam homesteading
ten acres of abandoned farmland near the Canadian
border. He felt that his Amish neighbors were teaching
him more of what he needed to know than he could
have learned at SUNY's fine schools of forestry and
agriculture.

Most parents are not enlightened enough—or affluent enough—to finance *anything* a college-age child
wants to do. Between "support for college only" and
"support for anything he wants" lies a vast no man's
land of parental policy. Some will shell out, parsimoni-
ously, for a holiday involving extended travel, often
legitimized as a high-school graduation present, but almost all become restive if the trip lasts more than a
year. Others would finance a worthy self-developmental
activity with subsistence (especially room and board at
home), such as painting or even volunteering to help on
a community service. Others would insist on at least a
part-time job. Very few would make an eighteen-year-
old pay room and board if he were not working, although some would put pressure on him to earn by
refusing him spending money. Almost all, it turned out,
would continue supporting an adult child "awhile," but
there is no set rule for how long is too long.

How about handing the capitalized value of a college
education over to an eighteen-year-old and letting him

spend it for college or not, as he thinks best? Families with substantial capital to leave their children often do it, if only to save on income and inheritance taxes. "All our children got their college money outright," Cameron Caswell, a management consultant told me. "They could have squandered it if they pleased, but they all knew there would be no more forthcoming if they did." None of them did squander it. One of them earned part of his way through college and invested part of his nest egg so well that he wound up with a substantial portion of the capital when he graduated. Families who hand capital over to their teen-agers usually have them programmed to deal with it like chips off the old block.

Parents who haven't carefully money-broken their young are shocked at the whole idea. "I would rather give my money to an institution, such as a college, than to a child who doesn't know what's good for him," one mother told us, and, to our surprise, we found undergraduates who didn't want the responsibility for handling $20,000 in one piece. William Irwin Thompson, a former professor at Massachusetts Institute of Technology, makes a more modest suggestion. Why not give an eighteen-year-old $3,000 to do with as he pleases? He might, says Thompson, use it to eat while writing a book, he might join with friends to start a farm, or he might just put it in the bank. If he lost it all, he would win at least a real life lesson in decision-making.

Parents are also concerned about time. How long is he going to do this "something else"? For some young people, "alternatives" are going to be stopout programs, a temporary break in the academic lockstep. But for others the same activity may turn out to last for years or even become a permanent way of life. It takes a little readjustment of perspective, especially for an adult committed to the academic timetable, but the validity of an activity should not be judged on the basis of whether it facilitates return to college and hence "normalcy." About all that can be usefully said about the permanence of any of the alternatives described in these pages is that people with few responsibilities are geographically and occupationally more mobile than they will be later on. Which is only as it should be.

WHAT ELSE IS THERE TO DO?

"I wouldn't go to college if I could think of something better to do."

Irritating as it is to parents and college administrators, the negative case for college is the least arguable. Though venturesome teen-agers are discovering a surprising range of alternatives, those who would like to work instead of going to school may find the going rough. In 1972 high-school graduates sixteen to twenty-one not enrolled in college were about twice as apt to be unemployed as workers of all ages. Of those who did get work, a quarter of the males were factory workers and more than half the females were clerical workers. In every occupation, young workers earned less. For instance, in 1969 the median earnings of male factory workers ("operatives except transport") eighteen to twenty-four years old were $5,561 compared with $7,599 for those twenty-five to thirty-four. One reason, of course, is that young people have less seniority. They try jobs and quit or are fired—evidence as much of their job status as their job attitude. Like explanations of discrimination against women and blacks, the reasons are less important to the victims than the fact.

Young people as well as women are restricted by obsolete "protective" labor laws. Eli Ginsberg, the Columbia University manpower specialist, thinks that employers are scared away from using young people by unduly restrictive child labor laws which they frequently do not understand. He points out that young people find it easier to get meaningful work experience in foreign countries, many of which have more extensive labor laws than we do. And he flatly charges American employers with "negative attitudes" towards young workers which reinforce their own lack of confidence in their ability to make a living.

Unions keep the young out of the high-paying skilled trades—particularly the black young—by restricting apprenticeships. A seventeen-year-old may operate a machine gun in the Marine Corps, but he is "too young" to operate a lathe in a commercial machine shop, even when he has been trained to do so in vocational high school. And unions have not taken kindly to vocational education programs or even to large-scale work–study programs which threaten to flood the market with young competitors.

Union opposition is only one of the reasons why the Census of 1970 found that only one in five young people sixteen to twenty-four had completed vocational training in a job skill. The sheer high cost of vocational training has discouraged school systems from offering it. Good courses in machine shop cost many times more than bad courses in social science which shunt the uncommitted to the community college. "Many students in my high school have been forced into college merely because we do not have classes in, say, auto mechanics or hair dressing, or good ones in woodworking, or complete print shop classes," a high-school student told an interviewer for the 1970 Sabine Youth Poll.

During the 1970s, high schools were increasingly criticized for short-changing the "terminal" students in an effort to upgrade themselves academically. A study of 1973 found that even affluent parents believe that the primary function of high school is to prepare students to earn a living, and parents complained that few graduates were trained to work. Career education had been proposed as a remedy. However, as of 1974 it was largely a program of teaching young people *about* jobs with field trips to places where young people could view actual workers and hopefully do a little themselves. But high-school graduates who want to enter the job market fast, do best with vocational training, and high-school guidance counselors are beginning to tell them so.

VOCATIONAL TRAINING

Postsecondary institutions offering formal training in job skills are growing faster than the four-year liberal arts schools which most people have in mind when they talk about "college." High-school graduates can take vocational interest tests, available free in most high schools and Ys, to discover specific occupations they might like to enter and then enroll for courses. Some occupations command earnings higher than the medians for graduates of four-year colleges. Among the highest paid are plumbers, construction electricians, locomotive engineers and firemen, long-distance truck drivers, air-conditioning mechanics, and bookbinders.

The trick is to make the training conform to the job market. One of the early experiments in separating skill training from the job itself was the land grant college system established more than a century ago in the United States. In the 1970s these colleges have far more elaborate resources for training farmers and home economists than the market for these skills warrant.

Vocational, or "grease," education is woefully split in the United States among public and private auspices. A high-school graduate who likes cars and wants to make a living repairing them can learn by working in a garage, the way most mechanics have learned in the past. Or he can enroll in one of the proprietary trade schools which charge steep tuition comparable to that of an elite college. Or he can head for the local community college which probably has an automotive course.

One of the best schools for automobile mechanics is Ferris State College in Big Rapids, Michigan. In 1974 students were willing to wait for a year in order to get one of the forty places in its eighteen-month automotive service course, whose graduates could count on starting at $700 a month. Facilities take so much space and money—each student gets a "laboratory," or car, of his own to work on—that they cannot be expanded easily or cheaply, and the school itself has to charge a substantial tuition, even though it is a state college. Graduates who want to go on can enter one of several B.S. programs. They can prepare for higher-paying supervisory jobs, for business careers, or for teaching the skills they have learned.

Most vocationally minded young Americans head for the community colleges which serve the high-school graduates of most population centers. While some are better than others and the many programs they offer vary widely, too, they have the signal advantage of being nearly free. Locally controlled, like the public school system, community colleges attempt to offer training in the skills needed by local employers. Offerings may be as staple as nursing and accounting skills or as special as marine diving, put on by Santa Barbara Community College in 1968 to train technicians for the underwater rigs of oil companies prospecting off the California shore.

It's hard to think of any activity which has not, at least for a time, been taught by some community college. A partial list offered in California includes courses in artificial insemination, baking, crime prevention, dry cleaning, escrow, floristry, gun smithing, horseshoeing, insurance adjusting, journalism, key punch operation, landscape design, manicuring, microwave electronics, nephrology, prosthetics, park work, quality control, resort management, sign art, television repair, travel agentry, undertaking, veterinary laboratory technology, warehousing, and X-ray technology.

Community college courses are cheap but they do not claim that they can place every single graduate in the field for which he or she has been trained, and many do not even make the attempt. In spite of advisory committees of local employers, they may temporarily "overproduce" specialists in well-paid, attractive fields which cannot employ large numbers.

And it isn't always easy to find the school that teaches the specific skill you want. Where, for instance, do you send a high-school graduate who wants to become a fireman, but does not live in a city which trains its own? Kevin Kennedy is one who had the luck to be the son of Jim Kennedy, a specialist in the executive job market, who as publisher of *Consultant News* researched the nation's fire-fighting courses and decided that the best fire school in the United States is at Oklahoma State University at Stillwater. That's where Kevin went in 1974. Most of his classmates go to work for fire insurance companies, but young Kennedy wants to fight real fires, and with his degree he should have no trouble in getting his choice of fire companies.

More flexible in meeting changing demands are the thousands of proprietary trade schools which spring up to teach computer programming, hotel management, air-conditioning repair, or anything else that appears in short supply. Since they are privately owned—hence "proprietary"—they have always advertised aggressively for students, and they spend a lot of money on high-pressure tactics to beef up their enrollments. They have been charged with promising job placement that they cannot deliver, but only a few schools of any kind, public or private, do a reliable job of placing their graduates.

John Bowers, a Chilean, chose the ITT Vocational School in Boston for automotive mechanics. This is one of twenty-six proprietary schools bought by ITT in the early 1970s when there was a resurgence of interest in vocational education. John was a racing-car enthusiast who had a job lined up with an automobile dealer in Roanoke, Virginia, which he intended to hold for a few years before going back to Chile to open up a dealership of his own. He doesn't expect to work as a plain mechanic, but as a diagnostician who can "diagnose what is wrong with the car before you get your hands on it."

Vocational training is, however, only one of the options taken by high-school graduates who do not want the liberal arts program of a traditional college. In the 1970s hard-pressed colleges tried to offer alternatives themselves by moving the curriculum out of the classroom and into the interests of prospective students. In 1974 it was possible, for a fee, to find some college somewhere which would give credit toward a diploma for doing anything a high-school graduate wanted to do.

COLLEGE WORK–STUDY PROGRAMS

Students who wanted to get out and earn in the "real" world could find jobs, and often more interesting ones, through the many colleges operating on the work–study, or "Antioch," plan, named for Antioch College in Yellow Springs, Ohio. During the past half century, Antioch has produced a long list of distinguished alumni who swear by the system.

A series of varying job experiences alternate with academic studies and can move a young person toward a congenial field he might never otherwise have discovered. David McConeghey, Antioch '72, describes himself as "not an academic person." In high school his main interest was flying. He learned to fly at sixteen, as soon as he could get a driver's license to take himself to flying lessons. He went to college because he wanted to be an aeronautical engineer, and he went to Antioch because he didn't think he could put up with classes for nine months on end without a break.

At school David decided that he wanted to work

more closely with people than engineers usually do, so
he tried sociology, and when that didn't satisfy his scientific standards, he tried psychology. On one of his
Antioch-sponsored jobs, he took care of the monkeys
and helped wherever he could as an assistant at the
Behavioral Research Laboratory in Boston. It showed
him what it was like to work as a psychologist, and "I
learned how to get money for a project by writing a
proposal." His next job wasn't related to his field at all,
but it did get him to Carson City, Nevada, albeit as a
dishwasher. He also worked in a computer research
laboratory in Washington, D.C.

All this time David was continuing to fly and to work
on his own as a flight instructor. Because of his interest
in this area, he joined the Association of Aviation
Psychologists. He wrote to the president and went down
to Texas to visit her laboratory. Through her he
learned of an aviation psychology project at the University of Illinois, where he now teaches and studies.

"I *could* have landed some of those jobs on my
own," David says, "but at the time I got them I
wouldn't have known where they were or how to
apply." Many of the jobs Antioch supplies are available
because the college keeps them filled with one student
after another so that the employer need not go to the
trouble of locating a replacement. The plan exposes
students to a variety of job settings in different parts of
the country. David's education cost his parents $13,000
for the four years, exclusive of the $6,000 that he
earned and spent maintaining himself on his work assignments.

TRAVEL–STUDY PROGRAMS

It's possible to combine college and travel. In addition
to traditional "junior year abroad" programs, many college departments offer courses which take the whole

class abroad. An eastern college has a seminar in Oriental religion that visits India. A graduate school of education takes a class in comparative school systems to Europe. Nathaniel Hawthorne College in New Hampshire has a fleet of airplanes for training fliers and stewardesses who get experience serving as alternates when the planes are used for field trips in liberal arts courses. Upperclassmen with a reasonable travel plan can often get college credit for an independent study project requiring it.

One of the easiest ways to combine travel and college is to enroll in one of the experimental colleges which require students to learn from life. Dr. Ronald D. Corwin, dean of the New York State Regents External Degree Program at Old Westbury, explains it this way: "If someone wants academic credit for having traveled and lived in Europe, we'll say, 'That's fine, what did you learn?' "

COLLEGE WITHOUT CAMPUS

Many of the new off-campus, external degree, or University Without Walls programs encourage students to undertake community projects, or to pursue their desire to "help people." Students at Kirkland College, for instance, have worked, for credit, with retarded children in Boston. Students at Queens College in New York have helped residents of a housing project organize a tenant's association.

While it is literally true that some institution of higher learning somewhere can be found to endorse (and collect tuition) for almost any activity a high-school graduate would prefer to traditional classes, it is also true that there is a real limit on the extent to which schools and colleges can provide *all* the growing up experiences that eighteen-year-olds want and need. One limit is expense. The other is administration.

Off-campus and experimental colleges tend to be expensive. Goddard, Bennington, Hampshire, Kirkland, and other experimental colleges have among the highest tuitions, in part because they are small, but mainly because there is a very high overhead involved in keeping control of a lot of people who are "doing their own thing." Choice and options cost. If the cheapest way to keep a surplus of eighteen-year-olds out of mischief is to incarcerate them in large classes and talk at them, the most expensive thing to do with them is to tutor them on individual projects. As one University Without Walls professor put it, individual projects mean "as much work for each student as I would normally have to do for a whole class."

On the other hand, projects and programs that take the student *off* campus look like money makers for straitened colleges because they put more students through existing professors and facilities, but the saving to the college often exports the expense to the student and, in some cases, the "community" whose facilities are exploited for educational purposes. It's cheap for a college to give you credit for a trip to Europe, but *you* have to find the cost of the trip. Even when a travel agent teams up with a college, the cost of the credit-bearing trip may be considerable. Less obvious, but even more critical, is the high and rising cost of letting inexperienced eighteen-year-olds do "real work." Work that is truly educational and developmental frequently does not contribute enough to an employer to provide even a minimum subsistence for a beginner. Supervising beginners is so expensive that they price themselves out of many labor markets even when they work at the minimum wage.

The basic elitism in seeking "real work" for young people comes through if you apply the categorical imperative; it won't work for everybody because there simply isn't enough interesting and educational "real work" to go around. Monitoring oil refineries for the

Audubon Society, clerking in Ralph Nader's office, feeding the rats in a biological laboratory, doing research for a historian writing a book are all developmental and mind-expanding jobs but they all take a lot of high-priced supervisory time. Workers in these fields get the individual attention from specialist-supervisors which they would not get as students in big university classes. This is one of the reasons young people like these jobs.

Work which could be self-supporting if undertaken individually becomes prohibitively expensive when it is administered through the double overhead of a university *and* an employer. A student who tutors in an elementary school for college credit is taking up the time not only of the elementary school administrators, but of the college administrators as well. It costs the Peace Corps more to train and administer a worker in the field than the frugal subsistence allowance for maintaining the worker.

Luckily, there are a lot of other ways to get started on a career without "learning" how to work in college.

A LEARNING JOB

Learning jobs are found or, more often, made on an individual basis, and the actual work itself is learned as it always has been learned—on the job. Some high-school graduates who go to work in the mailroom actually do move up the ladder to president, learning each job as they go. Fred L. Turner, a Drake University dropout, began frying hamburgers at the McDonald Corporation and became chief executive of the company by the time he was forty-one. "So long as I am here," he says, "McDonald's will be the kind of company where people will bubble up from the bottom."

Some individuals have a talent for extracting usable experience out of any job they find. Ruth Bates Harris, a black who became the first woman to reach the rank of deputy assistant administrator for the National Aeronautics and Space Administration, recalls with zest a stint she did in a typing pool as "a wonderful opportunity because I got a chance to work in every department of the company so that I could figure out just where I wanted to go." Many newcomers to the job market explore the opportunities by working with temporary help services.

APPRENTICESHIPS

Apprenticeship is the age-old system for formalizing a learning job, and, in spite of abuses aimed at limiting entry into desirable occupations, it is still the ideal way to go for a high-school graduate who likes working with his hands. If he gets into a program and sticks with it, he is very likely to outearn many of his classmates who go to college. A number of people earning more than $15,000 a year and who do not have a college degree are ōwners of construction firms, and a much larger number are executives and superintendents in construction companies, according to the Associated General Contractors of America.

Richard Husted is a teacher who will become a full-fledged journeyman in the International Association of Bridge, Structural, and Ornamental Iron Workers union after a three-year apprenticeship in 1976. Although at twenty-eight he was pushing the age ceiling for applicants, he was chosen as one of about 100 applicants who applied for 14 openings. Since then, Rick has been able to work on construction jobs with pay rising as he gains experience. He receives classroom instruction two nights a week given by members of the ironworkers union for which he pays $300 for a three-year course. The curriculum for ironworkers includes welding, use of tools, strength of materials, blueprint reading, orna-

mental iron work, and the basics of building construction and surveying.

Once you are in the union, you can work anywhere
you want to in the United States or Canada and as
much as you want. Rick likes it because, "It leaves you
free. If you feel like laying off, you have only your pay
to lose. And the pay is so good that you can take off."
In 1974 the union rate for ironworkers in Rick's area
was $8.70 an hour. As a second-year apprentice Rick
earned 80 percent or $7.00 an hour with additional
fringe benefits.

An apprenticeship is a job. Employers train apprentices only when, as, and if needed, which means that
those who stick it out and become journeymen should
not have trouble finding work. Competition for the
openings is keen. High-school graduation is preferred if
not required for most of the 350 registered apprenticeship programs administered jointly by employers, unions, and federal and state government agencies. There
may be other requirements, depending on the trade. A
carpenter's apprentice, for instance, must be good at
arithmetic, accurate in measuring, and neat. Husted
had no trouble scoring high on the competitive examination used to select applicants, but he had to be sponsored by members of the union and "pass" a personal
interview as well.

In the past openings have been kept quiet so that
they could be offered to relatives and friends of union
members, but government agencies now police the selection process to be sure blacks, women, and nonrela-
tives of members of the trade get an equal chance.
Rosane Menconi won a place in the carpenters apprenticeship program of the National Steel and Shipbuilding
Co. in San Diego when she heard that the company was
looking for women in some of its skilled trades to im-
plement the Affirmative Action Program required under
its government contracts.

Rosane's program is one of the many undertaken by

companies to train the skilled workers it needs. It is not registered with the state, but is operated by the company and the Shipwrights and Boat Builders union. In California, an apprentice in one of the 200 registered trades spends 6,240 hours of work and instruction over a four-year period and rotates from one employer to another to get different kinds of experience, but Rosane thinks she is getting the experience she needs in National Shipbuilding's two-year program, and when she gets her journeyman's card she wants to go into business for herself.

"I don't like doing piecework, the same thing all day, and the variety of work I'm doing while learning is interesting to me," she told us. "I've done the framing on a building, figured out where the windows go, put in the studs and floor joists. I think I could build my own house."

Rosane is already earning more than she could have made if she were not an apprentice. Apprentices earn an increasing proportion of journeyman pay as they progress. After one year, Rosane was earning $4.30 an hour, 89 percent of the pay of a shipyard carpenter. (Carpenters in the shipyard earn less than those outside, but the work is steady.) When she entered the program, three years out of high school, she was earning $2.87 as a salesgirl, cashier, and finally as an accounts payable bookkeeper with a furniture store in San Diego.

Each apprentice on Rosane's program works under the immediate direction of an experienced journeyman. "One of the men there really knows a lot," she says. "When I get a chance to work with him I feel I am really learning something." She had to spend $300 for tools but receives a $2 weekly allowance for their use. Halfway through her training she had acquired a hammer, two planes, a framing square, level, saws, an eggbeater drill, nail sets, combination squares, pry bars, clamps, chucks, screwdrivers, pliers, wire cutters, vise grips, and tin snips—and others will be needed before she is through. Every Wednesday afternoon there is a class in the theory of carpentry. The class built a small model house to demonstrate the various procedures of building.

Sherry Liddicoat became an apprentice meat cutter at age twenty-one after working for three years in her father-in-law's meat market in Madison, Wisconsin. In Madison the local community college gives courses in meat cutting for those whose apprenticeship is sponsored by a practicing meat cutter. The classes cover cutting theory, meat pricing, cooking temperatures and methods, and after classes are over the apprentices go back to their sponsors for on-the-job meat market training.

Apprentice meat cutters begin at $2.10 an hour in Wisconsin and earn $4 an hour after a three-year apprenticeship, when they become journeymen. "I love the work," says Sherry. "You can make an art out of meat cutting, if you take the time to make the cut something beautiful. People ask you questions in the market about meat, and you're qualified to answer them, so you feel sort of proud. You've told them something they were really interested in knowing. It can be fun— it's all in your attitude."

EMPLOYER TRAINING PROGRAMS

Apprenticeship for nonmanual jobs in large organizations is formalized in training courses, and here, too, the biggest problem is gaining admission to trainee status. Entry requirements change with supply and demand. If applicants are needed, schooling may not be required and applicants can qualify by taking an aptitude test. In the early days of the computer, for instance, high-school graduates who scored high on the programmer aptitude test were chosen by IBM for training in computer programming. When the demand became less urgent, a college degree was required.

Competitive examination is the route to employer training for policemen, firemen, telephone workers, and a long list of civil service specialists. Appliance companies use aptitude tests to recruit high-school graduates for training courses in servicing and repairing their products.

The retail business has traditionally trained its own. An easy way to get into a learning job right out of high school is to apply at one of the local grocery chains. Beginners who qualify for management training are systematically rotated through different jobs in the operation and given formal training too. Chains and franchise operations of all sorts have elaborate programs for training the relatively large number of managers retailing uses.

Commission selling jobs are easy to get. Anyone with an aptitude for selling—and there are vocational interest tests for this that can be given by high-school vocational counselors—can learn how to do it while earning. House-to-house distributors such as Fuller Brush, insurance companies, auto dealers, encyclopedia companies, magazine distributors, stockbrokers, and real estate brokers all provide extensive training courses for their commission salesmen.

Management training courses in large-scale manufacturing enterprises, banks, insurance companies, oil companies, and other blue-chip employers are almost wholly confined to college graduates, and fewer are being trained in the 1970s. So, too, with the "internships" established during the 1960s to show young college graduates how government works by assigning them at moderate pay for a year or so to help legislators or government officials at the federal, state, and even local level. Few of these internships were funded as of 1974, and those available to people without a college degree were short-term exposures carrying college or high-school credit rather than pay.

And in some fields experience is so hard for a newcomer to get that you may have to pay for it. In Scottsdale, Arizona, architect Paolo Soleri's "Cosanti Workshop 1973" charged budding young architects $250 tuition plus $72 board for the privilege of working for six weeks at common labor on the model city Soleri was building in the desert. The "apprentices" were attending two one-hour classes a week.

An organized pay-to-work enterprise expressly designed for high-school graduates who want a nonacademic experience is Dynamy, which provides "a series of full-time internships in the professions, crafts, businesses, government, labor unions, social agencies," group living arrangements, outdoor camping, and weekly seminars at annual fees ranging from $4,000 in Massachusetts to $2,250 exclusive of room and board in Minnesota.

THE ARTS

People born to be ballet dancers, baseball players, violinists, composers, poets, novelists, painters, and singers—all those whose work comes out of a special talent of mind or body—are far better off practicing those arts, with or without a private tutor, than they are sitting in a classroom—and most of them know it.

If music is more important to you than anything else, you may want to perfect your skill at an instrument, compose music, or play with a band. If you are both talented and lucky—and perhaps mainly lucky—you can manage to make a living at it.

People with an extraordinary talent are single-minded in their interest and remarkably ingenious in finding ways to pursue an art that may not have commercial possibilities. Actors and actresses, for instance, may stay in college primarily because colleges offer more opportunity for theatrical productions than the outside world. "Most drama students hang on to college because of its security," says Harold Harmon, a graduate of the Temple University Drama School. At Temple, as well as many other big universities, dramatic productions are better supported and financed than the amateur and off-Broadway productions beginning actors find on the outside.

THE CRAFTS

If you don't have an overwhelming talent, however, you may still want to make something with your hands—a pot, a blanket, a piece of jewelry. Handicrafts are satisfying, and quite a few manage to make it their life work. But most crafts take too much practice to learn well in spare time or in a college course. "All the course does is to give you a taste for it," says Michael Kurrier, a potter in Hatfield, Massachusetts, of a ceramics course he took. "The best way to learn is to serve an apprenticeship with a master potter." Apprenticeships in the handicrafts are not policed by regulation as are the building trades. Like the old medieval apprentices, those who want to learn have to work for little or nothing and often live with the master craftsman or in a commune of craftsmen. Michael works with other potters, silversmiths, and leatherworkers in a remodeled warehouse at Phoenix Farm, Hatfield, Massachusetts, which the owners, David and Jane Stemple, have opened for crafters. Each pays his light and heat, and if he succeeds in selling his product well enough, he might pay some rent. A simple lifestyle is one of the attractions of being a crafter, so many apprentices find it relatively easy to earn enough at odd jobs to keep going between sales of their product.

At twenty-one, Rosanna Risner is a silversmith. She

likes her work because it makes her "self-sufficient, self-supporting, and, most of all, gives me a chance to work for myself." Some silversmiths take apprentices on for a trial period without pay, but, according to Rosanna, "if you're really interested in what you're doing and it's a lot of fun, you don't really need the money if the craftsman is willing to give you room and board." Rosanna was a fine arts major who became an apprentice because it was the only thing she could do with fine arts except teach, and she didn't want to teach.

Not all handicrafters plan to make it their life's work. Many high-school graduates and college dropouts find it is easier to think out what they want to do with their lives while they are learning to be productive with their hands. Rosanna Risner says she may do something else if something else turns out to be more challenging. Marty Winn, son of a college English professor, went to an experimental open high school. When he was through, he didn't know where or whether he wanted to go to college. He thought he might be interested in writing or studio art. But while deciding, he thought it would be nice to learn how to build a guitar, and when he couldn't find anyone to take him on as an apprentice, he went to a community college woodworking class, where he started building banjos. After a year of craft work as his major activity, he went to Bennington College and then transferred to the Maryland Art Institute, where he studied to be a photographer.

Another way to go with your hands is to undertake one of the many worthwhile jobs that remains undone because no one is willing to spend the time and patience to do it. When Edward Hoe dropped out of Hamilton College, he undertook to refit a thirty-two-foot sailboat built in 1902 especially for his grandmother's elaborate "camp" on St. Regis Lake in the Adirondacks. The boat was one of fifteen raced by the very rich Victorian families who maintained summer places on the lake, but it had deteriorated, Egyptian long-staple cotton sails and all, to the point where it would have to be sunk or burned.

Ed moved into the summer cottage near the boat, kept warm with a wood stove, and taught himself how to repair the boat well enough so that it still sails St. Regis Lake with its original, much-mended sails.

OWN BUSINESS

Some people are born to build a business of their own. Alan Fastman is a good example of a growing number of the "new" or first-generation college students who try college, don't like it, and use the experience to discover where their real interests lie. Alan entered Pennsylvania State University because he had good grades in high school and neither his parents nor his high-school advisors could see any reason why he should *not* go. But Alan is not the sort of young man to follow the line of least resistance. His courses did not seem to be as interesting as the woodworking hobbies he shared with his father, who runs an unpainted furniture store, so Alan simply dropped out. He took his savings from part-time jobs and spent two months traveling across the continent with four friends. Back home, he thought about the woodworking and went down to the carpenters union to inquire about an apprenticeship.

"Can't talk to you now," the man at the desk told him. "Come back October 12 at 9 A.M."

On October 12, Alan found himself one of seventy young men waiting to fill out a long form. After an hour and a half in line, he explained he merely wanted to ask about apprenticeship.

"Can't talk to you until after you take the test," the man at the desk said. Alan passed the test, but still no conference. He passed another. Still no word.

Disgusted with waiting, he put an ad in the newspaper and went into the carpentry business on his own.

He was soon charging $8.00 an hour—more than he would have made as a carpenter's apprentice, but less than journeyman wages. In three years he had earned enough to buy a house of his own in Philadelphia. He is happily supporting himself as a skilled craftsman and wouldn't dream of going back to college.

Bruce Ampolsky is a young man with a dollar sign on his thumb. While still in high school, he built a small business in "buttons and advertising specialties" with $20 lent him by his parents. Over the years, he worked up to an order of 100,000 from a local politician. He was able to sell at prices so low that a major button distributor "500,000 times my size" persuaded his manufacturer not to sell to Bruce. He found another and went on. How did Bruce learn?

"When I was ten or eleven, instead of sitting around the house, I used to go out selling with my father."

Bruce continued the button business when he entered Brooklyn College, part of City University of New York, in the fall of 1974. He could easily make as much money as a college graduate by putting all his effort into buttons, but he now wants to be a lawyer, because he thinks it will help him in business. He has no illusions about undergraduate work, however. "People totally involved in school simply aren't with it in business," he says. "But I need the diploma to get into law school."

Bruce isn't a great student, but he's going along with college for a while, because it gives him another option. "I have college and the business, too," he says. Unlike many students, he finds business fascinating. "Everything in the world comes down to business of some kind," he says. "That's why I'm interested in it."

If you have a new idea you believe in and the talent for persuasion, you may find yourself literally too busy to go to college. That is what happens to some of the self-made young millionaires who hit it early in real estate, fast-food chains, or song writing—three disparate fields in which youth, inexperience, and incomplete academic credentials have not proved handicaps.

Succeeding on your own takes more than impatience with standing in other people's queues. The discouraging statistic is that eight out of ten who try it fail.

Can you manage your time? Start working without being told? Get along with almost anyone? See what has to be done first? Get people to go along with you? Stick with a project after the first enthusiasm for it declines? Do you get a second wind of energy and optimism when the going is rough? If your answer to most is yes, then you may be happier—and, more important, learn and grow best—by betting on yourself. Whether you succeed or not, is largely a matter of luck, but if you are a born entrepreneur, failure may only whet your appetite for another try. Many very successful businessmen fell flat on their faces the first time around.

Since most young people do not have capital and cannot establish credit at a bank, they are most likely to go into small business enterprises built on a bright new idea or a service. A high-school graduate whose parents will stake him not only to grub but to housing for his venture can take in typing, make household repairs, cater parties, tutor, raise animals for pet shops, or flowers for the florist shop, answer telephones, and run a clip service.

It sounds paradoxical, but an alternative to college could very well be a service aimed at college students your own age. Bancroft Avenue in Berkeley, California, is lined with street vendors selling tacos, beads, incense, and other items bought by students. Many of the little enterprises and others like them, such as typing services, are run by former students or young people who hope only to support themselves in studentry to enjoy the important nonacademic benefits of college. They run travel agencies, boutiques, newspaper distributorships, used book stores, furniture exchanges, health food shops, and occasionally tutoring services.

Services are naturals for beginners. House painting, lawn mowing, and local moving require relatively small capital. In New York City, Gary Ferguson started Cosmic Messengers, a motorcycle delivery service, when he was twenty-five; in four years he had built it into a million-dollar business enlisting people who have a motorcycle and want to make money at a part-time or short-term job. Bartending is another opportunity. Customers for all these services can be attracted inexpensively through classified ads.

If you are interested in a particular kind of business —such as a sporting goods store, automobile repair, or a nursery school—you should get a job in one or more establishments in the field to learn the ropes even if you have the money. You'll find that the most menial job in the place may be the best place to learn—and if your purpose is to get the real inside story about the industry, you won't find your chores dull.

THE ARMED FORCES

The armed forces turn many young people off, but now that the shooting war and the draft are gone, the military is a new deal and a better one. "I'm the type who likes to go out and do different things; that's why I joined," says twenty-one-year-old Lisa Tigar, shopkeeper, second class, U.S.S. *Sanctuary*, one of the first women to be a member of a ship's company in the navy. "I was accepted at college like everybody else I knew, but I'm glad I didn't go. All I would have had from college is a little piece of paper, and I would have learned a few things, but I could never compare it with the navy. You can go to school and they can tell you all they want, but unless you experience it, you don't know what's going on. I came in so I could learn at my job and know what I was doing."

"Parents think they're sending their kids to college to

grow up," she continues, "but they don't realize that they'll grow up in the same kind of society they've *been* in. What the parents should want is for them to grow up in the kind of society they're going to have to live in—where responsibility is important."

"I joined to go to school," Seaman Kathy Corbett told us. "I couldn't have afforded it at home; there are nine kids in our family, and I didn't have the marks to get a scholarship. So I had to do something—I couldn't just sit at home and waste away." Before going to the *Sanctuary*, where she works on deck crew, Kathy was a draftsman at Treasure Island, the naval base in San Francisco, where she received on-the-job training. "I'm not dependent on my parents anymore. I had to leave sometime, and this is the only way I could think of leaving, to be on my own and independent. The navy was the best offer."

"For me, coming in the navy was security," said another recruit. "I wouldn't go to college. You've got to pay for it, and then when you get out, you have to wonder if you're going to be able to get a job. If you go into the military, they send you to school, you can get college credits if you want, you're getting experience, you have a trade, and they're paying you. Why go to college? What is it, a status symbol? You can get a college education while you're in the navy if you want it. College is just expensive social life that's been organized for you. But after college, you can't call them up and say, 'hey, how about helping me out?' You can always call the military. You've got the G.I. Bill, discounts, and better interest rates, just because you've been in the military."

Many young people aren't sure they want a regimented life, but others welcome having decisions made for them.

"You give up your freedom. The government owns you, you have to recognize that," another sailor told us. "But once you do, there are advantages." In order to attract volunteers, the armed forces are trying hard to modernize. They've discarded outdated rules. Men can wear beards or a moustache and any hairdo that clears the uniform collar. Women may have long hair if they pin it up while on duty.

Benefits include a validated system of personnel selection and training. The services offer 237 occupational fields, most of which, except for combat-related jobs, are open equally to men and women. Recruits are tested for aptitudes, trained at no cost, and employed as specialists in jobs that include just about everything available in civilian life.

OUTDOOR AND PHYSICAL

It's easier to think things out when your body is active, and this is particularly true for young people who aren't sure what they want to do with their lives.

Beth McTavish left the University of New Hampshire at the end of her sophomore year because she couldn't decide what to major in and wanted to get closer to the "real, physical world." She taught riding in a summer camp in Maine, earning enough money to go to England in the fall, where she studied riding and horse training, gave lessons, and earned her room and board at the stable by "shoveling shit." Eight months later, she came back to the United States and got a job on a horse farm near Philadelphia where she supported herself on the same arrangement: subsistence pay and room and board for farm chores, giving riding lessons for pocket money. In the spring, she went to Steamboat Springs, Colorado, and worked as a maid in a hotel for $2.25 an hour from 7 A.M. to 1 or 2 P.M., giving her the afternoon on the ski slope.

A year of this picaresque life was enough, however. "I was having fun, but my mind was turning to rubber," she says. "I found I actually missed the intellectual stimulation of college. I still don't know what I want to do, but I think college will help me find out." This time, however, she is headed for a college close to the slopes.

During his year out of school, Roy Sheldon Marokus harvested fir boughs for Christmas ornaments in the mountains fifty miles from Portland, took care of animals for the University of Oregon medical school, "chopped a lot of firewood" in Ohio, and dug an outhouse pit for friends in Indiana, all odd jobs available to any high-school graduate. He reports going back to school with a "surge of enthusiasm."

Physical diversion from intellectual work helps many people over dry spells during their years of schooling, but there are some who will never be comfortable sitting down indoors. Temperamentally, physical activity is more meaningful for them than working with symbols. One of these is John Weeks.

Although both his parents are sedentary brain workers, they are both ardent skiers who took their children skiing every weekend, so when John was graduated from high school in Los Angeles he headed for Breckenridge, Colorado, where his older brother was working. Construction workers were needed to build new facilities for the expanding ski resort. John signed on as a common laborer at $4 an hour and found many other young people his age doing the same thing. By working every possible hour and saving every possible penny, he was able to save enough money to buy a season lift ticket and ski every day of the winter.

"It's wonderful for your skiing," John says, "but between earning money in the summer and skiing in the winter, you don't have time for much of anything else. And the novelty almost wears off."

Almost, but in John's case not quite. He knew at the end of a year that he did not want to go to college, and his parents, who had urged his brother to go, didn't push him. "I knew I wanted to ski," he said, "But I wanted to make a good living at it. I didn't want to be a ski 'bum.' So I looked over the possibilities. You can be a ski instructor. You can join the Ski Patrol. You can work in a ski shop."

John chose the ski shop. Starting wages as a clerk were $2 an hour, but during his second year he learned ski repair. By working at a construction job during the summer, he found he could live comfortably even if it meant taking some time off from the slopes to work in the ski shop. His third year, he headed the rental department. Now he's saving in order to buy a shop of his own. Before he does that, he's going to get experience working in all departments of the shop.

Outdoor physical activity does not have to be as social as the resort life of skiing. Steven Wing, Vassar '75, took a year out of college to rehabilitate an old farm his parents had bought near Chapel Hill. "I didn't drop out of college because I didn't want to go to college," he says, "It was more that I wanted to do something with that farm." He spent the year clearing the land, reestablishing the roads, building a pond, starting to build a house for himself, while living in a house with no running water and no heat except for a wood stove.

Steven went back to college after his year alone on the farm. "It was simply a tremendous experience," he summarizes. "I was very self-sufficient in a fairly physical way. The house didn't even have a furnace. It was a test of myself and what I could do."

Alexandra Forbes is another who proved she could survive in the wild. During her freshman year at the California Institute of the Arts she attended a lecture given by an American family living on the North Slope of Alaska with a minimum of gear, much as their Eskimo neighbors lived. The Meaders needed an extra hand and a companion for their growing son, whose only young friends were Eskimos. Alexandra wanted to see whether she could support herself on the game she could shoot through an Arctic winter.

In June 1971, at the age of nineteen, Alexandra flew to Bettles, Alaska, and from there by a small plane to the home of the Meaders, a tiny dot of blue on the large-scale map of Alaska appropriately named "Wild Lake." She took very little with her—salt, a good knife, a rifle, and heavy clothing. Once, when game ran low, Alex and the young Meader boy had to go up into the mountains to stalk and kill a Dall sheep—easier prey than the caribou which was their staple diet. "But the physical part of it was easy," she reports of her five months in the Arctic. "The Arctic isn't as forbidding as it sounds. The real test was facing myself. Because there are no intrusions, you have to come to terms with what you are really like. Some of the things may not be pleasant, but it is good to know them anyway. In the big quiet, you notice things you don't see in cities—and that includes things about the people on whom you depend for your life. It's a different relationship and more intimate."

In November, at the outset of the Arctic winter, the Meaders had to go back to the states, and Alexandra had no choice but to come back with them.

Back in New York City, Alexandra didn't consider returning to college, which seems to her as protected an environment as a nursery school, and she soon missed the "good feeling of using your body for survival." One summer she joined six friends in delivering a 60-foot sailboat across the Atlantic. The seven sailed from Madeira to Bermuda in twenty-nine days. In 1974 she was living in Vermont, learning to work with wood and to raise organic crops.

Most physical jobs are routine. It's the rhythm of activity and the environment that makes them attractive. But some are genuinely exciting, and those lucky enough to get them often find them through friends. Henry Sharpe III spent the year following his graduation from Exeter Academy mapping the Grand Canyon. A map maker on the Exeter faculty directed him to a map maker at the Boston Museum of Science who needed a young assistant.

Henry's job was to measure trail distances in the Canyon by pushing a measuring wheel and recording each mile on detailed aerial photographs. The work required him to spend five or six days at a time in the Canyon, hiking ten to twelve hours a day. "There are so many things that are neat, and nobody ever notices them because they're so busy getting educated—but not really getting educated at all," he says of his year off. He entered Brown University the following year.

TRAVEL

When a student says "I've been going to school all my life, now I want to do something else," he very often means that he doesn't care much *what* he does, providing he does it some *place* else.

Travel is the universal remedy. Many disenchanted students told us they wished they could take time off to travel until they found out what kind of work they wanted to do. A student working with a volunteer student counseling group at the University of California at Davis plans to quit and "travel around the country, looking for a nice place to stay." When he finds a community that he likes, he plans to settle down and see if there is some volunteer work he can do "with people."

A "wanderjahr" was the conventional "finishing" for Europeans of means, and in the heyday of the British Empire a trip around the world was an acceptable substitute for a university education. For an increasing number of young Americans, graduating from high school means taking off from home without any particular plan or destination for a journey as long as the checks relatives have given them for graduation will last.

Travel—particularly unscheduled travel—has the

salient advantage of motion without goal and change without commitment. It buys time. If you are traveling, no one expects anything of you. If you don't like the people you meet, you can get away from them. And it is, of course, the most direct way to "experiment with new lifestyles," "get away from home," and most of all "meet new people."

"But whatever would you *do* in Mexico?" a mother asked her son when he announced he was driving south of the border with friends, destination undecided.

"Why, I don't know," the young man answered. "I expect I'll just sit in the sun and drink wine."

"Doing nothing"—or apparently "nothing"—can be just what a young person needs, and many of them are afraid that they'll never get a chance to loaf when they are older.

Many organizations, some of them churches, have organized arrangements for young people to live and study abroad. Thousands of young Americans have lived with European families as foster children, working for their room and board "au pair," and thousands of American families have entertained a foreign young person on the same basis.

Steve Ono is a Sansei (third-generation Japanese) from Fresno, California, who spent a year in Holland after graduating from high school, where he was a big shot in school politics. The International Christian Youth Exchange found a host family for him, and the Wesleyan Methodist Church in Fresno put up the $1,500 and transportation costs required of the exchangees. Living with a Dutch working-class family was rough, partly because they had no common language, and his work-oriented Dutch foster parents couldn't understand why an able-bodied youth would like sitting around the house playing the guitar. The biggest culture shock—and the most rewarding part of the experience, Steve thinks—was getting over some illusions he felt he held about himself. "I'm not so cocksure about myself anymore. I hope I never get that way again."

Lucky high-school graduates have managed to wangle jobs with American firms in Hong Kong, on sheep farms in Australia and dairy farms in Switzerland. John Barkley took off from college with a spiritual goal in mind. He wanted to learn Indian philosophy and figured that the best place to learn that was in India. To get the money, he harvested watermelon in south Texas, a job at which a skilled worker, who knows how to stack them, can make as much as $450 a week by working practically every waking hour. John's year in India cost him $1,600. He flew to London, hitch-hiked to Istanbul on $45, sailed through the Black Sea to Trabzon in Turkey, thence by bus to Teheran, train to Meshad, Iran, and from there by bus to India. In India he traveled by train.

John spent two months studying meditation and a "very theoretical" brand of Indian philosophy with a philosopher who was living in a monastery in southern India. Although relieved to get back to "living fat" in the United States, he is enthusiastic about the spiritual growth he felt in his year of travel. "It was getting out on my own and away from set values that had been handed down to me, values I had just been assuming without question," he says. "It was wonderful just to get out of the whole linear progression from academic point A to academic point B." After graduating from college, he went back to the watermelons to earn enough in the summer of 1974 to study Zen in California.

Julia Bittman combined travel with physical work by spending eight months working on a kibbutz in Israel and in 1974 went back for more. "You make friends in a hurry. You get close to other people your age from all over the world, because you are all doing the same thing and all trying to fit into a totally new world at the same time." Most kibbutzes let foreign college students work with the kibbutz during the summer, and for as long as they are needed if they wish, so there is an international flavor to this experience. "Friendship is a more intense experience," Julia adds. "It isn't the same as in college, where one person is thinking about being a doctor and another a lawyer, all taking different courses and having different interests. While you're in the kibbutz, you are all pulling for the kibbutz."

Julia entered SUNY at Stony Brook intending to major in sociology, but she was turned off by the big classes and the impersonal atmosphere. She dropped out and worked in an office long enough to get the air fare for her trip to Israel.

"I'd worked, but I'd never worked like that before," Julia marvels. "Eight hours a day in the kitchen, six days a week, peeling vegetables and preparing food. But you feel different about the work. You have to get it done or the kibbutz won't eat that day." Later Julia planted apple trees and liked that job better.

American high-school students must be screened in the United States. They have to be healthy and able to take any kind of physical work assignment. Young people may apply to work in a kibbutz for periods ranging from a month on up to as long as the kibbutz is willing to have them. They get maintenance, including a small allowance for pocket money, but no medical care. There are lots of young people and a lot of good times, but only after the work gets done.

HELPING PEOPLE

If you're tired of school and don't like the kind of job a high-school graduate can get, you can do a lot worse, for a while, than give yourself away. Young people frequently turn away from saving the world through revolution to saving some small part of the human race on a one-to-one basis.

The superrich can afford to give themselves away full time. Most volunteer work, however, is organized to use people who can afford to give only part of their time. This works out well for those who are willing to clerk a few hours a week at the local supermarket providing they can find a meaningful job helping out in a school, hospital, park, playground, mental health center, social welfare office, or any of the private volunteer agencies such as the Red Cross, all of which are in desperate need of extra hands.

An enterprising high-school graduate who wants to stay at home for a while could learn a great deal about the world while volunteering to do some of the jobs for which other high-school and college students can now get academic credit. At the University of California at Davis, for instance, students have worked with the Sacramento County Probation Department, visiting kids in trouble with the law, sitting in on family counseling sessions, and with the Starr King Exceptional School for crippled children.

Working with juvenile delinquents is a challenge. "At first I believed that I would have to be really together in my head and respond to the kid correctly or I would further mess him up," one student reports. "But it's not true. Being together more and more often, we begin to know each other. By seeing the give and take in the relationship, I have furthered an appreciation for this with my own friends and new acquaintances."

Welfare programs are everywhere shorthanded, so most of them will find use for you even if you can't find a school or college program. For instance, hot lines are now prevalent, and they always need substitutes and replacements to keep going around the clock. In Battle Creek, Michigan, teen-age volunteers are trained by a professional counselor to staff a hot-line and drop-in center for age mates in trouble with drugs. Hot lines also exist in many communities for the elderly, the hard of hearing, potential suicides, and the emotionally disturbed, and all of them would welcome reliable and concerned volunteers. If there isn't a hot line for the people you worry about, you might try starting one.

Jeffrey Peda went to work for the experimental Program for Local Service (PLS) sponsored in Kent, Washington, by ACTION, the Federal agency overseeing all government-sponsored volunteer programs to find out how the talents of eighteen- to twenty-five-year-olds could be mobilized for volunteer work. A year after graduating from high school, Jeff signed up, at the subsistence allowance of $50 a week, to work as a teacher's aide in an elementary school, where he did all sorts of interesting things the teachers didn't have time to do. He built a fire engine for one class, a puppet theater for another. He played volley ball with the kids, and most of all he gave them individual attention. He helped a first-grader from Portugal learn English by reading fairy stories to her. He set up a library skills project for sixth graders, teaching them how to read a key on a map, how to draw a map of their route from home to school, how to read a phone book, use the Sears catalogue, fill out application forms. "The kindergarten kids are really neat, and I can get an ego trip out of them. When I'm out shopping in Woolworth's or something, here's one of the little kids who comes running up and says 'Mr. Jeff!' and gives me a big hug."

Social action groups are a rewarding way to do something about the "mess the world is in." Whatever your concern, there's an organized group which can use your help. Consumer advocate groups need volunteers in research, promotion, and office work. Someone must check the facts on complaints against offending merchants and manufacturers. Getting the message across to Congress, newspapers, and the public takes people who can make posters, walk in picket lines, stuff envelopes, make speeches, organize letters to editors and Congressmen, and knock on doors. Most needed of all is the office work for which activist groups seldom have money. If you are going to type, file, or answer phones, you might as well be doing it in a good cause.

Andy Lawrence thoroughly enjoyed a stint, at a subsistence $75 a week, as "general handyman" in consumer advocate Ralph Nader's Washington office. "There was no typical day," he reports. "Some days I ran messages up to Capitol Hill. I handled books and mail, proofread, got papers copied. Some days I was on my feet all the time. Once I took notes on a tape of one of Mr. Nader's old speeches so he could use it for a similar audience. I never knew what I was going to do until I got to work. Just answering the phone was an adventure in itself." Ideal spots like this are, of course, hard to find. Andy found out about the opportunity because his mother had applied for a job in Nader's office herself.

Helping jobs can teach you valuable lessons about yourself and the world you want to make better. "I learned I could get along with people different from myself and that you can't help a whole class of people without hurting some of them," a woman student reported of her stint with the United Farm Workers in Delano, California. "A social movement isn't going to make all the farm workers happy. Some of them are going to have to be sacrificed along the way." The United Farm Workers of America recruits college-age people from all over the country to help organize farm workers. Many hitch-hike from the East Coast. They are assigned office duties, helped to find lodgings, and are occasionally paid subsistence wages for their work. The experience is attractive to many young people who want to get into the movement to improve working conditions of some of the most depressed agricultural workers in the United States.

Volunteers may be perfectly selfish about giving themselves away. The only way to get your dream job may be to do it for nothing. Museums, archeological expeditions, and many research projects are able to get all the unskilled help they can use on a volunteer basis. At the Smithsonian Institution in Washington, now a complex of many museums, volunteers are piecing together shards of pottery brought back from the Tel Gemmeh site in Israel and transcribing manuscripts brought up from shipwrecks. If you want to learn about public affairs and can't get a paid job in the office of a Congressman or state legislator, ask a local elected official if there isn't a survey he would like to have done or a problem he would like to have researched. Your reward may be faster and more visible action than is available at the higher levels of government.

A young person can get much the same benefits from "giving himself away" as he can get from college. Like teachers, helpers cannot do a really good job of serving others without learning a great deal that is useful about themselves. Volunteering not only prepares for paid work in a field, but is often the best way for a newcomer to try out a career choice.

SUBSISTENCE JOB

Sometimes a nice, quiet, undemanding job helps you sort out your mind better than a high-powered college. "I didn't know what I wanted when I got out of high school, but I knew it wasn't more school," a nineteen-year-old told us. "What I really needed was a chance to think, and I figured I could do it better with money coming in than going out. For a while, at least, pumping gas is just fine."

For protected young people—and particularly girls —it can be important to learn that someone who doesn't love you values what you can do enough to pay you money for it, especially when it means making enough to live away from home. Waiting on table at a resort is popular because it provides room and board along with pay, but there are many options. During

1974, when lumber prices encouraged small logging operations to start up, several young women moved into an abandoned farm in the northeastern part of Vermont and worked in a sawmill at $2 an hour for cash. One of the Radcliffe dropouts of 1973 did much the same thing in Puget Sound. With several friends, she found a decrepit farm which they worked in exchange for rent, fixing up the house and clearing pastures. They grew their food and traded the surplus for the other things they needed.

Almost everyone faces some stretch in a lifetime when the most important thing is to be able to eat without getting involved. John Holt, author of *How Children Learn*, says he wandered around visiting schools and landed in a little boarding school in Colorado that "felt comfortable," so he said he wanted to work there. The school had no money, so he said he'd work for room and board and do anything for it—an offer institutions find hard to resist. He thinks it's an ideal arrangement for young people who want to learn about the world.

A self-supporting job is a discipline that can be therapeutic—although not nearly as often as older people imagine. One college professor told us his daughter had "authority" problems which she solved by taking a job clerking in a store. The job also convinced her, he added, that it was worthwhile learning how to add and subtract.

In our supposedly affluent society, young people are adept at surviving with very little cash outlay and find many ways of earning the little they need. Amy Van Doren, the architecture student who dropped out to build houses on her own, lived part of the time in an attic, baby-sitting for her landlord in lieu of rent.

PROTEST LIFESTYLE

"Live without dead time, love without reserve, enjoy without restraint."

The flower children have long since wilted out of the news, but a sign on a Berkeley, California, fence continues to proclaim their creed. There are many eighteen-year-olds who would like to try a "better way to live" than the compulsive, competitive "rat race" which drains their fathers and the "Mickey Mouse" activities which engage their suburban mothers.

A sizeable proportion of college-age people think of joining a commune—36 percent of those polled by Yankelovich in 1973—but less than 2 percent of the entering freshman class of 1973 thought they were likely actually to do it. Many others dream of heading for the woods, working in a factory to get to know "a different kind of person," bumming through Europe on a minimal nest egg, or scratching a bare living from the soil with as little reliance on civilized convenience as possible.

The Census of 1970 turned up tens of thousands of household heads sharing living quarters with unrelated partners of the opposite sex. These, however, are a drop in the statistical bucket, interesting largely, demographers speculate, because they are willing to tell the Census man that they don't fit into any of his boxes.

Protest lifestyles come in all colors. The most politically active gather in communes devoted to a specific cause. In Philadelphia, a group of self-styled revolutionaries have decided that it's more important to infiltrate labor unions and radicalize the workers than it is to go to college. They live together in a loose commune. More highly publicized are the communes which are trying to demonstrate the better way of life by creating a utopia free from competition, pollution, waste, and the "plastic" comforts advertised on television. During the early 1970s, several thousand Americans, mostly young, were living in organized communes reputed to average a "half life" of six months.

The decline of organized campus protest did not mean greater contentment with the lockstep of college, career, and family. It simply meant that the style of protest was more apt to be individual. Many young people who had been, or looked like, college students were rather pointedly thumbing their noses at what they were "sposed" to do, whether politically affiliated with revolutionaries or not.

The working-class world of factory and farm is a provocative frontier for middle-class young people. "I found I could learn a lot from Puerto Ricans and other people the Irish and Italians despised," the son of a physician says of his three months on the assembly line of a Philadelphia bakery. "Also, the job was routine, so it gave me a lot of time to think."

Manual labor with blue-collar fellow workers is a welcome new way of learning for many young people who have been "going to school" all their lives. A Harvard student who liked boats went to live for a term in a small fishing village, where he discovered that he had to work his way "up" the ranks and earn the trust of potential co-workers. He worked first in a factory, then on a ferry boat, and finally got a chance to work on a lobster boat. What did he learn? "Independence, survival, the ability to live life at its fullest,"—plus the realization that he didn't want to be a fisherman all his life.

Bob Larson, who dropped out of Rensselaer Polytechnic Institute in 1972, could have been found in early 1973 in a big college town. When asked what he was "doing," Bob replied, "vegetating." He prefers the "coolie labor" of odd jobs and living with friends to getting married and "supporting three children and a brown dog" at a nine-to-five job. "A good job in professional work is too steady and too permanent for what's happening now," he explains, although he is vague about what actually is happening now. "I want to live for the present rather than in the past or the future."

Bob takes a quiet pride in his ability to get by without "joining the establishment," by which he means subjecting himself to that good steady job for which college prepares. In 1973 he got by on $1,000 a year— the amount of the college loan he was awarded before he dropped out. He lived with a girl who is a musician and three other friends, one a graduate student with a grant and the other a welfare worker with a steady job. Expenses for the group were minimal—rent and utilities came to $30 a month for each; food cost, he said, only $10 a week apiece, and what else could you want?

The real savor of this life is its leisure. Bob gets up late, sits until eleven or twelve over breakfast, and then takes a ride on his bicycle. Around four o'clock, he comes home and engages in an activity he describes as "dreaming of Jeannie." "You can get used to doing nothing very easily," he reports. "Of course, I'm not going to continue doing nothing forever, but I don't know what is going to change me." Bob would like to have a research grant, like his housemate, who gets $120 a week for "doing nothing."

Protesters take pride in their ability to get along without the material comforts on which most of them have been reared. Young people who have no overhead —or access to the establishments kept up by their parents' generation—can get by very nicely on as little as $50 a week; although they may have to do a little scrounging to make it. One of the commune organizations actually offers a course in what is called "foraging." House-sitting for people on vacation is a good way to get free rent. Baby-sitting is another, and it is now open to both sexes. One student maintained herself while doing welfare work by holing up in an attic for which she paid $10 a week, then she moved in with a friend who had an apartment for which he paid the landlord by making repairs to it. Finally, she moved in with friends, each of whom paid $40 a month towards the rent. It's possible to live this way for three or four years on end, especially if you have parents with a washing machine.

A picaresque lifestyle works for some free spirits. Randall Scott is a sometime student at the City College of Santa Barbara. Deeply tanned, hair and beard bleached white from hitch-hiking in the sun, Randy looks like the illustrations of Robin Hood in old children's books.

"I have no ties and no goals," he announces, "but I don't blame people who are obsessed with money and prestige. They can't help it. It's their conditioning." Randy takes pride in having eluded this conditioning. "My thing is observation, trying to understand myself, my inner drives and fears, and to understand other people."

Randy left home right out of high school, heading for Canada to escape the draft, but he was turned back because he wasn't eighteen years old. For the next few years he drifted. In Santa Barbara he found work as a janitor and short order cook, but allowed his father to pay his expenses at college when he found that his night job interfered with seeing friends who were going to college during the day.

When college palled, he hit the road, winding up for a stay in a commune-type group in Eugene, Oregon, which he describes as "one of the best things I ever did." The commune was located in a big house with people drifting in and out. Some had dropped out of school, others had just quit working. Although there were no formal rules, a code of behavior was expected. For instance, whoever had money paid the bills. A central group of permanent residents more or less kept the place going.

Paul Asbell is a dropout from math and physics who has been living for four years in a geodesic dome he built in the middle of Vermont. He supports himself, between engagements of his guitar combo, by refinishing furniture and doing odd jobs of carpentry. With him in 1973 were two friends who worked at odd jobs too. Paul doesn't regard his lifestyle as a political protest, merely a comfortable way for him to do what he likes best to do. While good at theoretical math and obviously an intellectual (his father is an author), Paul felt that college was a kind of "existential vacation" that let him tinker at whatever interested him without forcing him to make real decisions. "Now playing the guitar—that's something you can't fake. And it's a thrill to feel yourself getting better and better at it," he says.

Most, of course, revert rather quickly to the striving, family-oriented, and materially comfortable life of their parents. But almost all who try an "alternative lifestyle"—whether communal or individual—find that the abrupt change of environment forces them to think through their values. Experience in a commune, especially a commune which fails, is a surefire way for a young person to confront the need for rules and, more importantly, unsuspected truths about himself.

12

Resources:
Where to Find
the Alternatives

NONTRADITIONAL EDUCATION

If you want the subject or the credential but can't stand the idea of a classroom or a campus, you can find colleges which will undertake to teach you by television, mail, telephone, and even through the newspaper that comes right into your home. If it's college *subjects* that turn you off, you can probably find some institution of higher learning somewhere in the United States that will arrange credit—for a fee—for anything you want to learn or do short of bank robbery.

They may be called nontraditional or external degree programs. Some are highly structured, such as the University of Oklahoma, which offers a traditional curriculum mostly by mail at your own pace. Others offer a custom-made curriculum built around your unique interests and goals, such as Goddard College in Vermont.

Most available and spreading widely in the 1970s is college credit for paid employment or volunteer work in a community agency. In many otherwise conventional institutions, you can get college credit for writing a book, creating a piece of sculpture, getting an idea patented, being an abortion counselor, editing a magazine, playing in a local orchestra or theater group, attending a business or government training course, serving as a student officer, and even unsupervised foreign travel. Some colleges will give you credit for these experiences even though you undertook them before you thought of asking for credit for them.

To find out where such programs exist, look through *Increasing the Options, Recent Developments in College and University Degree Programs*, by John R. Valley. Available from ERIC Document Reproduction Service, Post Office Drawer O, Bethesda, Maryland, 20014. Catalogue No. ED 073733; it costs $3.29.

For pointers on how to organize your own higher education, check out the pioneer book on alternatives to higher education, *This Way Out*, by John Coyne and Tom Hebert, 1972, E. P. Dutton & Co., Inc., 201 Park Avenue South, New York, New York, 10003. $4.95 for the paperback.

Most widely known of the new programs is the University Without Walls, a group of thirty-four colleges and universities which offer "an alternative form of undergraduate education making use of a variety of community-based and other learning resources." For more information on the University Without Walls, including the names of participating schools, write Dr. Samuel Baskin, Union for Experimenting Colleges and Universities, Antioch College, Yellow Springs, Ohio, 45387. In 1974 the Union announced two new programs, one providing for graduate degrees, and the other a High School–College University Without Walls which will admit high-school juniors as college students and lead toward a high-school and college diploma simultaneously.

You can get credit from many conventional institutions for "informal education" by taking an exam in a subject you already know. For more information contact the College Entrance Examination Board at Box 592, Princeton, New Jersey, 08540, and ask about the College Level Examination Program, CLEP. Or write the New York State Education Department at 99 Washington Avenue, Albany, New York, 12210, and ask for information about the College Proficiency Examination Program, CPEP. It is open to residents of all states, not just New Yorkers.

If you don't mind the classroom, but object to the system, consider one of the "free" (in curriculum, not necessarily money) universities which offer courses in things like folk music, encounter groups, and adopt-a-grandparent programs which you'd never get in a degree granting college. Write for *The Free University Directory* compiled by Jane Lichtman and published by the American Association for Higher Education, One DuPont Circle, Room 7800, Washington, D.C., 20036, $1.50. Or for more recent news, send for *The New Schools Exchange Newsletter*, Box 820, St. Paris, Ohio, 43072.

LEARNING JOB

If you want to learn a trade, but you don't know which one—or even if you have one in mind—find out what trades there are before you make your decision. Everything you need to know about any trade that strikes your fancy, from office machine operator to glass blower, is in the big fat *Occupational Outlook Handbook*, issued every two years by the Bureau of Labor Statistics of the U.S. Department of Labor, and available in most libraries. It describes more than 850 occupations, giving the nature of the work; places of employment; training and other qualifications; prospects for advancement; the employment outlook; earnings and working conditions. And don't ignore the fine print of the "additional information" on the trade which interests you. It usually lists associations and unions which can tell you where and how to train for the field.

A recent book which gives less formal leads to no-degree jobs is Muriel Lederer's *The Guide to Career Education*, 1974, Quadrangle/The New York Times

Book Co., 10 East 53 Street, New York, New York, 10022.

After deciding on a trade, you have to train for it. The best way to learn any skilled occupation is on the job, either through a formal apprenticeship program registered with the state or an unskilled entry job that involves working with skilled workers who can show you the ropes.

APPRENTICESHIPS

A formal or registered apprenticeship is essentially a learning job with legal safeguards protecting the learner, the employer, and the full-fledged craftsmen in the field. If the trade you want requires a formal apprenticeship, the *Occupational Outlook Handbook* will tell you so and describe the apprenticeship program. Material on the apprenticeable trades has been excerpted and published in a free leaflet you can get by writing to the Bureau of Labor Statistics, U.S. Department of Labor, 2220 GAO Building, Washington, D.C., 20212, for "Jobs for Which Apprenticeships Are Available." This leaflet lists over sixty occupations, the qualifications required and training available, and the employment outlook to 1980. Among the jobs described in detail are: photographers, cooks and chefs, asbestos and insulating workers, bricklayers, carpenters, cement masons, construction electricians, floor covering installers, glaziers, lathers, plumbers, sheet-metal workers, stonemasons, instrument makers, machinists, tool and die makers, automobile body repairers, bookbinders, electrotypers, lithographic craftworkers, photoengravers, blacksmiths, dispensing opticians, and jewelers.

You can find out about the legal nuts and bolts of apprenticeship, including addresses of local offices that supervise the programs, by writing to the Bureau of

Apprenticeship and Training, Manpower Administration, U.S. Department of Labor, Washington, D.C., 20212, and asking for their booklet, *The National Apprenticeship Program.*

TRADE SCHOOLS

Increasingly, however, skills are taught in schools. There is now even a school that will teach you how to be a truck driver. For most trades, you have a choice of a publicly supported vocational course at the high-school, community college, or four-year-college level or a private vocational school. If options are available, talk with a skilled craftsman in your field, or one of the associations in the "additional information" provided under the listing for your trade in the *Occupational Outlook Handbook*, about the pros and cons of each mode of training.

Schools differ, whether public or private, so investigate their standing before enrolling. Your local state employment service can advise you on training schools in your community, but for a glimpse of the national scene, go to the library and look up your trade in one of these books:

Directory of Postsecondary Schools with Occupational Programs, Public and Private, published by the National Center for Educational Statistics. Available from U.S. Government Printing Office, Washington, D.C., 20402.

Lovejoy's Career and Vocational School Guide: A Source Book, Clue Book, and Directory of Job Training Opportunities. New York, Simon and Schuster, 630 Fifth Avenue, New York, N.Y. 10020. Revised annually. Available in paperback at $3.95. Schools are listed under such headings as bookbinding, carpentry, ceramics, glassblowing, jewelry designing and decoration, sewing, silversmithing, and weaving. Apprenticeships are available in many of those fields.

Or write these agencies:

Engineers' Council for
   Professional Development Guidance
345 East 47th Street
New York, New York, 10017

National Association of
   Trade and Technical Schools
2021 L Street, N.W.—4th Floor
Washington, D.C., 20036

Association of Independent Colleges and Schools
1730 M Street, N.W.
Washington, D.C., 20036

Occupational Education Project
American Association of Junior Colleges
One DuPont Circle
Washington, D.C., 20036

The best way to decide on any school is to visit it and to talk with students and graduates. Since employment is the object of a trade school, it's a good idea to ask how and where graduates are placed, and then check with potential employers.

CRAFTS

If you want to try craft work, the local adult education programs at the Y or in the public schools may have courses or workshops. They'll have experienced craftsmen to get you started. Most libraries have useful "how to" books. A practical and lively book for beginners is the *Woodstock Craftsman's Manual*, edited by Jean Young and published in 1972 by Praeger, 111 Fourth Avenue, New York, New York, 10003. A comprehensive reference work is *Practical Encyclopedia of Crafts*, compiled by Louis and Maria Di Valentin, 1971, Sterling Publishing Co., 419 Park Avenue South, New York, New York, 10016.

If you're really serious about pursuing a craft, you should read *By Hand: A Guide to Schools and Careers in Crafts*, 1974, Dutton, 201 Park Avenue South, New York, New York, 10003. $8.95 in cloth, $3.95 in paper. It lists art centers, workshops, crafts cooperatives, apprenticeship programs, and college courses available by state. It also tells you how to start a crafts business of your own or form a crafts commune, and it has a good bibliography of books on crafts. You can also locate courses by consulting the standard trade school directories.

Once you get started, you should consider joining the American Crafts Council, 44 West 53rd Street, New York, New York, 10019. For an annual membership of $12.50 you get the beautifully illustrated bimonthly *Craft Horizons* which keeps you up to date on suppliers, markets, and people in the field, and advice from specialists. The Council also publishes an annual *Directory of Craft Courses* ($1.50 to members, $2 nonmembers) and *Craft Shops/Galleries, U.S.A.*, ($3 to members, $3.95 for nonmembers), a geographical directory of galleries and shops devoted to crafts.

Investigate also state crafts organizations. In New York, the New York State Craftsmen, Inc., 27 West 53rd Street, New York, New York, 10019, is a nonprofit educational group which runs community crafts workshops throughout the state, and publishes a monthly bulletin which contains a calendar of events and job listings.

Every craftsman should look at *The National Guide to Craft Supplies* by Judith Glassman, published by Van Nostrand Reinhold, 450 West 33rd Street, New York, New York, 10001. It is a comprehensive volume that tells you where to order what supplies, wholesale and retail, and also includes listings of fairs and shows, museums and galleries, craft societies and organizations.

There are several books in print on marketing your products. One of the best is *Selling Your Crafts*, by Norbert N. Nelson, published in cooperation with the American Craftsmen's Council in 1973. This helpful and all-inclusive guide is available in paperback for $3.95. The appendix lists buying offices, wholesale and trade publications of interest to craftsmen, and national craft markets.

Tips on selling your work are included in *How to Make Money with Your Crafts*, by Leta W. Clark, 1974, Morrow, 105 Madison Avenue, New York, New York, 10016, $7.95. Ideas to explore include craft fairs, renting a stall at flea markets, selling to local department stores, and craft exchanges. It is not necessary to live in the vicinity of a craft exchange to place your work with them on consignment. In the October, 1973, issue of *McCall's*, "Right Now" lists about forty such exchanges scattered all over the country.

OWN BUSINESS

If you are exploring the idea of going into business, head first for the library. There is plenty of advice available. While most of it emphasizes how hard it is to be successful, the books, pamphlets, and articles do tell you just about everything you need to know.

If your capital is limited and you don't know what you want to do, browse through *101 Businesses You Can Start and Run with Less Than $1,000*, by H. S. Kahm, 1973, Dolphin Books, Doubleday, Garden City, New York, 11530, $1.95. Although designed primarily for housewives, *The Family Circle Book of Careers at Home*, by Mary Bass Gibson, 1971, Popular Library, 600 Third Avenue, New York, New York, 10016, has a lot of small-business ideas you might adapt to your own circumstances. Ideas for businesses and reports of what other people have done can be gleaned from recent issues of a bimonthly periodical, *The Capitalist Reporter*, $1.00 an issue, 150 Fifth Avenue, New York, New York, 10001, or *Income Opportunities*, published fourteen times a year by Davis Publications, 229 Park Avenue South, New York, New York, 10003, 75¢ an issue.

For basic information on what it takes to succeed in any small business, check the handbook put out by the J. K. Lasser Tax Institute, 1963, McGraw-Hill, 1221 Avenue of the Americas, New York, New York, 10020, and also *Successful Management of the Small- and Medium-Sized Business*, by Franklin J. Dickson, 1971, Prentice-Hall, Englewood Cliffs, New Jersey, 07632. For some fast, general advice, look at the publication especially designed to help you make the decision put out by the Small Business Administration, the Federal agency set up to counsel and help those who run small businesses. *Starting and Managing a Small Business of Your Own* is the first of their *Starting and Managing Series*. It is written by Wendell O. Metcalf and is available from the U.S. Government Printing Office, Washington, D.C., 20402 for $1.50, stock number 4500–00123.

As soon as you choose a specific field, you will have scores of questions that can only be answered by someone who has made a go of it. If you haven't worked in the business, the quickest and cheapest way to learn is to get a job. When you start making plans for your own business, you might look up the association which covers your field and try some of your questions on them. You can find it in the *Encyclopedia of Associations*, 8th edition, 1973, Gale Research Co., Book Tower, Detroit, Michigan, 48226, available in the library. This is as good a time as any to confess your plans to the reference librarian in your community.

Most libraries make a special effort to keep information helpful to local businessmen. She will have directories of suppliers and wholesalers you will need when you start up.

You'll need some other fellow conspirators, too. The local bank has people who watch community marketing patterns closely, and their help comes free with their money if they decide to give you a loan. They'll probably give you valuable advice even if they have to turn you down. Big businesses employ marketing analysts to survey your market. This is one of the services provided by franchisers. But you can get some of the raw material marketers use directly from the U.S. Census: How many competitors in your area; average family incomes; number of homeowners; and other demographic data. Write the U.S. Census Bureau, Department of Commerce, Washington, D.C., 20233, or ask your librarian.

You'll find another friend—and free for nothing—at the nearest Small Business Administration field office. To find out where it is, look in your phone directory under U.S. Government. If it isn't there, write Small Business Administration, 1441 L Street, N.W., Washington, D.C., 20416.

While you're writing SBA, ask for two lists. One is Free Management Assistance Publications (SBA 115A). It includes booklets on such as "ABCs of Borrowing," "Loan Sources in the Federal Government," "Using Census Data in Small Plant Marketing," "Steps in Incorporating a Business," "Locating and Relocating Your Business," "Developing a List of Prospects," and even "Discover and Use Your Public Library."

The other SBA list is their For-Sale Booklets, SBA 115B. This lists the series "Starting and Managing a Small Business of Your Own," which includes separate guidebooks on starting and managing the most popular small businesses: service station; bookkeeping service; restaurant; dry-cleaning business; automatic vending business; car wash; swapshop; flower shop; pet shop; employment agency; building business; retail hardware store; retail drugstore; shoe service shop; retail camera shop; music store; retail jewelry store; drive-in restaurant. It also has a valuable "Handbook of Small Business Finance." If you're buying a business, you might want "Buying and Selling a Small Business." Once you're under way and encountering problems, you might find some help from "The First Two Years: Problems of Small Firm Growth and Survival."

A third source of reliable free advice is the Service Corps of Retired Executives (SCORE). These retired executives volunteer to give you the kind of coaching that highly paid consultants give big businesses for fancy fees. The nearest SBA office is the quickest way to find out whether there's a volunteer with experience specially valuable to your enterprise.

Is there a course you can take that will help? You can find out what is available in your community by writing the State Education Department in your state capital and asking them for a list of the small-business training programs sponsored by your State Board of Vocational Education or your State Agency for Community Service and Continuing Education. Since both of these agencies are funded by federal funds administered by the Department of Health, Education, and Welfare (Title I HEA 1965), you can also get information about where to find them by writing Director, Community Service and Continuing Education, U.S. Office of Education, Washington, D.C., 20202.

Finally, of course, you should rely heavily, particularly at the outset, on the paid advice from a good lawyer and a good accountant. A lawyer is not necessary, but probably helpful in incorporating. Level with him or her about your financial situation and don't hesitate to ask how he charges before you get in deep. If you don't have any business bookkeeping experience, get an accountant to set up the records you should be keeping. Even if you are good at the numbers yourself, you will need an accountant when tax time comes, so you might as well engage him before you make hash of the records.

THE ARMED FORCES

The military is one of the few ways a high-school graduate can get away from home, travel, and meet new people while earning a salary. Starting pay after basic training is $363.30 a month, not including medical, dental, food, and housing allowances. And though you have to sign up for three years in the army or navy, four in the Air Force and Coast Guard, and two in the Marine Corps, you can be sure all that time of a steady job.

All the services train recruits in their own specialized schools, help enlistees attend college in their spare time, and pay 75 percent of tuition costs. Enlistment bonuses for combat duty, as high as $2,500, are used to attract recruits. In all branches of the service, reenlistment bonuses may total as much as $2,000 during a twenty-year military career; at retirement, there's a pension of 50 percent of basic salary at the time you retire. In 1973 a Library of Congress study found that after all pay and extra benefits were counted, the average earnings for a career military man (both officers and enlisted men) could run as much as $1,500 a year more than average civilian earnings.

Detailed information on educational and occupational opportunities available through the armed forces and the enlistment procedures for each branch of the service are as close as your nearest post office, where the recruiters will be happy to fill you in. Available through them is a brochure entitled "Report: Basic Facts About Military Service," published by the Department of Defense, which can tell you everything you ever wanted to know about military service, from basic training to retirement plans, including detailed descriptions of each available job category.

OUTDOOR ACTIVITIES

You can play in the outdoors, you can live in the outdoors, and you can work in the outdoors, with jobs ranging from construction work to picking strawberries at the minimum wage.

The U.S. Department of Labor has prepared a special listing of outdoor jobs. It is called "The Outdoors and Your Career," and is available in most libraries, vocational guidance offices, and, if all else fails, from the Superintendent of Documents, Government Printing Office, Washington, D.C., 20402. A partial listing includes: agricultural workers, airport workers, amusement park workers, animal trainers, athletic coaches, auto mechanics, beekeepers, billboard erectors, blacksmiths, boat-dock and boat-ride operators, border patrolmen, bounty hunters, bricklayers, caddies, campground caretakers, carhops, carpenters, cement masons, cemetery workers, charter boat operators, circus workers, Coast Guardsmen, commercial fishermen, construction laborers, divers, dog catchers, dredge operators, electric power linemen and cable splicers, fish and game wardens, guards and watchmen, landscape architects, lifeguards, loggers, mail carriers, park rangers, parking attendants, racetrack workers, ranch hands, roofers, sheepherders, ski resort workers, smoke jumpers, steeplejacks, surveyors, telephone linemen, tour guides, vendors, window cleaners, zookeepers.

The government offers employment as well as advice. The Department of the Interior hires teen-agers to build trails, park facilities, fish hatcheries, plant trees, and gather air and water samples. For information write the U.S. Department of the Interior, Avenue C between

18th and 19th Street, N.W., Washington, D.C., 21240.

Other job-related government publications include "Careers in Resource Management," available from the Branch of Employment and Training, Bureau of Land Management, U.S. Department of the Interior, Washington, D.C., 20240; "Careers in Soil Conservation Service" from the Personnel Division, Soil Conservation Service, U.S. Department of Agriculture, Washington, D.C., 20250; "Careers in the National Park Service" from the Branch of Employment and Employee Relations, National Park Service, U.S. Department of the Interior, Washington, D.C., 20240; "Employment Opportunities in the Bureau of Sport Fisheries and Wildlife" from the Division of Personnel Management, Bureau of Sport Fisheries and Wildlife, U.S. Department of the Interior, Washington, D.C., 20240; "Women in the Forest Service" from the Division of Personnel Management, Forest Service, U.S. Dept. of Agriculture, Washington, D.C., 20250; and "Working for the Bureau of Outdoor Recreation" from the Bureau of Outdoor Recreation, U.S. Department of the Interior, Washington, D.C., 20240.

Living and playing outdoors can come at a high price (fancy ski resorts, oceangoing private yachts) or at a moderate price (grub stake for squatting on an abandoned farm, camper bus for a cross country jaunt) or, if that's too much, pocket money for hitch-hiking or backpacking.

Those who can afford the high-priced outdoors—from yachts to the hotel bills at Aspen—don't need advice from anyone; they can't get away from the salesmen.

But those who want to do it with a little bit of money need all the advice they can get. Camping is a high art, if not a cult, and a novice can get on to such tricks as cutting the labels out of underwear to lighten a backpack from "how to" books and classic memoirs of personal experience such as Colin Fletcher's *The Complete*

Walker, 1968, Alfred A. Knopf, 201 East 50 Street, New York, New York, 10022. He provides equipment checklists, lists of retailers of backpack equipment and freeze-dried foods. Another noted authority is Bradford Angier, author of such books as *How to Live in the Woods on Pennies a Day*, a classic on retreating to the north woods to find the good life ($3.95 in paperback). *How to Stay Alive in the Woods* and *Feasting Free on Wild Edibles*, by Euell Gibbons, are also full of information on how to cut your food bills, as are *Stalking the Good Life*, and *Stalking the Wild Asparagus*, all published by David McKay, 750 Third Avenue, New York, New York, 10017.

Several magazines specialize in outdoor activities. *Wilderness Camping* is published bimonthly, costs $4.00 a year, from 1255 Portland Place, Boulder, Colorado, 80302, and is devoted entirely to backpacking, canoeing, cycling, and related activities. *Fur-Fish-Game*, published monthly by A. R. Harding Publishing Company, 2878 E. Main St., Columbus, Ohio, 43209, for $4.00 a year, covers the same general topics but with the slant of earning your living from the outdoors.

Many mail-order firms specialize in selling sporting goods, camping equipment, outdoor clothing, and supplies to hunting and fishing enthusiasts, but the granddaddy of them all is L. L. Bean in Freeport, Maine, 04032. The Bean catalogue, issued four times a year, is sent free to anyone who writes for it.

The Sierra Club, with over forty chapters in the United States, organizes regional activities, works to preserve the wilderness, and publishes a series of guides and tote books of various wild areas. The club can be contacted at 1050 Mills Tower, San Francisco, California, 94104, or at 250 W. 40 Street, New York, New York, 10018.

For topographic maps of the wilderness area you choose, or for a folder describing topographic maps available, write U.S. Geological Survey, Washington,

D.C., 20242. For information on national parks, write the Office of Information, National Park Service, at Interior Building, Washington, D.C., 20240. Information on state recreational areas is available from the State Department of Environmental Conservation or each state's Park Service.

TRAVEL

Travel folders are alluring, but for realistic planning, turn to some of the organizations and publications geared to the needs of young people. While some discounts and other advantages are available only to bona fide students, any young person wanting to work, study, or travel independently in North America or abroad can benefit from the student-oriented guides listed below or the guides not slanted specifically towards youth which contain suggestions for low-budget travel.

Here is a sampling of the vast array of books and pamphlets available:

Youth Travel Abroad: What to Know Before You Go. Nineteen-page pamphlet of information on passports, visas, international driver's license, etc. Available at American Express offices, or send 20 cents to the U.S. Government Printing Office, Washington, D.C., 20402.

Student Travel Catalog. Invaluable, free 34-page booklet, describing the services of the Council on International Educational Exchange (CIEE). Contains applications and order forms for the International Student Identity Card, American Youth Hostel Pass and rail passes, and shows you how to save on museum fees, student hostels, restaurants, and transportation. Lists some of the best travel books, which are available from the CIEE in case your bookstore does not have them.

Write for the booklet to CIEE Student Travel Service, 777 United Nations Plaza, New York, New York, 10017, or 235 East Santa Clara Street #710, San Jose, California, 95113.

Whole World Handbook: A Student Guide to Work, Study, and Travel Abroad, published by CIEE at $3.50. Covering all continents, it lists U.S.-sponsored study programs around the world and opportunities to work or teach abroad, plus information for those on low budgets. Some are summer projects, but others are for longer periods.

Let's Go: A Student Guide to Europe, annual publication of the Harvard Student Agencies, 4 Holyoke Street, Cambridge, Massachusetts 02138. Paper, $3.95. Written for students by students, it covers Western and Eastern Europe, the Soviet Union, Turkey, Israel, and North Africa. For travel in North America, see their *Let's Go: A Student Guide to the United States and Canada.*

Europe on $5 to $10 a Day, by Arthur Frommer (paper, $3.95) Arhur Frommer, Inc., 70 Fifth Avenue, New York, New York, 10011. Not specifically for students but a useful guide to inexpensive places to eat, sleep, and shop. One of a series on many parts of the world. Annually revised. The author is a Yale University Law School graduate turned world traveler who recommends places frequented by natives rather than tourists.

More specialized titles include:

Bike Tripping, by Tom Cuthbertson, 1972, published by Ten Speed Press, Box 4310 Berkeley, California, 94704. Available in paperback at $3.00. Covers all aspects of cycling "from cross country racing to urban commuting, from short 'escape' trips . . . to long tours through the open countryside." Includes addresses of bike clubs, catalogs, magazines, etc.

Woodall's 1973–74 Travel Camping: The Four Seasons, 1973, Simon and Schuster, 630 Fifth Avenue, New York, New York, 10020. Paper, $2.45.

The traveler by sea might want to consult the *Worldwide Freighter Guide*, available for $1.75 from TRAVLTIPS, 40–21T Bell Street, Bayside, New York, 11361.

If you want to drive someone else's car, gas included, across the United States, consult the commercial notices in big city papers and go to one of the agencies advertising "Drive New Cars Free" or "Insured Auto Shippers." A young acquaintance of ours did this and tells us the only requirement was a valid driver's license. Other opportunities can be discovered in travel magazines such as *Holiday* or *Travel* or the travel section of *Saturday Review World*.

Organizations to investigate:

American Automobile Association, 8111 Gatehouse Road, Falls Church, Virginia, 22042. For the motorist, membership in the AAA is worth the price of the dues. They will plan your trip, give you excellent maps, and provide tour books of the U.S., Canada, and abroad which furnish detailed information about what to do and see. Their emergency road service is tops, too.

Appalachian Mountain Club, 5 Joy Street, Boston, Massachusetts, 02108. This mountaineering and conservation organization provides guidebooks and maps on the Appalachian Trail and other hiking trails in the Northeast. It also recruits staff to maintain eight huts in the White Mountains, and to cut, clear, and maintain trails throughout New Hampshire.

American Youth Hostels, National Census, Delaplane, Virginia, 22025. Sponsors inexpensive educational and recreational outdoor travel opportunities, primarily by bicycle or on foot along scenic trails and byways. Maintains 135 overnight accommodations (hostels) in the United States. AYH members are eligible to stay at hostels in forty-eight countries throughout the world for fees ranging from $1 to $3 per night. Two kinds of passes are available: junior at $5 and senior at $10.

Council on International Educational Exchange (CIEE), 777 United Nations Plaza, New York, New York, 10017. A dependable source for comprehensive information on student travel, work, and study. Its *Student Travel Catalog* describing its services is listed above.

Experiment in International Living, 4 Kipling Road, Brattleboro, Vermont, 05301. Write to them if you would like to live abroad with a foreign family, with or without academic credit.

Up with People, 3103 N. Campbell Avenue, Tuscon, Arizona, 85719. You can take part in original musical shows or help in a clerical, technical, or promotional capacity while traveling and receive high-school or college credit if you want it. *Up with People* says it aims to develop the potential of the individual participant and improve communications between people of varied cultures and ethnic backgrounds. It takes young people sixteen to twenty-five years old from the U.S. and abroad. The "Face to Face" section of *Seventeen*, July 1973, tells of the experience of one of these students, Karen Smith. A more general article by John Reddy appeared in the *Reader's Digest* for October 1972.

Commission on Voluntary Service and Action, 475 Riverside Drive, New York, New York, 10027. Publishes *Invest Your Self*, an annual listing of voluntary service opportunities in the United States and abroad. Send $1 with your request.

Kibbutz Aliya Desk, 575 Fifth Avenue, New York, New York, 10011. An organization recruiting and placing Americans who want to work in Israel.

HELPING PEOPLE

There are many organizations which can help you to find your niche as a part-time or full-time volunteer or worker at a subsistence level helping others. Locally you can get useful suggestions from such sources as your church, the office of your community fund, which acts as a clearing house for all the social agencies in the area, hospitals, nursing homes, homes for the elderly, mental health centers, libraries, and schools. Agencies which promote and stimulate local level voluntarism are:

Association of Volunteer Bureaus
    of America, Inc.
National Office; P.O. Box 7253,
    Kansas City, Missouri, 64113.
Local offices in over 225 communities.

National Center for Voluntary Action
National Office: 1785 Massachusetts Avenue,
    N.W., Washington, D.C., 20036.
Voluntary Action Centers in nearly
    200 communities.

United Way of America
National Office: 801 N. Fairfax,
    Alexandria, Virginia, 22314
Local offices in 2,430 communities.

If you see the need for a new program and wish to set it up yourself you can get help from the National Center for Voluntary Action listed above. The Center publishes a bimonthly *Voluntary Action News* and presents annual awards for exceptional achievement in voluntary action.

Letters to the editor of the local newspaper are often a good way to get in touch with like-minded neighbors —and, in smaller cities, the desk of a newspaper sometimes serves as a letterbox.

For a listing of opportunities part- or full-time, some at subsistence levels, outside your area, send $1 to The Commission on Voluntary Service Action, 475 Riverside Drive, Room 665, New York, New York, 10027, for *Invest Your Self: Involvement and Action: A Catalogue of Opportunities*. This is the most comprehensive listing of volunteer activities available to anyone in the U.S.A. both here and abroad. It reports on more than 150 organizations using volunteers for community services, institutional service and related programs in North America and abroad.

ACTION is the federal agency that operates both the Peace Corps, offering direct service in foreign countries, and VISTA (Volunteers in Service to America), its domestic counterpart channeling volunteers to direct service to underprivileged Americans. Both prefer college graduates or adults with established skills, such as card-carrying carpenters. In the mid 1970s, curtailment of their funds and a policy of pinpointing programs to very specific needs made it virtually impossible for them to take on high-school graduates who did not have work experience.

A new Youth Challenge Program was launched in 1974 to place young people ages fourteen to twenty-one in volunteer service in poor communities; planning grants were to be awarded to high schools, colleges, local agencies, and governments to enable them to design model volunteer programs. For information, write:

Youth Challenge Program, Action Education Program,
ACTION, 806 Connecticut Avenue, N.W., Washington, D.C., 20525.

Ralph Nader has been a hero to young people ever
since he launched his automobile-safety crusade. To
apply for work in his organization, send letters and
resumes to: Florence Dembling, Suite 711, 2000 P
Street, N.W., Washington, D.C., 20036.

Most people like to help other people on an individual basis, but if you want to save the world on a wholesale basis, you may be interested in volunteering for the
social action of your concern. If you want to find a way
to work with others "to build alternatives to institu-
tionalized forces that oppress us all," you can find
many opportunities listed in *Work Force*, a bimonthly
periodical published by Vocations for Social Change,
Inc., 4911 Telegraph Avenue, Oakland, California,
94609, which describes itself as a "tax-exempt, anti-
profit corporation/collective." They ask for a $5 dona-
tion for a six months subscription. They list communes,
research foundations, health groups, protest committees.

SUBSISTENCE JOB

Finding a job, particularly the "bread labor" kind of
subsistence job, is more fun if you use a little ingenuity.
If the neighbors are going away for the summer, would
they like a house-sitter? If you like to work outdoors,
does the local nursery need an extra hand? If you have
a friend working where you'd like to work, ask him to
keep an ear open for opportunities. Subsistence jobs are
often filled by word of mouth. Family contacts were the
biggest source of jobs for the Harvard dropouts studied
in 1974, followed closely by friends, former employers,
and want ads.

Jobs that support you without leading anywhere are

usually available without charge at the local state employment service. They should also have information on state and county civil service jobs. Check out the federal job openings at the local post office.

Occasionally you can find fascinating offers in the want ads, such as one that ran recently in New York's *Village Voice*: "Learning Experiments. Young adult subjects (17–30) needed for psychological experiments on learning, memory, perception. $2.50 an hour. . . ."

Most communities have branches of Manpower or other temporary help agencies listed in the phone book. This is a favorite device for job shoppers who want to look around before tying themselves up in a permanent job. The drawback is that you will be paid only about half of what the company pays the agency for your services.

PROTEST LIFESTYLE

There's a publication for every class of beef against the establishment, and the quickest way to find friends, advice, and news is to find one that covers your interests. A good place to begin is "Somewhere Else: A Living–Learning Catalogue," edited by the Center for Curriculum Design, published in 1973 by The Swallow Press, 1139 South Wabash Avenue, Chicago, Illinois, 60605, $3.00. It purports to be a "catalogue of places to learn for those who can't bring themselves to go to college." It tells you about communes, craft centers, free universities, and apprenticeship-type work opportunities.

Getting back to the simple life isn't so simple in the 1970s, U.S.A. *Mother Earth News*, P.O. Box 70, Hendersonville, North Carolina, 28739, published bimonthly and costing $8 per year, tells you such basics as how to get land, transportation, food, and housing free; how to organize a commune, how to homestead, and find like-minded partners, and generally survive doing exactly what you want to do. Gives detailed instructions for such important enterprises as building a tipi, growing a garden, milking a cow, and harnessing solar energy. Fascinating dreaming even if you don't intend to do any of it.

For an antiestablishment viewpoint on life problems from breast-feeding to dying, see Ernest Callenbach's *Living Poor with Style*, 1972, Bantam Books, 666 Fifth Avenue, New York, New York, 10019, $1.95. "People who really aren't ready to settle down," he writes, "should not kid themselves that they are going to fit into a commune." The chapter on the draft is obsolete and some others uneven, but it offers good advice on job-hunting, hiring lawyers, and many other topics.

Classified ads in the underground press are the quickest way to find kindred dropouts from the establishment. To find the underground paper nearest you, check out *From Radical Left to Radical Right*, by Robert H. Muller, Theodore Jurgen Spahn, and Janet M. Spahn, 1972, The Scarecrow Press, Inc., 52 Liberty Street, Metuchen, New Jersey, 08840. It may be obsolete today—counterculture publications are usually short-lived—but it gives an idea of the range. Described as a "bibliography of current periodicals of protest, controversy, advocacy or dissent, with dispassionate content—summaries to guide librarians and other educators," it has classified them under radical left, marxist-socialist left, underground, rock culture, anarchist, libertarian, utopian, liberal, civil rights, women's liberation, gay liberation, racial and ethnic pride, sexual freedom, peace, servicemen's papers, conservative, anticommunist, race supremacist, humanism, atheism, rationalism, metaphysical UFO's, and miscellaneous.

Communes come and go. To get an idea of what life in a commune is like, try one of the following firsthand reports. The communities they describe may be gone, but the pattern remains:

Communes, USA: A Personal Tour, by R. Fairfield, Penguin Books, Inc., 7110 Ambassador Road, Baltimore, Maryland, 21207. $7.95. A study of 2,000 communes in the United States.

Getting Back Together, by Robert Houriet. Available in paperback from Avon, 959 Eighth Avenue, New York, New York, 10019. It is a description of communes visited in Oregon, Colorado, California, and Vermont.

Notes

Chapter 1—The College Mystique

1. For evidence on the extent to which tax-supported colleges subsidize the rich, who would go to college anyway, at the expense of the poor, who don't utilize this public service as often, see pp. 90–92 of *Higher Education: Who Pays? Who Benefits? Who Should Pay?* A Report and Recommendations by The Carnegie Commission on Higher Education, June 1973, McGraw-Hill, New York. In California, students who come from families with incomes of more than $21,000 constitute 26 percent of the student body of the heavily subsidized University of California, and 27 percent of the student body of the state's private institutions.

2. Fritz Machlup made these estimates in "Matters of Measure," in *Universal Higher Education*, edited by Logan Wilson, American Council on Education, Washington, D.C., 1972, pp. 81–2.

3. During its six years of existence (1967–1973), the Carnegie Commission on Higher Education spent $6 million supplied by the Carnegie Foundation for the Advancement of Teaching on what Donald McDonald, editor of *The Center Magazine* (September–October 1973), criticized as "a strictly social science job on higher education—they climbed all over it, counting, measuring, describing, gauging, and projecting enrollment trends, demographic patterns, financing practices, student and alumni attitudes, governance procedures, and community relations." Any *facts* your heart desires is in one of its twenty statistics-bestuffed volumes. The Commission was neatly balanced. Headed by Clark Kerr, former president of the University of California, Berkeley, it included a black woman, lawyer Patricia Harris; a Catholic, Theodore Hesburgh; a southerner, William Friday; a businessman, Norton Simon, and others. In 1974 it continued as the Carnegie Council on Policy Studies in Higher Education, 2150 Shattuck Avenue, Berkeley, California, 94704.

4. Total and first time degree-credit enrollment in institutions of higher education rose from 8,265,057 in 1972 to an estimated 8,370,000 in 1973 according to Table 82 of *Digest of Educational Statistics*, 1973 Edition, U.S. Department of Health, Education and Welfare. Because the population is rising, enrollments will continue to rise but at a slower rate than anticipated. We refer to "nine million college students" in order to include students not enrolled for a degree. In 1972, degree credit and nondegree credit students totalled 9,214,860.

5. Evidence that money really does buy happiness comes from a survey by Paul Cameron, associate professor of Human Development at St. Mary's College, Maryland, reported in *Psychology Today*, August 1974.

6. My generalizations about students, and many of the statements I've quoted, come from talks with undergraduates at colleges where I spoke during 1973 and 1974. These included: University of California at Davis; Southwestern College, Chula Vista, California; Santa Monica College, Santa Monica, California; El Camino College, Via Torrance, California; Bakersfield College, Bakersfield, California; San Francisco City College, San Francisco, California; Modesto Junior College, Modesto, California; Canada College, Redwood City, California; American River College, Sacramento, California; University of Southern California at Los Angeles; Eastern Montana College, Billings, Montana.

Also, University of Missouri, Columbia, Missouri; Wichita State University, Wichita, Kansas; Hanover College, Hanover, Indiana; Wright State University, Dayton, Ohio; Allegheny Community College in Pittsburgh, Pennsylvania; Lafayette College, Easton, Pennsylvania; Vanderbilt University, Nashville, Tennessee.

Also, Kirkland College and Hamilton College in Clinton, New York; Ithaca College, Ithaca, New York; The New School for Social Research, New York City; Dowling College, Oakdale, New York; Barnard College, New York City; State University of New York at Oneonta; Marist College, Poughkeepsie, New York; Wellesley College and Babson College, Wellesley, Massachusetts; Green Mountain College, Poultney, Vermont.

I learned a great deal from class discussions with my own students at Russell Sage College and at The New School for Social Research. I also am indebted to students who undertook independent study with me on behalf of the book. Kathy Eisenmenger of Kirkland College looked for a sex difference, if any, between what men and women said that college did for them. Patty Coleman, also of Kirkland, provided skillful interviews of women students and alumnac. Larry Wingert, a Hamilton College senior, spoke with a number of young men at his institution. Claudia Hartung, Sharon Homan, Elizabeth Nordlund, Sheila Gualtieri and Karen Caudill, all of Wright State University, produced an impressive horde of interviewees from colleges in and around Dayton, Ohio, while Kathleen Johnson tackled students and alumni from her own Augsburg College.

We tried to find out why students went to college, how their parents felt about their going, and what the students felt they got out of it. We don't have a statistically representative sample, but we attempted to talk to many different kinds of students in different kinds of schools. Interviews came from Amherst College, Amherst, Massachusetts; Augsburg College, Minneapolis, Minnesota; Babson College, Wellesley, Massachusetts; Bennington College, Bennington, Vermont; City College of Santa Barbara, Santa Barbara, California; College for Human Services, New York City; Columbia University, New York City; Dayton Art Institute and Dayton University, both in Dayton, Ohio; Framingham State University, Framingham, Massachusetts; George Washington University, Washington, D.C.; Hamilton College; Harvard University; Hunter College, New York City; Kirkland College; Lewis and Clark College, Portland, Oregon; Nazareth College of Rochester, Rochester, New York; New York University, New York City; Ohio State University, Columbus, Ohio; Ohio University, Athens, Ohio; Queens College, New York City; State University of New York at Cortland; State University of New York at Stony Brook; University of Dayton, Dayton, Ohio; University of Denver; University of Iowa; University of Massachusetts, Amherst, Massachusetts; University of New Hampshire, Durham, New Hampshire; Vassar College, Poughkeepsie, New York; and Wright State University.

Nearly 250 young people, in and out of school, shared their feelings with me and with our interviewers. They are: Peter B. Ackerman; Guido Adelfio; Diane Adelstein; Jennifer Agnew; Regina Ahouse; Alberta Allen; Bruce Ampolsky; Ellie Anderson; Susan Anton; Paul Asbell; Maro Avakian; Heather Bacon; Richard Baloga; Tom Barber; Kathryn Bardsley; John Barkley; Liz Barrow; Denise Barton; Karen Beak; Susan Beaver; Kathryn Bedke; David Behnke; Linda Bell; Jane Bishop; Vera Bissell; Julia Bittman; Janice Blake; Victor Bobnick; Mike Borden; Nancy Borrell; Mike Boshart; Toby Bosniak; John Bowers; Susie Boyd; Steve Brace; Patricia Brady; Jane Brandfon; Herb Brown; Nellie Burlingham; Dave Caley; Louise Carberry; Marilyn Carol; Patrick Carr; Bradley Caswell; Lyn Chamberlin; Thomas E. Charbonneau; Patricia Chase; Candy Chayer; Elyn Cheney; Paul Chernick; Ann Christopher; Barbara Clavan; Susan Cogswell; Betty Cohen; Carol Cohen.

Also Diana Coleman; Paul Coleman; Kathy Collins; Betsy Congdon; Kathy Corbett; Sam Cordes; Chris Corey; Electra Cummings; Mary Lynn Dabney; Jerome Darring; Curt Davis; Joanne Davis; Peter Davol; Ira Deitch; Timothy Delaney; Hank DeLeo; Kathy Delle Fontane; Diane L. Denny; Melissa Drier; Jill Drinkwater; Anne Dumke; Jane Dunwoodie; Amy Eden; Cathy Elliott; Jeanne Ertel; Alan Fastman; Liz Feder; Laura Fehrs; Ruth Fein; Michelle Feldman; Kathleen Fish; Judith W. Fister; Michael S. Flynn; Pete Follansbee; Alexandra Forbes; Barbara Freshley; Laurey Galka; Fred Gardner; David Garfinkel; Bill Garrison; Rose Gladstone; David Goldmuntz; Susan Good; Carol Goodman; Craig Gudmundson; Donald Haggerty; Ronnie Halper; Alexander Hamilton; David Hanley; Harold Harmon; Judith Harris; Lorine Hartman; Karen Hayes; Tim Hill; Sharon Himmel; Edward Hoe; Barbra Hoffman; Fred Holender; Mark Holmes; Linda Homan; Audean Horgas, Rick Husted.

Also, Dean Johnson; Caroline Karp; Martha Katz; Collins Kellogg; Bob Kennerly; Susan E. Khobreh; Shirley Kidd; Juana King; Max Kirsch; Peter Kirschenbaum;

Pamela Kleinhenz; Nancy Klotz; James Krakowsky; Cheryl Kress; Michael Kurrier; Bob Larson, LaVerne Larson; Sue Laughlin; Melvin Lavender; Andy Lawrence; Carol Lazare; Irving LeBeau; Shirley Ann Lee; Debbie Lewis; Sherry Liddicoat; Susan Lilienthal; Janet Long; John Lopez; Michael Lovell; Susan Love; Ann MacKenzie; Dee McAnsipie; Linda McCloag; David McConeghey; Maura McDermott; Phil McKee; Beth McTavish; Andy Maddocks; Rich Mandelbaum; Stuart R. Malis; Marie Manning; Greg Marsello; Paul Marsh; Robert Martin; Susan Mead; Felice Meadow; Karen Meiselas; Rosane Menconi; Sharon Milano; Stephen Milford; Carole Ann Miller; Tim Miller; Mary Ellen Mitchell; Susan Monossan; Dale Nelson; Ellen O'Connell; Bill O'Hearn; John Oliverio; Steve Ono; Jim O'Neill; Paul Paganelli; Diane Parulis; Fran Paver; Jeffrey Peda; Chris Pengra; Darlene Polanka; Frederick Quirins.

Also, Paul Rainsberger; Rosanna Risner; Sherry Roach; Ellen Roberts; Brian Rokke; Alison Root; Robin Roseman; Gail Rosenblum; Mimi Ross; Jane Rouder; Robert Rowan; Alicia Ryan; Maribeth Salley; Anne Cary Sampson; Daniel Sanderson; Dick Saurber; Carrie Schmertz; Susan Schultz; Randall Scott; Lisa Sherman; Karen Signell; Melissa Silva; Joanne Sorrell; Brenda Mae Sowry; John Spangler; Marylou Spangler; Louise Spartz; Barbara Stanley; Sue Stephenson; Maggie Stern; Bob St. George; Bill Stowell; Jim Suslavich; William Swartz; Richard Tallman; Linda Tally; Mary Lou Thiebault; Marsha Thoma; Lisa Tigar; Valerie Tomaselli; Sharon Lee Tranka; Astrid Trostorff; Nikki Turner; Marty Tyksinski; Maren Valvik; Amy Van Doren; Michelle Vanni; Charles Verrill; Heidi Viemeister; Anita Voorhees; Mark Walpole; Kim Webster; John Weeks; Chip Whitely; Tobie Williams; Mykle Williamson; Sharon Williamson; Tobie Williams; Steve Wing; Marty Winn; Marlys Woesthoff; Jayne Wolford; Michael Woolley; Vicki Willard Yarwood; Robin Young; Jo Zabel; Kathy Zemberi; Dale Zunke.

7. "Parental encouragement is a powerful intervening variable between socioeconomic class background and intelligence of the child and his educational aspirations," according to William H. Sewell and Vimal P. Shah, whose

study of 10,318 Wisconsin high-school seniors was reported in "Social Class, Parental Encouragement, and Educational Aspirations," *American Journal of Sociology*, volume 73, 1967–1968.

The classic study on the characteristics of the college-bound is James W. Trent and Leland L. Medsker, *Beyond High School: A Psychosociological Study of 10,000 High School Graduates*, Jossey-Bass, San Francisco, 1968. The proportion of high-school graduates who enter college is higher now than it was in the class of 1965, which Trent and Medsker followed, but no study as comprehensive has been made since on a national basis.

Demographic information on a statistically representative sample of entering freshmen and their responses to a score of standard attitudinal questions ("Women should receive the same salary and opportunities for advancement as men in comparable positions," Agree Strongly, Agree Somewhat, Disagree Somewhat, Disagree Strongly) is gathered annually by the Cooperative Institutional Research Program of the American Council on Education under the direction of Alexander W. Astin, Margo R. King, John M. Light, and Gerald T. Richardson and published as *The American Freshman: National Norms*.

8. Joseph Katz and Associates, *No Time for Youth: Growth and Constraint in College Students*, Jossey-Bass, Inc., San Francisco, 1968, is a psychologist's interpretation of in-depth interviews with a relatively small sample of students in two California colleges. Katz gets down deep enough into his subjects to hit the basic motivations which do not change as quickly as the catch words with which students often answer probing questions.

9. Daniel Yankelovich, Inc. conducted studies of college youth in 1967, 1969, 1971, and 1973. *Changing Youth in the 70's: A Study of American Youth*, McGraw-Hill, 1974, summarizes the 1973 study. The results of earlier studies were published in *The Changing Values on Campus: Political and Personal Attitudes of Today's College Students* by Washington Square Press, Pocket Books, New York, 1972.

10. Leon Lefkowitz, "Our Newly Developing Waste Lands: The American Colleges," *Intellect*, March 1973.

11. The Carnegie Commission statement of "the main purposes of higher education in the United States today and for the prospective future" is so obviously a worked-over set of words that it deserves complete quotation. It appears in *The Purposes and the Performance of Higher Education in the United States Approaching the Year 2000*, June 1973, McGraw-Hill, New York. In the Commission's view, these purposes are:

The provision of opportunities for the intellectual, aesthetic, ethical, and skill development of individual students, and the provision of campus environments which can constructively assist students in their more general development growth

The advancement of human capability in society at large

The enlargement of educational justice for the postsecondary age group

The transmission and advancement of learning and wisdom

The critical evaluation of society—through individual thought and persuasion—for the sake of society's self-renewal.

Chapter 2—The Cost to Parents

1. In *Meeting College Costs in 1974–75, a Guide for Students and Parents*, the College Scholarship Service says it expected men students to save $400 and women students to save $300 from employment in the summer before their first year; higher earnings were expected for subsequent years.

2. *Student Expenses at Postsecondary Institutions* is issued in the spring of each school year by the College Scholarship Service and can be obtained by sending a check for $2.50 to Publication Order Office, College Entrance Examination Board, Box 592, Princeton, N.J. 08540. It lists the estimates of total costs made by each of 2,200 colleges. The estimates include subsistence at home for commuting students, which rose faster than room and board in residence colleges between 1973 and 1974. If this trend continued, the four-year cost for graduates of 1978 who "saved" by living at home would be $10,797,

compared with $10,656 for those who attended residence colleges. We have assumed that residence colleges will have to raise their board charges as well, and we have projected that the percentage of the four-year rise between 1970 and 1974 will continue for four years more, maintaining the historic differential between commuter and residence costs.

3. The estimate of 2.7 million students receiving financial aid during 1972–73 was made by Peter P. Muirhead, Deputy Commissioner for Higher Education in a speech delivered in May 1973.

4. The Carnegie Commission in the report cited above, *Higher Education: Who Pays? Who Benefits? Who Should Pay?* says that "Monetary outlays are borne about one-third by students and their parents, and about two thirds by public sources and philanthropy." But if you consider the total economic cost of a college education, which means including the money that a student would have earned if he had gone to work (see note 6 below), then, says the Commission, "the figures are reversed—students and their parents bear about two-thirds of the burden and public sources and philanthropy about one-third."

5. The estimate of 5 percent increase for 1975–76 in the Princeton costs sounds naïve in the face of "double-digit" inflation prevailing in 1974, but we have projected on the basis of an average of previous years.

6. For a discussion of foregone income as a cost of college, see Chapter 7, "Foregone Income," in *Higher Education: Who Pays? Who Benefits? Who Should Pay?*

7. The Panel on Student Financial Need Analysis chaired by Allan M. Cartter suggested that public programs "consider contributions to the low-income family as well as to the student" in order to compensate them for the income the family foregoes when a student attends college. See p. 95, *New Approaches to Student Financial Aid*, College Entrance Examination Board, New York, 1971.

8. Dr. Alexander Sidar, Jr., Executive Director of the College Entrance Examination Board, estimated that in 1972–73 1,020,000 Parents Confidential Statements, 200,000 additional Students Financial Statements, and 50,000 financial aid questionnaires were processed by the College Scholarship Service, another 300,000 were re-

viewed by the American College Testing Service, and 300,000 more by other systems for a total of 1,870,000 applications. Financial aid awards were made to only one-third of this number. A year later, because of the new Federal program of Basic Educational Opportunity Grants, Dr. Sidar estimated that 40 percent of the applicants for aid were actually receiving it.

Chapter 3—The Cost to Students

1. In 1972, the National Defense Student Loan Program, authorized by the National Defense Education Act of 1958, was renamed the National Direct Student Loan Program.

2. Most of the delinquent student loans and the student bankruptcies have involved trade schools rather than academic institutions. Information on the loans and bankruptcies is collected by the U.S. Office of Education, Reports and Data Analysis, in Washington.

3. In his 1973 book, *Beleaguered Minorities: Cultural Politics in America* (W. H. Freeman, San Francisco, 1973) S. J. Makielski of Loyola University, New Orleans, a political scientist, includes students because, like blacks, women, and other minorities, they find themselves in a hostile environment; have been historically subjected to discrimination and deprivation; and are relatively powerless to change their condition. When Professor Solon T. Kimball asked his anthropology students at the University of Florida at Gainesville to comment, four out of five agreed that students resemble other beleaguered minorities in their exclusion from full participation in society. Many pointed out, however, that the minority status of students is temporary.

4. Fringe benefits were estimated at 26 percent of overall compensation during 1970 by the Bureau of Labor Statistics, U.S. Department of Labor Report 419, "Supplementary Compensation in the PATC Survey Industries," 1973. PATC stands for Professional, Administrative, Technical, and Clerical occupations.

5. For case histories of dropouts, see Nancy Silver Lindsay, *Where Did You Go? Out!* a Descriptive Report on Leaves of Absences. Foreword by Dean K. Whitla,

Office of Instructional Research and Evaluation, Office of Career Services and Off Campus Learning, Harvard University, Cambridge, Massachusetts, 1974.

6. For analysis of the various institutional sources of financial aid to students, see Table 23, "Undergraduate Student Support by Federal Agencies, 1969–1973, on page 68 of *Higher Education: Why Pays? Who Benefits? Who Should Pay?* After the Veterans Administration, the Office of Education is the biggest source of student funding, followed by the Social Security Administration.

Chapter 4—The Dumbest Investment You Can Make

1. One of the best recent reports on student attitudes is *Youth and the Meaning of Work*, a study published in 1973 by David Gottlieb of the Institute for the Study of Human Development, Pennsylvania State University, for the Manpower Administration of the U.S. Department of Labor. The sample was composed of 1,860 male and female members of the class of 1972 at five colleges located in Pennsylvania. Data were collected by interviews and questionnaires. Gottlieb sees a work ethic emerging that "places a much greater demand on work while at the same time de-emphasizing the importance of money, power, and prestige." It has a valuable annotated bibliography.

2. Economists calculate the rate of return on a college education by computing the *difference* in lifetime income between the college and high school graduate and basing the rate on the net present value of that difference. The method of calculation is set forth in many of the references on investment in college. See note 10.

3. All of the lifetime earnings, as well as the gap between the income of a high school graduate and a man who had four years of college, were taken from Table 9, pages 26 and 28, "Expected Lifetime Income for all Males 18 to 64 Years Old with Income in 1972 by Years of School Completed, Age, Selected Discount Rates, and Selected Annual Productivity Increase," from U.S. Bureau of the Census, *Current Population Reports*, Series P-60, No. 92, "Annual Mean Income, Lifetime Income, and Educational Attainment of Men in the United States, for

Selected Years, 1956 to 1972," U.S. Government Printing Office, Washington, D.C., 1974. College graduate in our text means four years of college. We assumed a discount rate of zero and a zero percent productivity increase, unless otherwise noted in text. Since the Census has no way of predicting the lifetime earnings of any one young man, lifetime earnings are calculated by adding up the earnings of men of different ages at some base year, in this case, 1972. In order to allow for the chance of dying before retirement, the total earnings of all the men who are still alive and earning at each age are divided among the number of men alive and earning at eighteen. There are fewer fifty-year-olds than forty-year-olds, but those remaining make more money, so the pot of money earned by the fifty-year-olds isn't so much more than the pot of all the money earned by the more numerous but lower paid forty-year-olds.

4. For the cost of a Princeton education, class of 1976, see page 32 of the text.

Foregone income is an accepted cost of college and one which has to be considered in any comparison between investment in college, in a savings bank, or other income-producing alternative. It does, however, present some statistical problems. How do you count it? Is it appropriate to start the entire investment in college compounding at the age of eighteen, when the high-school graduate who decides to invest in the savings bank instead does not, in fact, forego the earnings but goes to work?

I think it is. If foregone income is part of the cost of college, then the *total* cost, as an investment must be considered when comparing alternative uses of the money, even though in one such alternative the income would not be foregone. It is true that the high-school graduate who goes right to work does not forego income, but after all he does work for the money and insofar as he does, he is worse off. The college student is supported while he is in college, a benefit which the high-school student who goes to work has a right to capitalize in assessing options.

The figures in this statistical exercise are, then, based on the assumption that the foregone income is banked at the outset, just as it would be if the hypothetical uncle included foregone income in his lump-sum gift.

A more realistic, but complicated way of counting foregone income would be to credit it to the bank account of the high-school graduate as it is earned. Figured this way, we would find $22,256 in the account at age eighteen. One year later, using the figures given in chapter 2, $2,575 would be added. At the end of the second year an additional $2,943 would be added, and so on until age twenty-two. At this rate the high-school graduate would have $43,578 in his bank account while the college graduate would be just starting to work. Forty-two years later the high-school graduate would have $1,062,106 in the bank while the college graduate would have $1,222,965.

5. Stephen G. Necel, a loan officer at Empire National Bank in Poughkeepsie, made all the calculations, compounding sums invested in a savings bank at the 1974 rate of 7.5 percent compounded daily.

6. College can't beat the savings bank unless you can get the total cost of college down to $8,445, the amount which, when invested in a savings account for forty-two years, will yield a net present value equal to the net present value of the incremental earnings of the college graduate over the high-school graduate between the ages of twenty-two and sixty-four when both are discounted at 7 percent.

According to Table 21 of *Current Population Report* No. 92, a high-school graduate eighteen years old in 1972 could have earned $19,363 if he had worked during nine months in each college year, so he is out $10,928 even if college tuition, fees, books, and the transportation to get to classes were absolutely free. Of course, most students living at home and attending state schools counted only the tuition costs and out-of-pocket expenses.

Their outlay would have been much higher if they had counted, in addition, the $2,085 the College Scholarship Service figured commuting students needed for room and board in 1974–1975. When foregone income is counted, students who live at home and go to a local state-supported institution don't do very much better than the Princeton student.

7. The average advantage in earnings of college graduates over high-school graduates was taken from Table A, p. 2, of *Current Population Report* No. 92, cited above.

8. For the influence of family income on the likelihood that a high-school graduate will attend college, see Table 13, "Income distribution of all families, families of the college-age population, and families of college attenders, Fall 1971," on p. 44 of *Higher Education: Who Pays? Who Benefits? Who Should Pay?* cited above.

9. We're indebted to banker Necel for what it costs—at least in Dutchess County, New York—to buy liquor stores, franchises, gas stations, and other investments a student could make with his college money.

10. Rates of return on the investment in a college education have been seriously calculated and compared with investments of other kinds since the development of the concept of human capital to account for the great expansion of the American economy after World War II. For a good overview, see the article "Capital, Human," in the *International Encyclopedia of the Social Sciences*, The Macmillan Company. Early contributions to the economic value of a college education were made by Dael Wolfle, *America's Resources of Specialized Talent*, Harper & Brothers, New York, 1954; Theodore W. Schultz, "Capital Formation by Education," *Journal of Political Economy*, December 1960, and by Gary Becker in his classic work, *Human Capital*, Columbia University Press, 1964. A good roundup of recent discussions and refinements as well as a bibliography are in chapters 10 and 11 of the Carnegie Commission report edited by Margaret S. Gordon, *Higher Education and the Labor Market*, McGraw-Hill, New York, 1974.

Chapter 5—College and the Job Market

1. Existing research on work satisfaction is summarized in *Work in America, Report of a Special Task Force to the Secretary of Health, Education and Welfare*, MIT Press, Cambridge, Mass., 1973. The list of occupations most frequently rechosen was quoted on p. 16 from "The Work Module" by Robert Kahn, 1972. Workers were asked,

"What type of work would you try to get into if you could start all over again?" Only 43 percent of white-collar workers would rechoose their jobs.

2. Joseph Katz, *No Time for Youth*, Jossey-Bass, Inc., San Francisco, 1968, is a valuable reminder in the 1970s that students don't change as fast as their fads. The Peace Corps would be popular today if it had a different name, an untarnished image, and the resources to employ young graduates.

3. The woman pushed ever onward and upward in school was quoted in The Carnegie Commission report authored by Joe L. Spaeth and Andrew M. Greeley, *Recent Alumni and Higher Education*, New York, McGraw-Hill, 1970.

4. The matching of job openings and graduates who might aspire to them was made by comparing the annual job openings in various occupations projected by the *Occupational Outlook Handbook*, 1974–75 edition, U.S. Department of Labor, Bureau of Labor Statistics, 1974, Bulletin 1785 with the number of graduates in 1973 projected by the U.S. Office of Education, in the 1973 edition of *Projections of Educational Statistics to 1982–83*, "Earned Bachelor's Degrees, by Field of Study: United States, 1961–62 to 1982–83."

5. U.S. Department of Labor, Bureau of Labor Statistics, "Employment of Recent College Graduates," *Special Labor Force Report* 151, 1973.

6. Dr. Kathleen Fisher of the Department of Genetics, College of Agricultural and Environmental Sciences, University of California at Davis, restructured the lecture-and-laboratory course in genetics so that it could be made available on tape and film.

7. The American Enterprise Institute, a private Washington-based research organization, was quoted on the coming surplus of physicians by Dr. Charles C. Sprague, in the chairman's address to the Association of American Medical Colleges on November 5, 1973.

8. Five percent of entering freshmen now say, on the Freshman Norms questionnaire, that they want to be doctors. Only a quarter of the population are college graduates, or 25,000 out of every 100,000. If 5 percent of the

entering freshmen actually graduated from college and became physicians, there would be 1,250 physicians for every 100,000 people, more than ten times the target ratio of 100 per 100,000.

9. The authority on the job prospects of college graduates is the Endicott Report issued annually by Frank S. Endicott, Director of Placement, Emeritus, Northwestern University, Evanston, Illinois, which surveys 196 "well-known business and industrial concerns" every spring on their hiring intentions and compares them with the previous year.

10. Most jobs done by "engineers" are learned on the job. The mean number of years of school completed by engineers was 15.2, less than four years of college, according to the 1970 Census of Population PC(2)-7C, Occupation by Industry, Table 3, "Mean Years of School Completed of Employed Persons According to Industry by Occupation: 1970," p. 129.

11. For a discussion of the relevance of education to specialized and managerial jobs, see V. Lane Rawlins and Lloyd Ulman, "The Utilization of College-Trained Manpower in the United States," in *Higher Education and the Labor Market*, a volume of essays sponsored by The Carnegie Commission on Higher Education, edited by Margaret S. Gordon, McGraw-Hill, New York, 1974.

12. J. Sterling Livingston's "Myth of the Well-Educated Manager," *Harvard Business Review*, January-February 1971, is a refreshing challenge to the notion that business enterprise can be "professionalized."

13. The failure of schools of education to test their own relevancy is reported in Edward F. Renshaw, "Estimating the Returns to Education," *Review of Economics and Statistics*, Vol. 42 (August 1960). We can only hope that the omission has been remedied since.

14. For an informed, first-hand account of Chinese medicine, see *Serve The People: Observations on Medicine in the People's Republic*, by Victor W. Sidel and Ruth Sidel, New York, Josiah Macy Jr. Foundation, 1974.

15. For a racy account of fake doctors, see "Strange Tales of Medical Imposters" by Ralph Lee Smith, *Today's Health*, October 1968. A more sober analysis of imposter-

ship was presented to the National Congress on Health Quackery in 1968 by Robert C. Derbyshire, a member of New Mexico's Board of Medical Examiners.

Chapter 6—The Liberal Arts Religion

1. "When alumni were forced to choose between a general education and a career-oriented education, they overwhelmingly endorsed the idea of a general education," Joe L. Spaeth and Andrew M. Greeley reported in *Recent Alumni and Higher Education*, a Carnegie Commission study published by McGraw-Hill, New York, in 1970. The study queried 40,000 graduates of the class of 1961 in 135 colleges in 1961, 1962, 1963, 1964, and 1968.

2. For a quick introduction to the slippery concepts involved in thinking about thinking, see the section "The Elements and Vehicles of Thought," pp. 188–237, in Berelson & Steiner, *Human Behavior, An Inventory of Scientific Findings*, Harcourt Brace, New York, 1964.

3. A dogged attempt to cope with the verbal foliage surrounding definitions of a liberal education, appears in Morris Keeton and Conrad Hilberry's *Struggle and Promise: A Future for Colleges*, McGraw-Hill, New York, 1969, p. 260. They identify several common elements including cultivation of the intellect; encouragement of "independent judgment" or "critical thought"; liberating the individual so that he can see the world in perspectives other than his own; evoking an integrated view of the world which can serve as an inner guide; equipping the individual to serve his society.

Chapter 7—The Diploma: America's Class Distinction

1. The advantages enjoyed by the college-educated population were summarized by Stephen Bassett Withey for the Carnegie Commission in his report *A Degree and What Else?* McGraw-Hill, New York, 1972, beginning on p. 74. Berelson & Steiner, *Human Behavior* reports better prognosis in psychotherapy, fewer divorces, and greater likelihood of voting. Longevity of college graduates is reported in "Socioeconomic Characteristics of Deceased Persons," National Center for Health Statistics, Series 22, Number 9, U.S. Department of Health, Education, and Welfare, 1969.

The health record of college graduates is available from Table 3, "Duration of Work Disability for Persons 18 to 64 Years Old with Disability by Years of School Completed, Vocational Training, Race, Sex, and Age, 1970," from the 1970 Census of Population, PC(2)-6C.

Psychological tests and the results of public opinion polls are frequently reported by years of schooling. The Gallup Opinion Index of 1970, for instance, found that 52 percent of college-educated respondents thought that Communist China should be admitted to the United Nations, compared with only 32 percent of the high-school-educated and 26 percent of those with eight years of schooling or less.

2. Characteristics of the collegebound over the years are neatly packaged in the annual *Digest of Educational Statistics* issued by the National Center for Educational Statistics, Office of Education, and available from the U.S. Government Printing Office.

3. James W. Trent and Leland L. Medsker, *Beyond High School: A Psychosociological Study of 10,000 High School Graduates*, Jossey-Bass, San Francisco, 1968, is the most authoritative study whose design permits a measure of the impact of college, rather than the characteristics of college graduates. Another way to do it is to compare graduating seniors with entering freshmen, such as The American Council on Education Report prepared by Alan E. Bayer, Jeannie T. Royer, and Richard M. Webb, *Four Years After College Entry*, March 1973, Publications Division, American Council on Education, One DuPont Circle, Washington, D.C. 20036. Comparing the collegebound with the noncollege-bound introduces sampling problems, while longitudinal studies can't account for normal development that might have happened to collegebound individuals anywhere.

You can see how widely the results vary from study to study from the extremely useful summary of early studies in *The Impact of College on Students*, by Kenneth A. Feldman & Theodore M. Newcomb, San Francisco, Jossey-Bass, San Francisco, 1969, Volume 2.

An interpretive study by a psychologist is Mervin B. Freedman's *The College Experience*, Jossey-Bass, San

Francisco, 1967. One of the first scholarly attempts to assess the effect of college was the widely quoted Mellon Foundation study of Vassar College students and alumnae in the 1950s. The studies of alumnae are summarized in chapter 25 of *The American College: a Psychological and Social Interpretation of the Higher Learning*, John Wiley & Sons, New York, 1962, and edited by Nevitt Sanford.

4. For the experience of Vietnam veterans with their educational benefits, see "Report of Educational Testing Service, Princeton University, on Educational Assistance Programs for Veterans," 93d Congress, 1st Session, House Committee Print No. 81, U.S. Government Printing Office, Washington, 1973.

5. Christopher Jencks was quoted as saying that college was "a hell of an expensive aptitude test" in *Fortune*, November 1970, page 100.

6. David Riesman gave the origin of the word "diploma" on p. 26 of the book he wrote with Christopher Jencks, *The Academic Revolution*, Doubleday, Garden City, 1968.

7. Margaret Gordon's definition of "credentialism" appears in her introduction to *Higher Education and the Labor Market*, cited above.

8. Ivar Berg, Professor of Sociology at the Columbia University Graduate School of Business Administration, brought the emptiness of the college credential to public attention in *Education and Jobs: The Great Training Robbery* in 1970. It is widely available in a 1971 paperback from Beacon Press, Boston.

9. The skill and education required to do jobs has been extensively studied by manpower and employment agencies of the government as well as the armed forces. Evidence that the skill levels required for jobs have not changed materially comes from "Changes in the Skill Requirements of Occupations in Selected Industries," by Morris A. Horowitz and Irwin L. Herrnstadt, in Appendix Volume II, *Technology and the American Economy*, a Report of the National Commission on Technology, Automation and Economic Progress, Washington: U.S. Government Printing Office, 1966.

10. Private communication from W. J. Reusch, Man-

ager of Management Development and Manpower Planning at the Bethlehem Steel Corporation, Bethlehem, Pennsylvania.

11. On the national differences in educational requirements for jobs, see Peter Drucker, *The Age of Discontinuity*, New York, Harper & Row, 1969, p. 279.

12. The variability of the education required for hotel clerks, orderlies, bank tellers, and cashiers was established by a U.S. Department of Labor study reported by Daniel E. Diamond and Hrach Bedrosian, "Job Performance and the New Credentialism," *California Management Review*, Summer 1972.

13. See *The New York Times* front-page article on July 1, 1973.

14. Private communication from W. T. Hudson, Chief, Office of Civil Rights, United States Coast Guard.

15. The study of the two-year nursing course was conducted by Mildred Montag and completed in 1959. Her findings were reported in a book published by McGraw-Hill in 1959 entitled *Community College Education for Nursing*.

16. Colin Greer has shown that economic considerations played a major role in extending high school to all. See his book *The Great School Legend, A Revisionist Interpretation of American Public Education*, New York, Basic Books, 1972.

17. Willie Griggs and twelve other black employees of Duke Power found they could not advance to better jobs unless they earned a high-school diploma or scored well on two intelligence tests. Represented by NAACP lawyers, they contended in a suit that these requirements were not relevant. The Supreme Court agreed 8–0. Chief Justice Warren Burger said that no test or educational requirement can keep a person out of a job unless the test measures the specific talents needed to do that job. "What Congress has commanded," he explained, "is that any test used must measure the person for the job and not the person in the abstract. . . . Diplomas and tests are useful servants, but Congress has mandated that they are not to become the masters of reality." For repercussions, see *Psy-*

chology Today, December 1973, and Donald J. Petersen, "The Impact of Duke Power on Testing," *Personnel*, March-April 1974.

Chapter 8—A Place to Grow Up . . . Or Not
1. The National Survey of Faculty and Student Opinions, directed by Martin Trow, was taken in 1969 and its findings reported in *The Purposes and the Performance of Higher Education in the United States Approaching the Year 2000*, A Report and Recommendations by the Carnegie Commission on Higher Education, McGraw-Hill, New York, 1973.

2. The great theory builder of modern sociology, Talcott Parsons, delivered his interpretation of the student revolts of the 1960s in "Higher Education and Changing Socialization," a paper he wrote with Gerald M. Platt for Volume III of *Aging and Society: A Sociology of Age Stratification*, edited by Matilda White Riley, Marilyn E. Johnson, and Anne Foner, Russell Sage Foundation, New York, 1972.

3. Mental health and suicide in colleges are documented in a question-and-answer leaflet, *Facts About College Mental Health*, issued by the National Institute of Mental Health, 5600 Fisher Lane, Rockville, Maryland, 20852, as Department of Health, Education and Welfare Publication No. (HSM) 72-9154 in 1972.

4. Student suicides have always attracted study and press attention. For the California scene, see *Suicide in California, 1960–1970*, a study made by the State of California Department of Public Health written by Nancy H. Allen, 1973. See also "The Turned-Off World of Student Suicide," by Andy Olstein, *College*, n.d.

5. Studies on attrition rates comparing the number of entering freshman with graduating seniors as far back as 1913 have been summarized by J. Summerskill, "Dropouts from College," in an anthology, *The American College*, edited by Nevitt Sanford, Wiley, 1962. Because their study was longitudinal, following the same group of students over the four years of college, Trent and Medsker were able to get very accurate information on the dropout rate for students entering college between 1959 and 1963.

6. The new, benign attitude of colleges to dropping out is evident in the interpretations in a study of Harvard and Radcliffe dropouts cited earlier.

7. Dr. Nicholi's study is available from ERIC Reports, published by the U.S. Department of Health, Education & Welfare, Educational Resources Information Center, Washington, D.C. 20202. It is entitled "An Investigation of Harvard Dropouts," ED 042 068, 1970.

8. The study of college dropouts in the Berkeley community was made by David Whittaker. His "Vocational Dispositions of the Nonconformist, Collegiate Dropouts" was published in proceedings of the 1968 Annual Forum of the Association for Institutional Research, San Francisco, Calif., May 6–9, 1968.

9. John Coleman's *Blue-Collar Journal: A College President's Sabbatical*, J. B. Lippincott Company, Philadelphia and New York, 1974, makes many of the same points as this book. It's a delightful book to read, even if you don't agree.

Chapter 9—The Anatomy of Success

1. Malcolm Bricklin's challenge to the automobile industry was headed "Don Quixote of Detroit" by *Time*, May 27, 1974.

2. The statistics on the relationship between college and earnings are neatly packaged in Indicators of Educational Outcome, Fall 1972, p. 10, Department of Health Education and Welfare Publication No. (OE) 73-11110. Statistics for the year 1972 are available from *Current Population Report*, Series P-60 No. 92.

3. For the college records of people in *Who's Who*, see "Majority in Who's Who not top students," *Phi Delta Kappan*, 1965, 46, 441.

4. A review of studies on grades and success is in Donald P. Hoyt, "The Relationship between College Grades and Adult Achievement: A Review of the Literature: *ACT Research Reports*, September 1965, No. 7, American College Testing Program, P.O. Box, Iowa City, Iowa 52240.

5. Walters and Bray studied approximately 10,000 AT&T employees who had been graduated before 1950 and

had gone to work for the company no more than five years after graduation. As reported in "Today's Search for Tomorrow's Leaders," *Journal of College Placement*, 1963, 24, 22–23, they found 45 percent of employees who graduated in the top third earned salaries which were in the top third, while only about 25 percent of the lowest third academically earned comparable salaries. Of this, Hoyt wrote: "It is possible that advancements . . . are based in part on an employee's cumulative record, which includes his college grades. This practice would also produce an artificial correlation between grades and salary."

6. Berelson & Steiner, *Human Behavior*, p. 223, gives the mean I.Q. scores and ranges of scores by civilian occupations for nearly 10,000 white Army Air Force enlisted men.

7. For an account of the tragic career of William James Sidis, see "Twilight of a Genius," by Frances Velie and Caroline Menuez, *Coronet*, February 1945.

8. *The Young Millionaires* is an anthology of business success articles from *Fortune, Signature, Finance, New York, Forbes, The National Observer*, and other publications edited with comment by Lawrence A. Armour, associate editor of *Barron's*, published by Playboy Press, Chicago, 1973.

9. Lear, the inventor, did not get beyond the eighth grade in school. See Ronald Schiller, "Bill Lear: Inventor of the Impossible," *Reader's Digest*, August 1971.

10. For an account of Resnick's success, see Arthur Herzog's *True* article reprinted in *Instant Millionaires*, edited by Max Gunther, Playboy Press, Chicago, 1973.

11. For stories about Evinrude and Drew, see Joseph C. Keeley, *Making Inventions Pay*, Whittlesey House, New York, 1950, pp. 7–8.

12. Tilly Lewis was the only company founder in a *Fortune*, 1973, feature on leading American businesswomen. Her career was reported by Ruth Winter in the *San Francisco Sunday Examiner & Chronicle*, January 6, 1974.

13. C. Kemmons Wilson's career is reported in *The Young Millionaires*.

14. The study was published in Metropolitan's *Statis-*

tical Bulletin, February 1974, and summarized in *Psychology Today*, August 1974, p. 30.

15. All the generals are listed along with their graduating class rank in *Ike*, a pictorial biography by William F. Longgood, New York, Time-Life Books, 1969, pp. 24–5, with the comment: "In most cases a cadet's standing was not a barometer of how well he would do later on. Ike, for example, was 61st and [Omar] Bradley 44th; John Keliher stood 159th but became a brigadier general."

16. Marilyn Wellemeyer and Chandley Murphy analyzed the 1949 Harvard Business School graduates in "The Class the Dollars Fell On," *Fortune*, May 1974.

17. Newcomb's views were recorded at length by Carol Tavris, " 'What Does College Do for a Person? Frankly. Very Little,' " *Psychology Today*, September 1974.

18. Matthew Josephson gives a vivid account of the inventor's youth in *Edison, A Biography*, McGraw-Hill, New York, 1959.

19. His father took Edsel to the bank and showed him the money in gold, according to Booton Herndon, *Ford*, Weybright and Talley, New York, 1969, p. 387.

20. Fred C. Kelly, authorized biographer of the Wright brothers, wrote: "Wilbur gave up the idea of going to college. Neither his nor Orville's formal education went beyond high school, and though each spent the time for a full course, neither ever received a diploma." See *Miracle at Kitty Hawk*, Farrar, Straus and Young, New York, 1951, p. 10.

21. The most revealing of the many Truman books are Margaret Truman, *Harry S. Truman*, William Morrow, New York, 1973; and Merle Miller, *Plain Speaking*, an oral biography of Harry S. Truman, Berkeley Publishing Corp., New York, 1974.

Chapter 10—Student Liberation

1. None of these suggestions is particularly original with the author. Many authors of the Carnegie Commission reports would agree with them, and a number of specific proposals are made in the Carnegie Commission volumes, *Less Time, More Options: Education Beyond the High School*, McGraw-Hill, 1971, and *Reform on Campus:*

Changing   Students,   Changing   Academic   Programs,
McGraw-Hill, New York, June 1972. See also the report of
a study group set up by The Department of Health, Education, and Welfare under the chairmanship of Frank C.
Newman, Professor of Law at the University of California
at Berkeley, to explore the Federal role in higher education. Its report of 1973 made thirty recommendations.

Suggestions for breaking the lockstep of college have
been made by Ernest L. Boyer, Chancellor, State University of New York; Blanche Blank, Professor of Political
Science at Hunter ("Degrees Who Needs Them?" *AAUP
Bulletin,* Autumn 1972); Peter Caws, Professor of Philosophy at Hunter College; Paul Woodring, a psychologist
and former editor of *The Saturday Review* ("The Higher
Learning in America," 1968), and many others.

2. National service as an alternative to the draft attracted wide attention during the Vietnam War. People as
different as David Eisenhower and Margaret Mead have
suggested it.

3. In 1973, the Committee for Economic Development,
a research organization for the business community,
shocked both colleges and parents by recommending that
Federal and state governments target aid directly to students and that colleges raise tuition.

4. The difficulties that can be created when more able
students are given more desirable financial aid packages
are discussed on p. 78 of the College Entrance Examination Board publication *New Approaches to Student Financial Aid* cited above.

5. Both Peter Drucker and Blanche Blank think that
equal-opportunity laws will one day be extended to bar
discrimination on the basis of education. See Drucker's
The Age of Discontinuity, Harper & Row, New York,
1968, p. 332.

Bibliography

The literature on education—and young people—is volumi-
nous. It would take another volume to report on all the
books, pamphlets, and articles that came across my desk
while I was researching this consumer report on college.
Some of the works that were valuable and helped shape my
thinking are cited in the text itself, in the chapter notes, and
in the resource section on alternatives. Listed below, for
those who would like to explore further, is a small selection
of other sources that were helpful.

On Higher Education:

Blaug, Mark, ed., *Economics of Education. Selected Read-
ings*, Penguin, Middlesex, England, 1968.
Blaug, Mark, *An Introduction to the Economics of Educa-
tion*, Penguin, Middlesex, England, 1970.
Carnegie Commission on Higher Education, *Any Person,
Any Study*, McGraw-Hill, New York, 1973.
Carnegie Commission on Higher Education, *Governance of
Higher Education; Six Priority Problems*, McGraw-Hill,
New York, 1973.
Carnegie Commission on Higher Education, *The More
Effective Use of Resources: An Imperative for Higher
Education*, McGraw-Hill, New York, 1972.
Carnegie Commission on Higher Education, *Toward a
Learning Society; Alternative Channels to Life, Work
and Service*, McGraw-Hill, 1973.
Eurich, Alvin C., ed., *Campus 1980: The Shape of the Fu-
ture in American Higher Education*, Delacorte, New
York, 1968.
Glenny, Lyman, "Pressures in Higher Education," *College
and University Journal*, vol. 12, no. 4, September 1973.
Handlin, Oscar and Mary, *The American College and
American Culture: Socialization as a Function of Higher
Education*, McGraw-Hill, New York, 1970.
Rosen, David; Brunner, Seth; and Fowler, Steve, *Open Ad-
missions, The Promise and the Lie of Open Access to*

American Higher Education, University of Nebraska, Lincoln, Nebraska, 1973.

Trow, Martin, *The Expansion and Transformation of Higher Education*, General Learning Press, Morristown, New Jersey, 1972.

United States Department of Health, Education and Welfare, *Toward a Social Report*, Government Printing Office, Washington, D.C., 1969.

On Financing College:

College Entrance Examination Board, "Report of the Committee on Student Economics," New York, 1972.

College Entrance Examination Board, *Toward Equal Opportunity for Higher Education*, New York, 1972.

Committee for Economic Development, *The Management and Financing of Colleges*, New York, 1973.

Carnegie Commission on Higher Education, *Tuition; A Supplemental Statement to "Who Pays? Who Benefits? Who Should Pay?"* McGraw-Hill, New York, 1974.

Cox, Claire, *How To Beat the High Cost of College*, Dial Press, New York, 1971.

National Commission on the Financing of Post-Secondary Education, *Financing Post-Secondary Education in the United States*, United States Government Printing Office, Washington, D.C., 1973.

On Human Capital and Rates of Return:

Koch, J. V., "Student Choice of Undergraduate Major Field of Study and Private Internal Rates of Return," *Industrial and Labor Relations Review*, October 1972.

Parsons, Donald O., "The Cost of School Time, Foregone Earnings, and Human Capital Formation, *Journal of Political Economy*, vol. 82, no. 2, part 1, March-April 1974.

Schultz, Theodore W., *Investment in Human Capital*, The Free Press, New York, 1971.

Taubman, Paul and Wales, Terence, "Higher Education, Mental Ability and Screening," *Journal of Political Economy*, vol. 81, no. 1, January-February 1973.

On College and the Labor Market:

Blank, Blanche D., "College Competency and Credentializing: An Odd Couple," paper prepared for Symposium on

Competency Module Development, Northern Illinois University, 1973.

Carnegïe Commission on Higher Education, *College Graduates and Jobs*, McGraw-Hill, New York, 1973.

Dunnette, Marvin, "Strategies for Measuring and Predicting Human Work Performance," paper prepared for Conference on the Use of Psychological Tests in Employment, University of Rochester, 1972.

Freeman, Richard B., *The Market for College Trained Manpower*, Harvard University Press, Cambridge, Mass., 1971.

Holmen, Milton G., and Docter, Richard, *Educational and Psychological Testing; A Study of the Industry and Its Practices*, Russell Sage Foundation, New York, 1972.

Kaufman, Jacob J., and Lewis, Morgan V., "The High School Diploma: Credential for Employment?," Institute for Research on Human Resources, Pennsylvania State University, University Park, 1972.

Mincer, Jacob, *Youth, Education and Work*, National Bureau of Economic Research, Inc., New York, 1973.

Sheppard, Harold L., and Herrick, Neal Q., *Where Have All the Robots Gone? Worker Dissatisfaction in the Seventies*, The Free Press, New York, 1972.

Tarnowieski, Dale, "The Changing Success Ethic," AMA Survey Report, AMACOM, New York, 1973.

On the Impact of College:

The Advocates: "Would the Nation be Better Off if Fewer People Went to College?" WGBH Boston, Mass., Transcript of program aired January 1974.

Astin, Alexander W., *The College Environment*, American Council on Education, Washington, D.C., 1968.

Astin, Alexander W., and Panos, Robert J., *The Educational and Vocational Development of College Students*, American Council on Education, Washington, D.C., 1969.

Baird, Leonard L., *The Graduates, A Report on the Characteristics and Plans of College Seniors*, Educational Testing Service, Princeton, New Jersey, 1973.

Cort, Stewart S., "Education for What?," *Journal of College Placement*, April-May 1973.

Kahn, E. J., Jr., *The American People. The Findings of the 1970 Census*, Weybright and Talley, New York, 1973.

Keats, John, *The Sheepskin Psychosis*, Dell, New York, 1965.

Sabine, Gordon, *When You Listen, This Is What You Can Hear . . .* , American College Testing Program, Iowa City, 1971.

Sanford, Nevitt, *Where Colleges Fail*, Jossey-Bass, San Francisco, 1968.

Solmon, Lewis C., and Taubman, Paul J., ed., *Does College Matter? Some Evidence on the Impact of Higher Education*, Academic Press, New York, 1973.

United States National Center for Educational Statistics, *Indicators of Educational Outcome, Fall 1972*, Government Printing Office, Washington, D.C., 1973.

Woodring, Paul, *Who Should Go to College?*, Phi Delta Kappa Foundation, Bloomington, Indiana, 1972.

On Student Leaves of Absence:

Babbott, Edward J., "Postponing College, Alternatives for an Interim Year," *College Board Review*, no. 80, College Entrance Examination Board, Summer, 1971.

Bachman, Jerald, *et al.*, *Youth in Transition: Dropping Out —Problem or Symptom?*, vol. 3, Institute for Social Research, Ann Arbor, Michigan, 1971.

Brown, Newell, *After College . . . Junior College . . . Military Service . . . What?*, Grosset and Dunlap, New York, 1971.

Dunnette, Marvin, *et al.*, "Why Do They Leave?" *Personnel*, May-June 1973.

Wright, Erik, Olin, "A Study of Student Leaves of Absence," *Journal of Higher Education*, vol. 44, March 1973.

Index